CASH & CREDIT
Accounting

tutorial

NVQ LEVEL 2
ACCOUNTING

David Cox
Michael Fardon

OSBORNE
BOOKS

Published by Osborne Books Limited
Unit 1B Everoak Estate
Bromyard Road
Worcester
WR2 5HN
Tel 01905 748071

Printed by the Bath Press, Bath.

British Library Cataloguing in Publication Data
A catalogue record for this book is available from the British Library

ISBN 1 872962 03 3

CONTENTS

ACKNOWLEDGEMENTS

The authors wish to thank the following for their help with the reading and production of the book: Jean Cox, Michael Gilbert, Jon Moore and Anita Sherwood. Particular thanks go to Roger Petheram for his guidance, to the staff and students of Worcester College of Technology and to the many college tutors who have advised on the length, breadth and format of this new text. Thanks are also due to the Association of Accounting Technicians for their generous help and advice and to the Lead Body for Accounting for permission to reproduce extracts from the Standards of Competence for Accounting, to Barclays Bank for the illustrations of a Barclaycard and a Connect Card, to the Royal Mint for permission to use images of coins and to Marks & Spencer plc for the use of a photograph of a till.

THE AUTHORS

David Cox has had more than twenty years' experience teaching accountancy students over a wide range of levels. Formerly with the Management and Professional Studies Department at Worcester College of Technology, he now lectures on a freelance basis and carries out educational consultancy work in accountancy studies. He is author and joint author of a number of textbooks in the areas of accounting, finance and banking.

Michael Fardon has extensive teaching experience of a wide range of banking, business and accountancy courses at Worcester College of Technology. He now specialises in writing business and financial texts and is General Editor of the Osborne Books GNVQ series. He is also an educational consultant and has worked extensively in the areas of Key Skills and GNVQ development.

INTRODUCTION

Osborne tutorials

Cash & Credit Accounting Tutorial has been written to provide a study resource for students taking courses based on the NVQ Level 2 Accounting standards such as the AAT Foundation and ACCA technician level course. As the title suggests, it covers the first two NVQ units. The area of payroll is covered by its companion Osborne text *Payroll Accounting Tutorial* and the *Payroll Accounting Workbook.*

Cash & Credit Accounting Tutorial also covers Unit 24 'Communicating for Accounting' in Chapter 18, as this skill is essential to the assessment material for the other units. For similar reasons Chapter 19 'Business Contracts' has also been included in this tutorial.

The chapters of *Cash & Credit Accounting Tutorial* contain:

• a clear text with worked examples and case studies
• a chapter summary and key terms to help with revision
• a wide range of student activities

Cash & Credit Accounting Tutorial provides the student with the theoretical background to the subject while at the same time including plenty of opportunity to put theory into practice. The aim has been to introduce the right amount of material at the right level, avoiding the temptation to overburden the student with unnecessary detail. The tutorial text is therefore useful for classroom use and also for distance learning students. It is with the latter type of student in mind that the answers to all the student activities have been included at the back of the book.

Osborne workbooks

Cash & Credit Accounting Tutorial has been written to be used alongside the *Cash & Credit Accounting Workbook,* which contains

• extended student activities
• AAT Devolved Assessments
• AAT Central Assessments

The answers to these tasks and Assessments are included in a separate *Tutor Pack* which also includes a range of photocopiable documents.

If you would like a workbook, please telephone Osborne Books on 01905 748071 for details of ordering by credit card, or by cheque.

COVERAGE OF NVQ SPECIFICATIONS

UNIT 1: RECORDING AND ACCOUNTING FOR CASH TRANSACTIONS

element 1

record and bank monies received   chapter

❏ *monies are banked in accordance with organisation's policies, regulations, procedures and timescales*   *13*

❏ *incoming monies are checked against relevant supporting documentation*   *12*

❏ *cash is correctly counted and correct change given where applicable*   *12*

❏ *monies received are correctly and legibly recorded*   *12*

❏ *written receipts are correctly issued where required*   *12*

❏ *totals and balances are correctly calculated*   *12*

❏ *paying in documents are correctly prepared and reconciled to relevant records*   *13*

❏ *documentation is correctly filed*   *12*

❏ *cash handling, security and confidentiality procedures are followed*   *12,13*

❏ *discrepancies, unusual features or queries are identified and either resolved or referred to the appropriate person*   *12,13*

element 2

make and record payments

❏ *payments are made and recorded in accordance with the organisation's policies, regulations, procedures and timescales*   *14*

❏ *payments are properly authorised*   *14*

❏ *cheques are prepared correctly and are signed by designated person(s) prior to despatch*   *14*

❏ *standing orders and other inter-bank transfers are correctly documented*   *14*

❏ *remittance advices are correctly prepared and despatched with payments*   *14*

❏ *totals and balances are correctly calculated and checked against documentation*   *14*

❏ *available cash discounts are identified and deducted*   *14*

❏ *documents are correctly filed*   *14*

❏ *safety and security procedures for the handling of cash and cheques are followed*   *14*

❏ *discrepancies, unusual features or queries are identified and either resolved or referred to the appropriate person*   *14*

element 3

maintain petty cash records   chapter

- ❏ *transactions are accurately recorded and analysed to the correct expenditure heads*   *16*
- ❏ *cash withdrawals from the main cash account are accurately recorded*   *16*
- ❏ *claims are properly authorised, are within prescribed limits and are supported by adequate evidence*   *16*
- ❏ *totals and balances are correctly calculated*   *16*
- ❏ *the balance of cash in hand is reconciled with the petty cash records at appropriate intervals*   *16*
- ❏ *documentation is correctly filed*   *16*
- ❏ *analysed totals of petty cash expenditure are transferred to the correct ledger accounts*   *16*
- ❏ *cash handling, security and confidentiality procedures are followed*   *16*
- ❏ *any discrepancies, unusual features or queries are identified and either resolved or referred to the appropriate person*   *16*

element 4

account for cash and bank transactions   chapter

- ❏ *entries in the cash book are accurately transferred to correct ledger accounts*   *15*
- ❏ *bank reconciliation statements are accurately prepared and are presented within specified timescales*   *17*
- ❏ *recorded transactions are supported by properly authorised primary documentation*   *15*
- ❏ *details for the relevant primary documentation are recorded in the cash book and analysed accurately*   *15*
- ❏ *totals and balances are correctly calculated*   *15*
- ❏ *security and confidentiality procedures are followed*   *15*
- ❏ *the organisation's policies, regulations, procedures and timescales are observed*   *15*
- ❏ *any discrepancies, unusual features or queries are identified and either resolved or referred to the appropriate person*   *15,17*

UNIT 2 RECORDING AND ACCOUNTING FOR CREDIT TRANSACTIONS

element 1

process documents relating to goods and services supplied on credit   chapter

- ❏ *invoices and credit notes are correctly authorised and coded, and
     despatched to customers*   2
- ❏ *the calculations on invoices and credit notes, including discounts and VAT,
     are correct*   2
- ❏ *invoices and credit notes are correctly entered as primary accounting
     records in a form acceptable to the organisation*   5
- ❏ *the analysis and totalling of the primary record is completed accurately* 5
- ❏ *documentation is correctly filed*   2
- ❏ *the organisation's procedures and timescales are observed*   2
- ❏ *discrepancies, unusual features or queries are identified and either resolved
     or referred to the appropriate person*   2

element 2

process documents relating to goods and services received on credit

- ❏ *suppliers' invoices and credit notes are correctly checked against ordering
     documentation and evidence that goods/services have been received*   3
- ❏ *suppliers' invoices and credit notes are correctly coded*   3
- ❏ *calculations on suppliers' invoices and credit notes are correct*   3
- ❏ *documents are correctly entered as primary accounting records in a
     form acceptable to the organisation*   6
- ❏ *documents are correctly filed*   3
- ❏ *the organisation's procedures and timescales are observed*   3
- ❏ *discrepancies, unusual features or queries are identified and either
     resolved or referred to the appropriate person*   3

element 3

account for goods and services supplied on credit

- ❏ *entries in the primary records are correctly transferred to the correct ledger
     accounts*   5
- ❏ *adjustments involving debtors' accounts are properly authorised and
     documented, and are correctly transferred to the correct ledger accounts*   9,11
- ❏ *the control account in the general ledger is reconciled with the total
     of balances in the sales (debtors) ledger*   10
- ❏ *where required, statements of account are sent to debtors promptly*   9

element 4

account for goods and services received on credit

UNIT 24 COMMUNICATING FOR ACCOUNTING

element 1

supply information for a specific purpose

element 2

draft routine business communications

Note
For the 'Knowledge and Understanding' requirements of the course, please refer to the index for individual subjects, eg contract, double-entry, organisational structures, security, and so on.

1 INTRODUCTION TO ACCOUNTING

this chapter covers . . .

Before studying cash and credit transactions and payroll in detail it is important to understand the varied contexts in which they take place. Every organisation is unique, and therefore no one accounting system will be exactly the same as another. This chapter provides a brief introduction to the different types of business organisation, the types of transactions they will carry out and the different ways in which they set up their accounting systems.

Set out below are the NVQ competences covered by this chapter. As you will see they involve the "Knowledge and Understanding" content of the course.

NVQ PERFORMANCE CRITERIA COVERED

KNOWLEDGE AND UNDERSTANDING – THE ORGANISATION

❑ background understanding that the accounting systems of an organisation are affected by its organisational structure, its administrative systems and procedures and the nature of its business transactions

KNOWLEDGE AND UNDERSTANDING – ACCOUNTING TECHNIQUES

❑ calculation facility, including use of equipment provided

❑ methods of coding data

❑ operation of manual and computerised accounting systems

KNOWLEDGE AND UNDERSTANDING – ACCOUNTING PRINCIPLES AND THEORY

❑ distinction between capital and revenue (in general terms)

❑ principles of internal check

BUSINESS ORGANISATIONS

There are three main types of business organisation:

sole trader

A sole trader is an individual trading in his/her own name, or under a trading name.

The majority of businesses are sole traders. A sole trader is likely to be a 'jack of all trades'; he or she will be in charge of buying and selling of goods and services, hiring and firing of staff and will often, unless an outside book-keeper is employed, 'keep the books' – ie maintain the accounts. This is important because if the sole trader becomes bankrupt – ie s/he owes more than s/he has – the sole trader's personal belongings may have to be sold to pay off the business debts.

partnership

A partnership is a group of individuals trading in business, aiming to make a profit.

The partnership is clearly a step up from the sole trader: more people are involved in the business and so more expertise and money will be available. Examples of partnerships (normally from 2 to 20 people) include solicitors, accountants, dentists and small building firms. Like sole traders, partners in a partnership are fully liable for business debts. If the business becomes bankrupt, so do all the partners. The need for maintaining the accounts therefore becomes very important. Often one of the partners will take responsibility for the financial management of the business. As with a sole trader, a book-keeper may also be employed.

limited company

A limited company is a separate legal body, owned by shareholders and managed by directors.

The largest business organisations are usually limited companies. A limited company is quite different from a sole trader and a partnership in that it exists as a business in its own right. It exists separately from its owners, the shareholders, who will not be called upon to pay up if the company goes into liquidation (goes 'bust'). The shareholders have what is known as *limited liability*: all they can lose is the money they have invested in the company. The need for the keeping of accounting records by limited companies is strictly regulated in law. Many limited companies will have an Accounts Department which will carry out all the accounting functions.

ORGANISATIONAL STRUCTURES AND ACCOUNTING

We have just seen that in a small sole trader business the owner is likely to carry out all the 'bookwork' as well as all the other functions of running the business. This is why small business owners work such long hours and also why they are motivated by their work – it is so varied. The diagram below shows the organisational structure of the functions of a typical sole trader. The structure is known as a 'flat' structure.

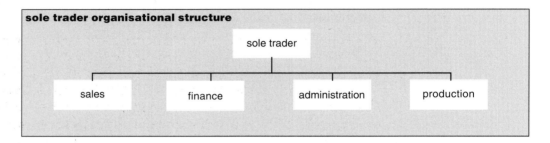

The organisational structure of a larger business such as a limited company is far more complex and 'taller', and as you will see from the diagram below, involves many more staff. Accounting jobs in a larger organisation may therefore be less varied but will allow greater specialisation. Nevertheless, as we will see in the Case Study on the next page, the transactions carried out are essentially the same: buying, selling, settling expenses, paying wages.

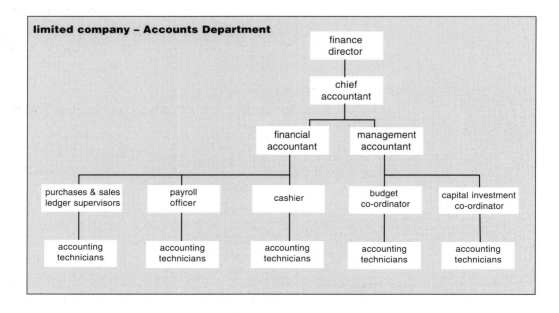

ACCOUNTING TRANSACTIONS

All businesses carry out transactions which need to be recorded in some form of manual or computerised accounting system. The most common transactions include:

- selling goods and services
- making purchases and paying expenses
- paying money into the bank and making payments from the bank account
- paying wages

If you consider all the activities undertaken during a working day, you will see that there are many different transactions taking place, all of which need recording accurately. Read through the following Case Studies which present two businesses: Stan Taylor Plumbing – a small 'one-person' business (which employs two assistants) and Osborne Electronics Limited – a larger limited company business which supplies computers and business machines and employs eight people.

CASE STUDY

STAN TAYLOR – PLUMBER

sale of goods and services
- installation of lavatory for Fred Lush, £250 paid in cash, receipt given by Stan
- repair of burst pipe at City Architect's office, invoice for £95.50 issued to City Council, payment to be made in 30 days' time (normally a cheque will be posted to Stan)

purchases and payment of expenses
- settle account with builders merchant, a £1,750 cheque issued by Stan for items bought over the last six weeks
- buy new van, pay £12,000 by cheque
- buy diesel fuel for van, pay £18.50 by cheque

visit to the bank
- pay in cheques totalling £1,753.95
- cash a cheque, £250, for wages for employees
- query charges on the bank statement

pay wages
- complete documentation, including wage slips, and pay employees £250

CASE STUDY

OSBORNE ELECTRONICS Limited

sale of goods and services

- sale of fax machine to Merton Textiles, for £750, cheque received with order
- installation of photocopier for Mereford Tourist Office, cost £2,450, invoice issued to Tourist Board, payment to be made in 30 days' time (normally a cheque will be posted to Osborne)

purchases and payment of expenses

- pay for colour laser printer for use in the office, a £2,750 cheque is issued by Osborne Electronics
- settle account with Nippon Importers for computer software, a £5,675 cheque issued
- issue cheque for £3,500 for insurance premium due

visit the the National Bank plc

- pay in cheques totalling £10,645.50, money received from customers
- cash a cheque, £2,500, for the week's wages

pay wages

- complete documentation, make up pay packets, totalling £2,500

RECORDING FINANCIAL TRANSACTIONS

Although the two businesses in the Case Study are very different in size and in what they do, the types of transactions fall into distinct catagories:

- *Cash transactions* – transactions which involve immediate payment, eg Fred Lush's loo and the sale of a fax machine to Merton Textiles. Note that 'cash' payment means 'immediate' payment and can include payment by cheque as well as payment using banknotes.
- *Credit transactions* – transactions which involve payment at a date later than the original transaction, eg the City Architect's burst pipe and the installation of the photocopier for Mereford Tourist Office.

The following transactions can be for cash or for credit:

- *Capital transactions* – the purchase (or sale) of items which are permanently used by the business, eg Stan's van and Osborne's colour laser printer.
- *Revenue transactions* – items of income or expense which occur on a day-to-day basis, eg Stan's diesel bill, Osborne's insurance premiums.

As you will see from the very varied items in the Case Study, recording financial transactions is a complex business. You have to keep track of:

- who owes you what, and when the payment is due

- amounts that you owe, and when the payment is due

You have to record what you pay into the bank and what you draw out. You need to record the amounts paid in wages to each employee. We will not at this stage explore in any detail how these transactions are recorded – such areas will be covered later in the book – but it is worth noting that if these transactions are not recorded accurately, the owner of the business and other interested parties such as the bank manager and the tax authorities will not know how the business is progressing!

ACCOUNTING SYSTEMS

The accounting system of a business is the system for recording information from documents (such as invoices and receipts) into the accounting records, checking that the information has been recorded correctly, and then presenting the information in a way which enables the owner(s) of the business and other interested people to review its progress.

Most businesses use an accounting system based on the double-entry book-keeping system, whereby each financial transaction is recorded in the accounts *twice*. Some small businesses will use a single-entry system, where each transaction is entered once only in a cash book, which records receipts and payments of money.

Accounting records are usually kept in one of two forms:

- handwritten records

- computer records

written accounting records

This is the traditional method of keeping 'the books', particularly for the smaller business. The main record is the ledger which, many years ago, would be a large leather-bound volume, neatly ruled, into which the book-keeper would enter each business transaction in immaculate handwriting into individual accounts. In modern times, the handwritten ledger is still used, and stationery shops sell ledgers and other accounting books, designed especially for the smaller business.

computer accounting records

Nowadays, computers have come down in price so much that they can be afforded by most businesses. With computer accounting programs, such as

Sage™, business transactions are input into the computer and stored on disk. The major advantage of computer accounting is that it is a very accurate method of recording business transactions; the disadvantage is that it may be cumbersome and time-consuming to set up, particularly for the smaller business. Interestingly, the word 'ledger' has survived into the computer age and refers to data files held on computer disk.

double-entry book-keeping and coding

Double-entry book-keeping involves making two entries in the accounts for each transaction: for instance, if you sell some goods and receive a cheque, you will make an entry in the sales account to record the sale, and an entry in the bank account to record the receipt of a cheque. If you are operating a manual accounting system you will make the two entries by hand, if you are operating a computer accounting system you will make one entry on the keyboard, but indicate to the machine where the other entry is to be made, by means of a numerical code. Accurate coding is important in the efficient operation of any accounting system.

accounts

The sources for the entries you make are the financial documents. The ledger into which you make the entries is normally a bound book (in a non-computerised system) divided into separate accounts, eg a separate account for sales, purchases, each type of business expense, each customer, each supplier, and so on. Each account is given a specific name, and a number code for reference purposes. In a computer system, the accounts are held as data files on a disk, and each account becomes a computer record with its own reference number code.

the different ledgers

Because of the large number of accounts involved, 'the ledger' is divided into a number of different ledgers:

- *sales ledger* – records of sales made to customers, and payments received at a later date (ie not cash sales) – each record shows the amount owed by a particular customer (debtor)
- *purchases ledger* – records of purchases from suppliers, and payments made at a later date (ie not cash purchases) – each record shows the amount owed to a particular supplier (creditor)
- *cash book* – a record of cash and bank transactions (a cash book is the main accounting record for the single-entry system mentioned earlier)
- *general (or nominal) ledger* – a record of all other transactions of the business, such as assets (things owned), expenses (the overheads of the

business, eg wages, rent paid), drawings (the amount taken out of the business by the owner), loans to the business (eg by a bank), and the owner's capital (the amount invested in the business by the owner)

The same division of the ledger is seen in computer accounting programs.

trial balance

Double-entry book-keeping, because it involves making two entries for each transaction, is open to error. What if the book-keeper writes £45 in one account and £54 in another? The trial balance effectively checks the entries made over a given period of time and will pick up most errors. The trial balance sets out the balances of all the double-entry accounts, ie the totals of the accounts for a certain period. As well as being an arithmetic check, it is used to help in the preparation of financial statements – the final accounts of the business.

financial statements (final accounts)

The financial statements (final accounts) of a business comprise the profit and loss statement and the balance sheet.

WHAT THE PROFIT AND LOSS STATEMENT SHEET SHOWS

income *minus* **expenses** *equals* **profit**

The profit and loss statement of a business shows the day-to-day ('revenue') income, a business has received over a given period for goods sold or services provided. It also sets out the expenses incurred – the cost of producing the product, and the overheads (eg wages, administration, rent, and so on). The difference between income and expenses is the profit of the business. If expenses are greater than income, then a loss has been made. The profit (or loss) belongs to the owner(s) of the business. The figures for sales, purchases, and expenses are taken from the double-entry system.

WHAT THE BALANCE SHEET SHOWS

| **assets** what a business owns | *minus* | **liabilities** what a business owes | *equals* | **capital** how a business has been financed |

The balance sheet of a business gives a 'snapshot' of the business at a particular date – eg the end of the accounting period of the business. It is prepared from the accounting records and shows:

assets	what the business owns – eg premises, vehicles, computers, stock of goods for resale, debtors (money owed by customers), money in the bank
liabilities	what the business owes – eg bank loans, creditors (money owed to suppliers)
capital	where the money to finance the business has come from – eg the owner's investment. profits made by the business

The equation shown on the previous page –

assets minus liabilities equals capital

is known as the 'accounting equation.' Now study the diagram below which summarises the way the accounting system operates from documents through to profit and loss statement and balance sheet.

prime documents

processing of documents relating to purchases, sales, payments and receipts

accounting records

recording financial transactions in the accounting system using primary accounting records (eg day books) and the double-entry book-keeping system

trial balance

the extraction of figures from all the double-entry accounts to check their arithmetical accuracy in the form of a list, known as the trial balance

financial statements

production from the double-entry accounts of:

• profit and loss statement

• balance sheet

together known as the 'final accounts'

ACCOUNTING – CHECKING AND AUDITING

the importance of checking

Complete accuracy is essential in accounting. Mistakes in money amounts can result in suppliers being paid too much, the record of the bank balance in the cash book being wrong and, very importantly, employees' wages being wrong! An efficient business will therefore institute checking procedures for all calculations and listings of figures.

The checking may be carried out by employees at the same level of seniority, or it may be carried out by a supervisor. This type of checking will form part of the day-to-day procedures of the business, and will often be shown by the initials of the checker and date of checking.

auditors

Another form of checking is *auditing* this is carried out by *auditors* – people who do not normally carry out the job in question, and may not even be employees of the business.

Auditors are normally employed by larger limited companies and similar - sized organisations, eg local authorities, because they are required to do so by law. Smaller businesses such as sole traders and partnerships do not have this legal obligation and so they rarely use auditors.

There are two types of auditor:

• internal auditors

• external auditors

Internal auditors are employees of the business being audited. They are concerned with the internal checking and control procedures of the business: for example control of cash, signing of cheques, authorising of purchases. In a limited company the internal auditors normally report directly to the Finance Director.

External auditors are independent of the business which is being checked (audited). External audit is still the 'bread and butter' business of many firms of accountants. The most common form of external audit is the audit of larger limited companies which is required by the Companies Acts. The auditors, when they have completed the audit, have by law to sign a declaration stating that the accounts represent a 'true and fair view' of the state of the company. The external auditors report to the shareholders (owners) of the limited company, and are appointed by them.

ACCOUNTING – TOOLS OF THE TRADE

An accounting technician will need to deal competently with a wide variety of figures and must be familiar with the various types of calculator. There will be the need, for example, to calculate percentages – VAT amounts, discounts, tax due – and to add up columns of figures.

pocket calculator

This type of calculator is very familiar and is in common use in many professions and occupations. It is excellent for 'one-off' calculations such as percentages, multiplication, division and scientific functions (if you have a scientific calculator). A hint: it is advisable to perform each calculation *twice* as a check on accuracy.

tally-roll desk calculator

The tally-roll calculator will print out on a paper roll all the figures you input. This type of calculator is very useful when you have long columns of figures to add up, for example totalling 250 cheques received in the post. It operates very easily and rapidly and lists on the tally-roll all the figures you key in. This machine is particularly useful if you have to locate an error – because you can tick back the tally-roll record of the figures against the original figures and trace any mistakes you may have made.

- There are three main types of business organisation: sole trader, partnership and limited company.

- Small businesses tend to have 'flat' organisational structures – the owner carries out most functions, including running the accounting system.

- Larger businesses tend to have more complex and 'taller' organisational structures – the accounting jobs will be carried out by a greater number of specialised staff.

- All types of business carry out the same basic types of financial transaction – buying, selling, banking, paying wages; all these transactions need to be accurately recorded and coded.

- Accounting systems within a business may be handwritten (manual) or computerised; they may be single entry (for the smaller business) or, more commonly, double entry – which involves two entries being made for each transaction.

- Financial transactions are recorded in separate 'accounts' which are grouped in 'ledgers'; this system is true of both handwritten and computerised accounts. The accuracy of the system is checked in a listing of balances known as the 'trial balance.'

- The accounting system is used to produce the financial statements of the business – the profit and loss statement and the balance sheet.

- The accuracy of the accounting records should be checked regularly by the accounting staff. In the case of larger businesses it may also be checked by internal and external auditors.

- Accounting staff must be competent in the use of pocket and tally-roll calculators.

sole trader	an individual trading on his or her own
partnership	a group of individuals trading in business
limited company	a separate legal body, owned by shareholders
cash transactions	transactions which involve immediate payment
credit transactions	transactions which involve payment at a later date
capital transactions	purchase (or sale) of items which are in permanent use by the business
revenue transactions	items of income or expense which occur on a day-to-day basis
double-entry book-keeping	an accounting system which involves two entries being made in the accounts for every transaction

	**coding**	an identifying reference number or letter code given to accounting transactions, eg an account number, a supplier reference
	ledger	a sub-division of the accounting system (strictly speaking a 'ledger' is a book, but the term is still used in computer accounting systems)
	trial balance	a listing of the accounts in the accounting system, used to check the accuracy of that system
	profit and loss statement	a financial statement showing the profit or loss made by the business in a given period
	balance sheet	a financial statement showing what a business owns and owes
	assets	items the business owns
	liabilities	items the business owes
	capital	where the money used to finance the business comes from
	accounting equation	assets minus liabilities equals capital
	auditor	a person who independently checks the accuracy of the accounting records

STUDENT ACTIVITIES

1.1   A business which is owned by shareholders is known as:

(a)   a sole trader business

(b)   a partnership

(c)   a limited company

(d)   a limited partnership

Answer (a) or (b) or (c) or (d)

1.2 In each of the following cases, state whether the transaction is a **capital** transaction or a **revenue** transaction:

(a) payment of wages by a bus company

(b) purchase of a car by an advertising company

(c) purchase of a car for a customer by a Ford dealer

(d) sale of a table by a furniture store

(e) sale of office furniture by a Ford dealer moving premises

1.3 State whether the following are **cash** transactions or **credit** transactions:

(a) an office buys stationery and settles immediately by cash

(b) an office buys stationery and settles immediately by cheque

(c) an office buys stationery and pays thirty days later on an invoice

(d) a petrol station sells petrol and is paid by cheque

(e) a business sells goods and is paid thirty days later in cash

1.4 A person starting a new business is not clear about the meaning of the word 'ledger.' What exactly does it mean?

1.5 Write out the accounting equation. Explain the items which make up the two sides of the equation. What would happen to the capital of the business if the assets increased and the liabilities stayed the same (eg if a company revalued its premises)?

1.6 Explain in two short paragraphs:

(a) why it is important to check financial transactions

(b) what auditors do

1.7 The three examples set out below are mistakes that can and do happen in business. Read them through and state in each case what the consequences of each error might be.

(a) The overtime sheet given to the accounting assistant who calculates the wages has not been checked. Jo Isback's fifteen hours of overtime have not been recorded on it.

(b) Because of a computer input error a customer has been billed for 1,000 computer disks instead of 100 computer disks.

(c) The bank has deducted £5,000 from the business bank account by mistake and has not noticed the error.

2 DOCUMENTS – SELLING ON CREDIT

this chapter covers . . .

This chapter examines the procedures involved when a business sells goods or services on credit. The essential point here is that the business wants to get its money on time and it wants to get the right amount. It can achieve these aims through the efficient use and monitoring of business documents. The chapter covers the areas of:

- the use of business documents – purchase order, invoice, delivery note, returns note, credit note, statement

- the calculation of document totals, discounts and Value Added Tax (VAT)

- the coding of documents

- the checking and authorisation of documents

- filing of documents

NVQ PERFORMANCE CRITERIA COVERED

unit 2: RECORDING AND ACCOUNTING FOR CREDIT TRANSACTIONS
element 1
process documents relating to goods and services supplied on credit

- ❑ invoices and credit notes are correctly authorised and coded, and despatched to customers
- ❑ the calculations on invoices and credit notes, including discounts and VAT, are correct
- ❑ documentation is correctly filed
- ❑ the organisation's procedures and timescales are observed
- ❑ discrepancies, unusual features or queries are identified and either resolved or referred to the appropriate person

PURCHASES AND SALES DOCUMENTS

the documents used

When a business sells goods or services it will use a number of different documents (shown in the diagram below). A single sales transaction of course involves both seller *and* buyer. In this chapter we look at the situation from the point of view of the *seller* of the goods or services; the next chapter deals with the situation from the point of view of the buyer. Documents used in the *selling* process include:

• the *purchase order*, which the seller receives from the buyer

• the *delivery note* which goes with the goods from the seller to the buyer

• the *invoice*, which lists the goods and tells the buyer what is owed

• the *credit note*, which is sent to the buyer if any refund is due

• the *statement*, sent by the seller to remind the buyer what is owed

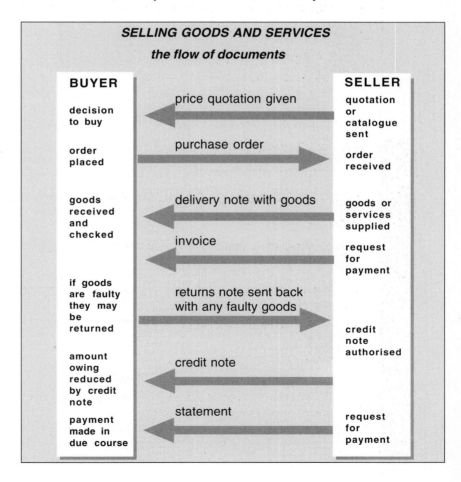

SELLING GOODS AND SERVICES
the flow of documents

BUYER		SELLER
decision to buy	price quotation given	quotation or catalogue sent
order placed	purchase order	order received
goods received and checked	delivery note with goods	goods or services supplied
	invoice	request for payment
if goods are faulty they may be returned	returns note sent back with any faulty goods	credit note authorised
amount owing reduced by credit note	credit note	
payment made in due course	statement	request for payment

the flow of documents

Before you read the Case Study, examine the diagram set out on the previous page. Down the columns representing the buyer and the seller are various activities which lead to transactions which in turn generate documents.

CASE STUDY

COOL SOCKS – A SALES TRANSACTION

situation

Cool Socks Limited manufactures fashion socks in a variety of colours. It supplies a number of different customers, including Trends, a fashion store in Broadfield. In this Case Study, Trends, a fashion shop, places an order for 100 pairs of socks with Cool Socks. The socks are delivered, but some are found to be faulty, so some of the socks have to be returned. The Case Study looks in detail at the documents involved.

the price quotation

In this Case Study, Trends orders some socks from Cool Socks. Before placing the order the buyer at Trends will need to find out the price of the socks. This can be done by consulting Cool Socks' catalogue, or by means of a written or telephoned enquiry, or, if Cool Socks has a web page, by an on-line enquiry. Cool Socks *may* provide a written quotation for the socks if they are requested to do so, although this procedure is more common with higher value orders. A written quotation might look like this:

——— QUOTATION ———

COOL SOCKS LIMITED

Unit 45 Elgar Estate, Broadfield, BR7 4ER
Tel 01908 765314 Fax 01908 765951 Email toni@cool.u-net.com
VAT REG GB 0745 4672 76

Trends 4 Friar Street Broadfield BR1 3RF	date 19 09 97

Thank you for your enquiry of 19 September 1997. We are pleased to quote as follows:

100 pairs Toebar socks (blue)@ £2.36 a pair, excluding VAT.

M Arnold

Sales Department

CASE STUDY

cool socks

PURCHASE ORDER – THE SOCKS ARE ORDERED

The buyer at Trends, once she has accepted the quoted price will post or fax the authorised purchase order shown below. The order will have been typed out in the office, or produced on a computer accounting program.

Note the following details:

- each purchase order has a specific reference number – this is useful for filing and quoting on later documents such as invoices and statements
- the reference number is an example of *coding* in accounting
- the catalogue number of the goods required is stated in the product code column – this number can be obtained from the supplier's catalogue – this number is a further example of coding
- the quantity of the goods required is stated in the quantity column – socks are obviously supplied in pairs!
- the description of the goods is set out in full
- the price does not need to be stated, although some purchase orders will include a price
- the purchase order is signed and dated by the person in charge of purchasing – without this authorisation the supplier is unlikely to supply the goods (the order will probably be returned!)
- if Trends had a separate warehouse for storage of its clothes the purchase order will state the address of the warehouse so that the goods could be sent there; in this case the socks will be delivered direct to the shop

---

Trends   **PURCHASE ORDER**

4 Friar Street
Broadfield
BR1 3RF
Tel 01908 761234 Fax 01908 761987 Email nic@trends.u-net.com
VAT REG GB 0745 8383 56

Cool Socks Limited, Unit 45 Elgar Estate, Broadfield, BR7 4ER	purchase order no 47609 date 25 09 97

product code	quantity	description
45B	100 pairs	Blue Toebar socks

AUTHORISED   signature................*D Signer*................date................*25/09/97*

DELIVERY NOTE – THE SOCKS ARE DELIVERED

A delivery note is despatched with the goods when the order is ready. It is normally either typed in the office or printed out by a computer accounting program, often at the same time as the invoice (see next page).

In this case, the delivery note travels with the socks, and a copy will be signed by Trends on receipt. Note the following details:

- the delivery note has a numerical reference, useful for filing and later reference if there is a query – this is an example of coding
- the method of delivery is stated – here the delivery is by parcel carrier
- the delivery note quotes the purchase order number – 47609 – this enables the buyer to 'tie up' the delivery with the original purchase order – this is another example of the use of coding
- the delivery note quotes
  - Cool Socks' catalogue reference 45B
  - the quantity supplied
  - the description of the goods

  these details will be checked against the goods themselves straightaway so that any discrepancies can be reported without delay
- no price is quoted on the delivery note – it is not relevant at this point
- the delivery note will be signed and dated by the person receiving the goods
- a signed copy of the delivery note is normally retained by the carrier as proof of delivery; this is so that the buyer cannot say at a later date "We are not paying for these goods, we never received them!"

DELIVERY NOTE

COOL SOCKS LIMITED

Unit 45 Elgar Estate, Broadfield, BR7 4ER
Tel 01908 765314 Fax 01908 765951 Email toni@cool.u-net.com
VAT REG GB 0745 4672 76

Trends 4 Friar Street Broadfield BR1 3RF	delivery note no delivery method your order date	68873 Lynx Parcels 47609 03 10 97

product code	quantity	description
45B	100 pairs	Blue Toebar socks

Received
signature.........*V Williams*.........name (capitals).*V WILLIAMS*....date...*5/10/97*

CASE STUDY

cool socks

INVOICE – THE SELLER REQUESTS PAYMENT

The invoice is the trading document which is sent by the seller to the buyer stating how much is owed by the buyer for a particular delivery of goods.

The invoice, like the delivery note, is prepared in the supplier's (seller's) office, and is either typed or produced on a computer printer using a computer accounting program. Invoices produced by different organisations will vary to some extent in terms of detail, but their basic layout will always be the same. The invoice prepared by Cool Socks Limited – illustrated on page 23 – is typical of a modern typed or computer printed document. An invoice will normally be printed as part of a multiple set of documents which might include the delivery note, possibly an advice note sent by post to the buyer, and always a copy invoice for the seller's own records. The copy invoice will normally be filed in numerical order (see 'references' below). If a computer accounting program is used, the invoice can, of course, be called up on screen, referenced by its invoice number.

Note the following details, and refer to the invoice on page 23.

addresses

The invoice shows the address:

- of the seller/supplier of the goods – Cool Socks Limited

- where the invoice should be sent – to Trends

- where the goods are to be sent – if it is different from the invoice address

references

There are a number of important references on the invoice:

- the numerical reference of the invoice itself – 787923

- the account number allocated to Trends by the seller – 3993 – possibly for use in the seller's computer accounting program

- the original reference number on the purchase order sent by Trends – 47609 – which will enable the shop to 'tie up' the invoice with the original order

- the VAT registration number (if the business is registered for VAT)

date

The date on the invoice is important because the payment date (here one month) is calculated from it. The invoice date is often described as the 'tax point' because it is the transaction date as far as VAT calculations are concerned, ie it is when the sale took place and the VAT was charged.

Note: VAT (Value Added Tax) is a tax on the supply of goods and services. At the time of writing the VAT rate is 17.5%.

the goods

As the invoice states the amount owing, it must specify accurately the goods supplied. The details – set out in columns in the body of the invoice – include:

- *product code* – this is the catalogue number which appeared on the original purchase order and on the delivery note
- *description* – the goods must be specified precisely
- *quantity* – this should agree with the quantity ordered
- *price* – this is the price of each unit shown in the next column
- *unit* is the way in which the unit is counted and charged for, eg
    - boxes of tights
    - single items, eg designer dresses
- *total* is the unit price multiplied by the number of units
- *discount %* is the percentage allowance (known as trade discount) given to customers who regularly deal with the supplier ie they receive a certain percentage (eg 10%) deducted from their bill; discounts are explained in more detail on page 26 – in this case no trade discount is given
- *net* is the amount due to the seller after deduction of trade discount, and before VAT is added on

totals and VAT

Further calculations are made in the box at the bottom of the invoice:

- *Goods Total* is the net amount due to the seller (the total of the net column)
- *Value Added Tax (VAT),* here calculated as 17.5% of the total after deduction of any cash discount. VAT is added to produce the invoice final total.
- Total is the VAT added to the Goods Total; it is the amount due to the seller

terms

The terms for payment are stated on the invoice. In this case these include:

- *Net monthly* – this means that full payment of the invoice should be made within a month of the invoice date
- *Carriage paid* means that the price of the goods includes delivery
- *E & OE* stands for 'errors and omissions excepted' which means that if there is a error or something left off the invoice by mistake, resulting in an incorrect final price, the supplier has the right to rectify the mistake and demand the correct amount

Other terms (not shown here) include:

- *COD* stands for 'cash on delivery' – payment is due when the goods are delivered
- *Cash Discount* – a further discount given when payment is made early, eg '2.5% cash discount for payment within 7 days'. See page 28 for further details
- *Ex-Works* – the price of the goods does not include delivery

INVOICE

COOL SOCKS LIMITED

Unit 45 Elgar Estate, Broadfield, BR7 4ER
Tel 01908 765314 Fax 01908 765951 Email toni@cool.u-net.com
VAT Reg GB 0745 4672 76

invoice to

Trends
4 Friar Street
Broadfield
BR1 3RG

invoice no	787923
account	3993
your reference	47609
date/tax point	03 10 97

deliver to

as above

product code	description	quantity	price	unit	total	discount %	net
45B	Blue toebar socks	100	2.36	pair	236.00	0.00	236.00

terms
Net monthly
Carriage paid
E & OE

goods total	236.00
VAT	41.30
TOTAL	277.30

CREDIT NOTE – A REFUND IS DUE TO THE BUYER

A *credit note* is a 'refund' document. It reduces the amount owed by the buyer. The goods, remember, have not yet been paid for. The credit note is prepared by the supplier and sent to the buyer. For example:

- the goods may have been damaged, lost in transit or they may be faulty
- not all the goods have been sent – this is referred to as 'shortages'
- the unit price on the invoice may be too high

In this Case Study, when the staff of Trends unpack the socks in the stock room they find that ten pairs are faulty. They telephone Cool Socks to report the problem and Cool Socks authorise the return of the socks for credit. These socks will be sent back to Cool Socks with a returns note (see page 47) asking for credit – ie a reduction in the bill for the 10 faulty pairs. Cool Socks will have to issue the credit note for £27.73 shown below. Note the following details:

- the invoice number of the original consignment is quoted
- the reason for the issue of the credit note is stated at the bottom of the credit note – here 'damaged' goods
- the details are otherwise exactly the same as on an invoice

---

CREDIT NOTE

COOL SOCKS LIMITED

Unit 45 Elgar Estate, Broadfield, BR7 4ER
Tel 01908 765314 Fax 01908 765951 Email toni@cool.u-net.com
VAT Reg GB 0745 4672 76

to

Trends
4 Friar Street
Broadfield
BR1 3RG

credit note no	12157
account	3993
your reference	47609
our invoice	787923
date/tax point	10 10 97

product code	description	quantity	price	unit	total	discount %	net
45B	Blue toebar socks	10	2.36	pair	23.60	0.00	23.60

REASON FOR CREDIT:

10 pairs of socks received damaged
(Your returns note no R/N 2384)

goods total	23.60
VAT	4.13
TOTAL	27.73

CASE STUDY

cool socks

STATEMENT – THE SELLER REQUESTS PAYMENT

A supplier will not normally expect a buyer to pay each individual invoice as soon as it is received: this could result in the buyer having to make a number of payments during the month. Instead, a *statement of account* is sent by the supplier to the buyer at the end of the month. This statement, which can be typed out, or printed by the seller's computer accounting program, shows what is owed by the buyer to the seller. It contains details of:

- any balances (amounts owing) at the beginning of the month
- payments received from the buyer (if any)
- invoices issued for goods supplied – the full amount due, including VAT
- refunds made on credit notes – including VAT
- the final amount due

The statement issued by Cool Socks to Trends for the period covering the sale and refund is shown below. You will see that it includes a balance owing ('b/f' means 'brought forward') on 1 October, a payment received to clear that balance, and then the invoice and credit note to Trends.

STATEMENT

COOL SOCKS LIMITED

Unit 45 Elgar Estate, Broadfield, BR7 4ER
Tel 01908 765314 Fax 01908 765951 Email toni@cool.u-net.com
VAT Reg GB 0745 4672 76

to

Trends 4 Friar Street Broadfield BR1 3RG	account 1040 date 31 10 97

date	details	debit	credit	balance
01 10 97	Balance b/f			1040.70
02 10 97	Payment received		1040.70	Nil
03 10 97	Invoice 787923	277.30		277.30
10 10 97	Credit note 12157		27.73	249.57

	AMOUNT NOW DUE	249.57

DISCOUNTS

In the Case Study the invoice (see page 23 and also the opposite page) showed a column for *trade discount*.

We also saw that the terms at the bottom of the invoice can allow for *cash discount*.

We will now explain these terms and show how the discount is calculated.

trade discount

It is common practice for suppliers to give businesses that order from them on a regular basis an agreed discount – a percentage reduction in the invoiced amount. This is commonly known as *trade discount* because it applies to businesses rather than to the general public. Discount may also be given by sellers to buyers who purchase in large quantities. Discount may also be offered as a 'carrot' to new buyers whose custom the seller is trying to attract.

In the example on the next page 10% discount has been given to Trends. Note how the discount percentage is shown in the discount column and the net amount is the amount after deduction of the discount.

The calculations on the invoice are as follows:

Step 1	Calculate the total price before discount 100 x £2.36 = £236.00
Step 2	Calculate the trade discount £236.00 x 10% (ie 10/100) = £23.60
Step 3	Calculate the net price before VAT £236.00 - £23.60 = £212.40
Step 4	Calculate the VAT £212.40 x 17.5% (ie17.5/100) = £37.17
Step 5	Calculate the total invoice price £212.40 + £37.17 = £249.57

INVOICE

COOL SOCKS LIMITED

Unit 45 Elgar Estate, Broadfield, BR7 4ER
Tel 01908 765314 Fax 01908 765951 Email toni@cool.u-net.com
VAT Reg GB 0745 4672 76

invoice to

| Trends |
| 4 Friar Street |
| Broadfield |
| BR1 3RG |

invoice no	787923
account	3993
your reference	47609
date/tax point	03 10 97

deliver to

as above

product code	description	quantity	price	unit	total	discount %	net
45B	Blue toebar socks	100	2.36	pair	236.00	10.00	212.40

terms
Net monthly
Carriage paid
E & OE

goods total	212.40
VAT	37.17
TOTAL	249.57

an invoice with 10% trade discount deducted

cash discount

Cash discount is a discount offered by the seller to the buyer to encourage the buyer to settle up straightaway or in a short space of time rather than waiting the thirty or more days specified on the invoice. For example, the terms on the bottom of the invoice may include the phrase: *"Cash discount of 2.5% for settlement within seven days"* This means that the seller will allow 2.5% off the net invoice price (ie the price before VAT is added on) if the invoice is settled within seven days of the invoice date.

There are two important points to remember:

1   VAT charged on an invoice with cash discount offered is calculated *on the invoice amount after deduction of cash discount.*

2   The invoice total is the sum of this reduced amount of VAT and *the goods total before deduction of cash discount.*

If we take the Cool Socks invoice on the previous page, the calculations for a cash discount of 2.5% are as follows:

Step 1	Calculate the total price before trade discount (as before) 100 x £2.36 = £236.00
Step 2	Calculate the trade discount (as before) £236.00 x 10% (ie 10/100) = £23.60
Step 3	Calculate the net price/Goods Total (as before) £236.00 - £23.60 = £212.40
Step 4	NOW calculate the cash discount £212.40 x 2.5% (ie 2.5/100) = £5.31
Step 5	Calculate the reduced goods total (this is not written on the invoice) £212.40 - £5.31 = £207.09
Step 6	Calculate the VAT on this lower amount £207.09 x 17.5% (ie17.5/100) = £36.24
Step 7	Calculate the total invoice price (using the goods total before deduction of cash discount) £212.40 + £36.24 = £248.64

INVOICE

COOL SOCKS LIMITED

Unit 45 Elgar Estate, Broadfield, BR7 4ER
Tel 01908 765314 Fax 01908 765951 Email toni@cool.u-net.com
VAT Reg GB 0745 4672 76

invoice to

```
Trends
4 Friar Street
Broadfield
BR1 3RG
```

invoice no	787923
account	3993
your reference	47609
date/tax point	03 10 97

deliver to

```
as above
```

product code	description	quantity	price	unit	total	discount %	net
45B	Blue toebar socks	100	2.36	pair	236.00	10.00	212.40

terms

2.5% cash discount for settlement within 7 days, otherwise net monthly
Carriage paid
E & OE

goods total	212.40
VAT	36.24
TOTAL	248.64

an invoice with 10% trade discount deducted and 2.5% cash discount allowed for quick settlement

VALUE ADDED TAX (VAT)

VAT (Value Added Tax) is a government tax on the selling price charged to buyers at every level of sales, from the first supplier to the final consumer.

As we have seen on some of the business documents illustrated in this chapter, VAT is added to the purchase price of items sold. VAT is a tax on the consumer and, along with income tax, is an important source of revenue for the government.

registering for VAT

In Britain most businesses with a sales turnover (ie the total amount of sales in a given period) of more than a certain figure (increased from time-to-time by the government's budget) must be registered for VAT. The figure set in November 1996 was £47,000.

Once registered, a business is issued with a VAT registration number which must be quoted on all invoices and on other business documents. It charges VAT at the standard rate (currently 17.5 per cent) on all taxable supplies, ie whenever it sells goods, or supplies a service. From the supplier's viewpoint the tax so charged is known as *output tax*.

Businesses registered for VAT must pay to the VAT authorities (H M Customs and Excise Department):

• the amount of VAT collected on sales (output tax)

• less the amount of VAT charged to them (input tax) on all taxable supplies bought in

If the amount of input tax is larger than the output tax, the business claims a refund of the difference from H M Customs and Excise.

Every three months a form known as a VAT return (Form VAT 100) has to be completed, although some smaller businesses submit a VAT return on an annual basis. Payment of VAT due (if the business is not claiming a refund) is made with the VAT return.

zero-rated and exempt supplies

A number of items are zero-rated and no tax is charged when they are supplied: for example, food and children's clothing are zero-rated.

Some goods and services (such as postal services, loans of money, sales or lettings of land) are neither standard-rated nor zero-rated for VAT: instead they are exempt. The effect of this is that the supplier of such goods cannot charge VAT on outputs (as is the case with zero-rated goods) but cannot claim back all the tax which has been paid on inputs.

VAT – a tax on the final consumer

VAT is a tax which is paid by the final consumer of the goods. If we take, for, example, a member of the public buying a computer for £705, the amount paid includes VAT of £105 (ie 17.5% of £600). The buyer stands the cost of the VAT, but the VAT is actually *paid* to H M Customs & Excise by all those involved in the manufacturing and selling process. This procedure is illustrated by the flow chart shown below. You will see that the right hand column shows the amount of VAT paid to the Customs & Excise at each stage in the process.

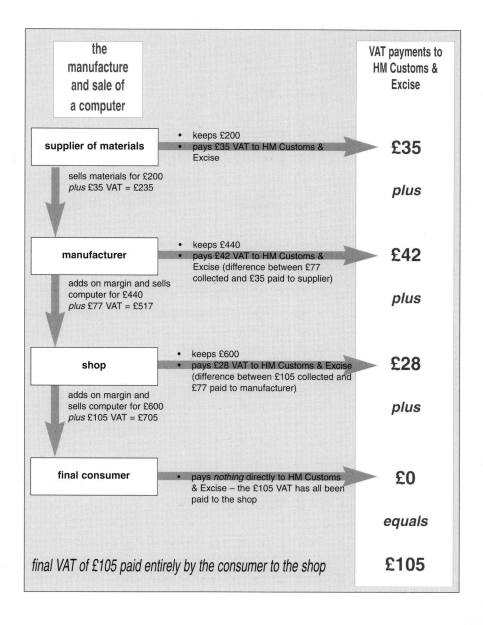

the manufacture and sale of a computer

VAT payments to HM Customs & Excise

supplier of materials
- keeps £200
- pays £35 VAT to HM Customs & Excise

£35

sells materials for £200
plus £35 VAT = £235

plus

manufacturer
- keeps £440
- pays £42 VAT to HM Customs & Excise (difference between £77 collected and £35 paid to supplier)

£42

adds on margin and sells computer for £440
plus £77 VAT = £517

plus

shop
- keeps £600
- pays £28 VAT to HM Customs & Excise (difference between £105 collected and £77 paid to manufacturer)

£28

adds on margin and sells computer for £600
plus £105 VAT = £705

plus

final consumer
- pays *nothing* directly to HM Customs & Excise – the £105 VAT has all been paid to the shop

£0

equals

final VAT of £105 paid entirely by the consumer to the shop

£105

VAT records

Organisations must keep careful records of VAT paid and collected. This means filing documents such as invoices and credit notes for a minimum period of six years. H M Customs & Excise VAT inspectors visit businesses from time to time to ensure that:

- VAT is being charged and claimed correctly
- there are no VAT 'fiddles' taking place
- VAT records are being maintained correctly

If, for example, a business has been trading and not charging VAT, the VAT authorities can claim back payment of all the tax that should have been paid. Traders have been put out of business in this way because they have not been able to afford the VAT due.

some VAT calculations

You may be asked to carry out a variety of calculations involving VAT. Here are some of the more common ones.

what is the VAT to be charged?

If you need to work out the VAT on a given amount you apply the formula:

$$\text{amount} \times \frac{17.5 \text{ (ie the VAT rate)}}{100} = \text{VAT payable}$$

VAT chargeable on £100 is therefore $£100 \times \frac{17.5}{100} = £17.50$

what is the VAT exclusive amount?

If you are given a total amount, for an example a shop till receipt which does not show the VAT amount, you may need to work out both the VAT content and also the amount before VAT is added (the 'VAT exclusive' amount). The formula for working out the amount before VAT is added is

$$\text{total amount including VAT} \times \frac{100}{117.5} = \text{amount excluding VAT}$$

The VAT exclusive amount in a receipt for £117.50 is therefore

$$£117.50 \times \frac{100}{117.50} = £100$$

A quick way to calculate the VAT exclusive amount on a calculator is to divide the total amount by 1.175.

VAT amounts – rounding down

When calculating VAT, the VAT amounts should always be rounded *down* to the nearest penny. VAT amounts should not be rounded up.

AUTHORISING INVOICES

bad debt problems

All businesses like to sell goods and services because sales lead to profits. It is important however that sales are made to customers who will be able to pay their invoices. If a customer cannot pay its invoices – perhaps because it has gone 'bust' – the seller loses the money, which becomes a *bad debt* which will reduce its profits. A seller can help to avoid this unfortunate situation by means of *credit control*. We will deal with this in detail in Chapter 9. At this stage you should appreciate that credit control involves:

• 'vetting' new buyers

• chasing up buyers who do not pay their invoices on time

• setting up credit limits for buyers

We will now explain credit limits.

credit limits

A credit limit of a customer is the maximum amount which the seller will allow the customer to owe at any one time.

Part of the accounting control system of a business is to set credit limits for its established customers and to establish limits for new customers. Each time therefore that an invoice is issued, a check should be made against the credit limit of that customer.

authorisation of invoices

Most invoices issued will be within the credit limit and processed with the authority of the person in charge of invoicing. What if the credit limit will be exceeded? No business is going to be foolish enough to refuse to supply a good customer. It may be that a cheque will soon come in from the buyer, or the amount involved is relatively small. In these cases the invoice will need authorisation from a more senior person in the accounts department. It is quite possible that a credit limit may have to be raised if a customer is buying more goods or services, and, of course, is paying invoices on time.

checking invoices

Few things are more annoying to a buyer than an incorrect invoice – the wrong goods, the wrong price, the wrong discount, and so on. It wastes the buyer's time and often leads to an adjusting credit note being issued. It is essential that the following details are checked by the seller before invoices are sent out:

- is the correct customer being invoiced? – there are often customers with similar names
- are the correct goods being sent? – the product coding on the purchase order must be checked carefully against the description – it is quite possible that the buyer has quoted an incorrect code!
- is the quantity correct?
- are the goods being sent to the correct place? – sometimes the delivery addresses can be different from the address normally held on file
- is the price right?
- is the discount allowed to the customer (if any) right? – do any special terms apply?
- are the calculations on the invoice correct? – this is especially relevant to invoices which are not produced on a computer

checking invoices – manual accounting

As you will see from the above list, the person processing the invoice will need to consult:

- the purchase order (this is very important)
- the seller's own record of any price quoted (this may be as simple as looking at a catalogue or stock list)
- the seller's file record of the buyer (which will normally give the credit limit and the discount allowed)
- a calculator!

checking and coding – computer accounting

Clearly, if the business uses a computer, many of these processes, particularly the calculations, will be automated. If a computer is used, *checking of coding* will be very important. There will be codes for

- the buyer (which will bring up the buyer's address on the invoice screen)
- the buyer's purchase order number (normally input in a 'reference' field on the invoice screen)
- the seller's product code (which is normally quoted in the catalogue and which will be input on the invoice screen to bring up the product details and price)

You will see from this that computerised invoicing is much easier than producing the documents manually. Accurate checking, however, is critically important.

- When a business sells goods or services on credit it will deal with a number of business documents, including the purchase order, the delivery note, the invoice, the credit note and the statement (see key terms below).

- The seller of the goods or services will request payment by means of an invoice and then remind the buyer by means of a regular statement (normally monthly).

- Any refund due to the buyer will be acknowledged by means of a credit note.

- All documents and goods and services are normally coded (given a numerical code) both for reference purposes and also for input into the accounting systems of the seller and the buyer.

- All documents should be checked carefully both by the originator and by the recipient to make sure that the right goods or services have been supplied, and at the right price. It is essential that items such as discounts, VAT and totals are calculated correctly.

- All documents generated in the sales transaction are normally filed away for reference purposes.

- Some documents, eg the purchase order, will need to be authorised before issue – this is part of the control system of the accounting function.

purchase order	a document issued and authorised by the buyer of goods and services, sent to the seller, indicating the goods or services required
delivery note	a document sent by the seller with the goods
invoice	a document issued by the seller of goods or services indicating the amount owing and the required payment date
credit note	a document issued by the seller of the goods or services reducing the amount owed by the buyer
statement	a document issued by the seller to the buyer summarising invoices and credit notes issued and payments received
trade discount	a percentage reduction in the selling price given to the buyer because of the trading relationship
cash discount	a percentage reduction in the selling price given to the buyer if the buyer pays within a short space of time
Value Added Tax (VAT)	a government tax on spending, calculated on invoices and credit notes

STUDENT ACTIVITIES

2.1 What type of business document would normally be used when goods are sold on credit:

(a) to accompany goods from the seller to the buyer?

(b) to accompany faulty goods sent back by the buyer?

(c) as a formal notification of the amount owed?

(d) to remind the buyer of the amount owed to the seller?

(e) as a formal notification from the seller of a refund made to the buyer?

(f) to order the goods from the seller in the first place?

2.2 Compudisk sells computer floppy disks and has a special sales offer. A box of ten formatted disks normally sells at £8.00 (excluding VAT). Compudisc is offering to give a 20% discount for orders of ten boxes or more. It receives in the post one morning the following orders:

(a) 20 boxes ordered by Osborne Electronics Limited

(b) 50 boxes ordered by Helfield College

(c) 5 boxes ordered by Jim Masters

(d) 1000 boxes ordered by Trigger Trading Limited

Calculate in each case

- the total cost before discount

- the discount

- the cost after discount

- the VAT at the current rate

- the total cost

2.3 Recalculate the totals in Question 2.2 allowing for a cash discount of 2.5%.

2.4 Explain what is meant by the invoice terms 'net monthly'and 'E & OE' and 'carriage paid.'

2.5 Give three examples of coding on business documents. Why is coding important?

2.6 You work as one of three assistants in an accounts office. Your supervisor is off sick. You receive an urgent and large purchase order and find that the product code and goods description do not match up. The goods have to be despatched on the same day. What *exactly* is the problem and what would you do about it?

2.7 • Check the invoice extracts shown below.

• State what is wrong with them.

• Calculate the correct final totals.

Note: VAT is always rounded down to the nearest penny.

invoice (a)

description	quantity	price	total	discount %	net
Cotton shirts (red)	10	9.50	95.00	20	85.50

goods total	85.50
VAT @ 17.5%	14.96
TOTAL	100.45

invoice (b)

description	quantity	price	total	discount %	net
'Crazy Surfin' T-shirts (yellow)	50	5.00	225.00	10	202.50

goods total	202.50
VAT @ 17.5%	35.44
TOTAL	237.94

2.8 The following amounts include VAT. What is the VAT content and the amount before VAT is added in each case? Remember that VAT must be rounded down to the nearest penny.

(a) £47.00

(b) £40,670.98

(c) £39.98

(d) £94.00

(e) 47p

(f) £1.20

3 DOCUMENTS – BUYING ON CREDIT

this chapter covers . . .

The last chapter looked at the selling of goods and services on credit from the point of view of the supplier. This chapter examines the transaction from the point of view of the purchaser and describes the procedures and documents involved. The chapter covers the areas of:

- the use of business documents – purchase order, invoice, delivery note, goods received note, returns note, credit note, statement, remittance advice

- the checking of sthe upplier's documents against the purchaser's documents

- the calculation of document totals, including discounts and VAT

- the coding and filing of documents

- the checking and authorisation of documents and dealing with discrepancies

NVQ PERFORMANCE CRITERIA COVERED

unit 2: RECORDING AND ACCOUNTING FOR CREDIT TRANSACTIONS
element 2
process documents relating to goods and services received on credit

- ❏ suppliers' invoices and credit notes are correctly checked against ordering documentation and evidence that goods/services have been received
- ❏ suppliers' invoices and credit notes are correctly coded
- ❏ calculations on suppliers' invoices and credit notes are correct
- ❏ documentation is correctly filed
- ❏ the organisation's procedures and timescales are observed
- ❏ discrepancies, unusual features or queries are identified and either resolved or referred to the appropriate person

BUSINESS DOCUMENTS – THE PURCHASER'S POINT OF VIEW

When a business *sells* goods and services its main concern is that it provides what has been ordered and that it gets paid on time. When a business, on the other hand, *orders* goods and services it will want to ensure that:

• the correct goods and services are provided

• they are provided on time

• they are charged at the right price

Businesses vary in the way they achieve this. The normal procedure is for the purchaser to accumulate on file – normally stapled together – a series of documents which will be checked against each other as they are produced or come into the office, eg copy purchase order, delivery note, invoice, a copy of any returns note, any credit note, statement, and so on. These will often be kept in a 'pending invoices' file until payment is finally made, when they will go into a 'paid invoices' file. The diagram below shows this flow of documents.

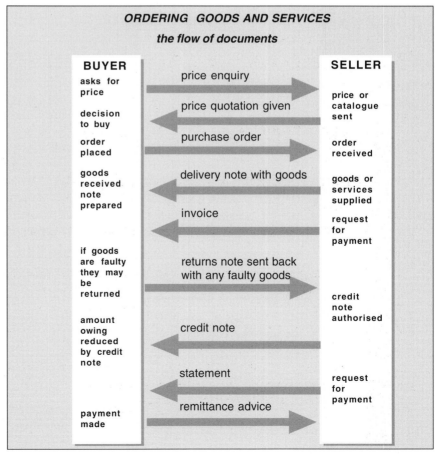

ORDERING GOODS AND SERVICES

the flow of documents

BUYER		SELLER
asks for price	price enquiry →	
		price or catalogue sent
decision to buy	← price quotation given	
order placed	purchase order →	order received
goods received note prepared	← delivery note with goods	goods or services supplied
	← invoice	request for payment
if goods are faulty they may be returned	returns note sent back with any faulty goods →	credit note authorised
amount owing reduced by credit note	← credit note	
	← statement	request for payment
payment made	remittance advice →	

AUTHORISATION OF PURCHASE ORDERS

A purchaser, once the price of the product(s) has been agreed, normally issues a *purchase order*. It is essential that this purchase order is *authorised* by the appropriate person. This authority is shown on the document in the form of a signature and date. Some businesses will insist on more senior staff in the buying department signing larger orders. A business will keep a copy of every purchase order it issues and will often file them in numerical order (each will have a numerical code). The purchase order from the Case Study in the last chapter is shown here.

It should be noted that a business may not *always* issue a purchase order: if the order is small, or if the buyer knows the seller well, the order may be made by telephone.

Trends		**PURCHASE ORDER**

4 Friar Street
Broadfield
BR1 3RF
Tel 01908 761234 Fax 01908 761987 Email nic@trends.u-net.com
VAT REG GB 0745 8383 56

Cool Socks Limited, Unit 45 Elgar Estate, Broadfield, BR7 4ER	purchase order no 47609
	date 25 09 97

product code	quantity	description
45B	100 pairs	Blue Toebar socks

AUTHORISED   signature...... *D Signer* ....date.......... *25/09/97*

CHECKS AND CONTROLS: PURCHASES

When an organisation purchases goods, it is important that the accounting system includes checks and controls to ensure that:

- the correct goods have been received in an acceptable condition
- the correct terms and price have been applied
- the goods are only paid for once (paying for goods twice does occur!)

The three main documents involved in the checking process are the *purchase order* (a copy of which will be kept by the purchaser), the *delivery note* and the *invoice,* received from the seller.

You should note that some organisations use an internal document known as a *goods received note* on which the buyer records the receipt of the goods and the details set out on the delivery note or advice note sent by the supplier. Most businesses, however, rely on the delivery note as a record of the goods received, and we will concentrate on this document in this chapter.

CHECKING INVOICE, DELIVERY NOTE AND PURCHASE ORDER

The checking process involves two separate procedures carried out in the Accounts Department:

- checking the three documents – the invoice, delivery note and copy purchase order – with each other
- checking the calculations on the invoice

We will deal with these in separate stages, starting with the checking of the three documents:

check 1 – goods received and delivery note

When the goods are received they should be checked against the delivery note – the quantities should be counted and the condition of the goods checked. Any discrepancies or damage should be notified immediately to the supplier, usually on a *discrepancy note*, so that replacements can be sent or the buyer credited with the value of the missing or damaged goods (ie the bill reduced by the issue of a credit note).

check 2 – delivery note and purchase order

The delivery note should then be checked in the Accounts Department against a copy of the original purchase order. The illustration on the next page shows the details that should be checked:

- catalogue number (ie the supplier's catalogue) – has the right type of goods been delivered?
- quantity – has the right number been delivered?
- specifications – are the goods delivered to the same specifications as those ordered
- purchase order reference number – do the goods relate to the purchase order being examined?

If all is in order, the delivery note will be filed with the copy purchase order under the purchase order reference number, ready for checking against the invoice when it arrives.

check 3 – invoice, delivery note and purchase order

When the invoice arrives from the supplier, it should be checked against the delivery note and the purchase order (which should be filed together). The specific points to look at are:

- *invoice and delivery note*
  Are the details of the goods on the invoice and delivery note the same? The product code, description and quantity of the goods should agree.

- *invoice and purchase order*

  Has the correct price been charged? The unit price quoted by the supplier or obtained from the supplier's catalogue will be stated on the purchase order, and should agree with the unit price stated on the invoice. If there is a difference, it should be queried with the supplier.

student task

Look at the invoice below and the purchase order and delivery note on the next page. They all relate to the same transaction. Can you spot any discrepancies? The answers are set out at the bottom of the page.

━━ INVOICE ━━

Stourford Office Supplies
Unit 12, Avon Industrial Estate, Stourford SF5 6TD
Tel 0807 765434 Fax 0807 765123
VAT Reg 0745 4672 76

invoice to

| Martley Machine Rental Ltd |
| 67 Broadgreen Road |
| Martley |
| MR6 7TR |

Invoice No	652771
Account	MAR435
Date/tax point	30 March 19-9
Your Reference	47780

deliver to

as above

product code	description	quantity	price	unit	total	disc %	net
3564748	80 gsm white Supalaser	15	3.50	ream	52.00	0	52.00

	GOODS TOTAL	52.00
Terms	SUBTOTAL	52.00
Net monthly	VAT	9.01
Carriage paid	TOTAL	42.99
E & OE		

The purchase order and delivery note agree, but the invoice has a number of discrepancies:

- the order reference differs (47700 and 47780)
- the product code differs (3564749 and 3564748)
- the product description differs (100 gsm and 80 gsm)
- the price differs (£4.00 and £3.50 per ream)

PURCHASE ORDER

MARTLEY MACHINE RENTAL LTD

67 Broadgreen Road
Martley MR6 7TR
Tel 090655 6576 Fax 090655 6342

```
Stourford Office Supplies          No          47700
Unit 12                            Date        13 March 19-9
Avon Industrial Estate             Delivery    to above address
Stourford SF5 6TD
```

catalogue	quantity	description	price
3564749	15 reams	100gsm white Supalaser paper	£4.00 per ream

authorised   signature......*C J Farmer*...................   date..*13 March 19-9*

catalogue number	quantity	specifications	purchase order reference number

━━ DELIVERY NOTE ━━

Stourford Office Supplies
Unit 12, Avon Industrial Estate, Stourford SF5 6TD
Tel 0807 765434 Fax 0807 765123

```
Martley Machine Rental Ltd        Delivery Note No   26754
67 Broadgreen Road                Date               26 March 19-9
Martley                           Order No           47700
MR6 7TR                           Delivery           Van Delivery
```

product code	quantity	description
3564749	15 reams	100 gsm white Supalaser paper

received
signature......*G Hughes*......................print name (capitals)......*G HUGHES*..........
          30 March 19-9

date...

details to check on the purchase order and delivery note

CHECKING THE CALCULATIONS ON THE INVOICE

Another important step is for the Accounts Department to check the calculations on the invoice. If any one of these calculations is incorrect, the final total will be wrong, and the invoice will have to be queried with the supplier, so accurate checking is essential. The checks to be made are:

quantity x unit price
The quantity of the items multiplied by the unit price must be correct. The result – the total price or *price extension* – is used for the calculation of any trade discount applicable.

trade discount
Any trade discount – an allowance given to approved customers – must be deducted from the total price worked out. Trade discount is calculated as a percentage of the total price, eg a trade discount of 20% on a total price of £150 is calculated

$$£150 \ x \ \frac{20}{100} \ = \ £30$$

The net price charged (before VAT) is therefore

$$£150 \ - \ £30 \ = \ £120 \ = \text{net total}$$

cash discount
Any cash discount – an allowance sometimes given for immediate payment – is deducted from the net total before VAT is calculated. Cash discount, when it is offered, is usually included as one of the terms at the bottom of the invoice. It is not normally, however, deducted from the invoice total, so it will be up to the buyer to settle early and to adjust the invoice total down.

VAT
Value Added Tax is currently charged at the rate of 17.5%. To calculate VAT, the total after the deduction of any cash discount is treated as follows

$$\text{Total} \ x \ \frac{17.5}{100} \ = \ \text{VAT amount}$$

If you are using a calculator, all you need to do is to multiply the total by 0.175 to give the VAT, which is then added to the total.

Remember that any fractions of a penny are ignored. For example if the total price is £55.75, the VAT will be

£55.75 x 0.175 = £9.75625

£9.75625 then loses the last three digits – the fraction of a penny – to become £9.75.

For the purpose of your studies you must assume that the calculations on all invoices must be checked. In practice, invoicing programs perform the calculations automatically, and in principle should be correct.

Now check the calculations on the invoice on page 42. You should be able to detect a large number of errors:

*   quantity x unit price should be £52.50, not £52.00

*   the VAT is wrongly calculated £52.00 x 0.175 = £9.10, not £9.01 (it would be £9.18 on £52.50)

*   the VAT has been deducted instead of added: the total should be £52.50 + £9.18 = £61.68

AUTHORISING THE INVOICE FOR PAYMENT

In most organisations checked invoices are passed to the person in the Accounts Department who deals with making payments to suppliers. First, however, an invoice will have to be *authorised* for payment. It will then, as long as no credit notes are due, be paid after the statement arrives and the date for payment is reached. Clearly only correct invoices can be passed forward for payment. Invoices with errors will need to be queried with the supplier.

authorising correct invoices

When an invoice is checked and found to be correct, the person carrying out the check will usually mark the document and authorise it for payment. This authorisation can take a number of forms:

*   the checker can initial and date the invoice, and tick it or write 'pay' as an authorisation

*   the organisation may have a special rubber stamp which can be used in the authorisation process (see next page)

This procedure of authorisation obviously helps the efficiency of the organisation:

*   only authorised invoices will be passed forward in the Accounts Department for payment

*   the checker's initials will be there in case of any future query on the invoice, eg an undetected error

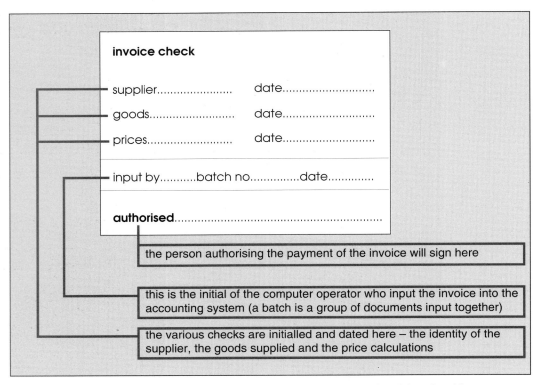

authorisation stamp placed on an invoice received for checking

GOODS RECEIVED NOTES (GRNS)

As mentioned earlier in the chapter some purchasers use a document known as a *goods received note* (GRN). This is essentially a checklist on which is recorded the name of the supplier and details of the goods ordered. As the goods are received and are checked in, the GRN is ticked and initialled to indicate that the right quantity and description of goods have been received. The GRN forms part of the payment authorisation process: only when a completed and correct GRN is approved by the Accounts Department can the relevant invoice be paid. As you will see, the GRN fulfils the same checking function as the entries on the invoice authorisation stamp shown above.

Shown on the next page is the goods received note relating to the Case Study in the last chapter in which the shop 'Trends' ordered some fashion socks from Cool Socks Limited. Note that the receipt of the 100 pairs of socks has been recorded, and also the fact that 10 pairs are damaged.

Trends   **GOODS RECEIVED NOTE**

Supplier

Cool Socks Limited, Unit 45 Elgar Estate, Broadfield, BR7 4ER	GRN no date	1871 06 10 97

quantity	description	order number
100 pairs	Blue Toebar socks	47609

carrier	Lynx Parcels	consignment no	8479347

received by	*V Williams*	checked by	*R Patel*

condition of goods	good condition damaged ✓ (10 pairs) shortages	copies to Buyer Accounts ✓ Stockroom

RETURNS

As you can see from the goods received note above, a purchaser will sometimes have to return faulty or incorrect goods and request a credit note from the seller to reduce the amount owed. Note that a purchaser should *never* for this reason change figures on an invoice – this would cause havoc with the accounting records! When the goods are sent back – the socks in the case of the Case Study – they will be accompanied by a *returns note*.

When the goods are received back by the seller and checked, a *credit note* will be issued to reduce the amount owing. This is illustrated on the next page.

Trends   **RETURNS NOTE**

4 Friar Street
Broadfield
BR1 3RF
Tel 01908 761234 Fax 01908 761987 Email nic@trends.u-net.com
VAT REG GB 0745 8383 56

Cool Socks Limited, Unit 45 Elgar Estate, Broadfield, BR7 4ER	returns note no date	2384 7 10 97

product code	quantity	description
45B	10 pairs	Blue Toebar socks

REASON FOR RETURN: *faulty goods; credit requested*

signature.........*R SINGH*..date......*07/10/97*............

```
──────────────────── CREDIT NOTE ────────────────────
                  COOL SOCKS LIMITED
                Unit 45 Elgar Estate, Broadfield, BR7 4ER
        Tel 01908 765314  Fax 01908 765951 Email toni@cool.u-net.com
                      VAT REG GB 0745 4672 76
```

to		
Trends	credit note no	12157
4 Friar Street	account	3993
Broadfield	your reference	47609
BR1 3RF	our invoice	787923
	date/tax point	10 10 97

product code	description	quantity	price	unit	total	discount %	net
45B	Blue Toebar socks	10	2.36	pair	23.60	0.00	23.60

Reason for credit
10 pairs of socks received damaged
(Your returns note no. R/N 2384)

GOODS TOTAL	23.60
SUBTOTAL	23.60
VAT	4.13
TOTAL	27.73

CHECKING THE CREDIT NOTE

When the credit note is received by the purchaser it will have to be checked carefully to make sure that the quantity of goods, the price, discount and VAT are correctly calculated. If it is correct, the document will be filed with (stapled to) the appropriate copy purchase order, delivery note, invoice and copy returns note, awaiting the arrival of the statement.

PAYING SUPPLIERS' INVOICES

There are two common ways of setting up a system for paying invoices:

1   Many businesses pay on receipt of a statement, not on receipt of the invoice. As most statements tend to go out at the end of the month, paying of invoices often then becomes a monthly routine. In this case payments due can be put on diary for a set day of the month, eg the 27th.

2   Some businesses will pay invoices after the maximum number of days allowed – normally 30 days. In this case a diary system will be set up and the checked/authorised invoices filed in payment date order.

MAKING PAYMENT – REMITTANCE ADVICES

Although making payments is covered in full in Chapter 14, it should be mentioned here that the cycle of documents is completed by the issue of a remittance advice by the supplier when payments is made.

Payment can either be made by *cheque* or by *electronic transfer* through the bank using a system known as BACS (Bankers Automated Clearing Services).

Illustrated below are remittance advices for both types of payment.

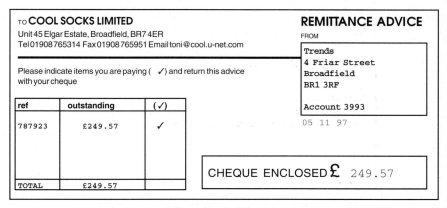

remittance advice sent with a cheque payment

```
BACS REMITTANCE ADVICE

                                                    FROM: Trends
                                                      4 Friar Street
                                                         Broadfield
                                                            BR1 3RF

TO: Cool Socks Limited
Unit 45 Elgar Estate,
Broadfield, BR7 4ER                                 05 11 97

Your ref    Our ref                                        Amount

787923      47609        BACS TRANSFER                      249.57


                                            Total           249.57

THIS HAS BEEN PAID BY BACS CREDIT TRANSFER DIRECTLY INTO YOUR BANK ACCOUNT
ALBION BANK NO 11451226 SORT CODE 90 47 17
```

remittance advice sent to advise of a BACS payment

- A business purchasing goods or services will request the goods or services by means of an authorised purchase order.

- A business purchasing goods or services will need to ensure that the right goods have been supplied, at the right price, before payment is made.

- When the goods arrive they should be checked against the delivery note which accompanies the goods. The delivery note is then checked against the purchase order and attached to it.

- Some businesses will prepare a goods received note to check off the goods when they arrive and to record any subsequent returns.

- When the invoice arrives it will be checked against the purchase order and delivery note and attached to the documents.

- The calculations and terms on the invoice will be checked carefully, particularly if it is not a computerised invoice.

- If any goods have to be returned they will be sent back with a returns note.

- Any credit notes issued to the purchaser (including any for returned goods) will have to be checked carefully on receipt.

- When the invoice and any relevant credit notes have been found to be correct the invoice can be authorised for payment.

- Authorised invoices are filed in a diary system until the appropriate payment date (normally after receipt of a statement).

- Payment is normally advised to the seller by means of a remittance advice.

purchase order	a document issued and authorised by the buyer of goods and services, sent to the seller, indicating the goods or services required
delivery note	a document listing and accompanying the goods sent to the purchaser
goods received note	a document sometimes used by purchasers to record receipt of stock and any returns made
invoice	a document issued by the seller of goods or services to the purchaser indicating the amount owing and the required payment date
returns note	a document sent with goods returned by the purchaser to the seller, requesting credit
credit note	a document issued by the seller of the goods or services reducing the amount owed by the buyer

statement

a document issued by the seller to the buyer summarising invoices and credit notes issued and payments received

remittance advice

a document sent by the purchaser to the seller advising the amount and date of payment of money due

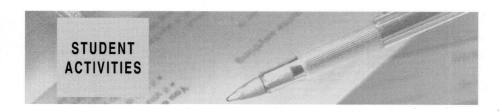

STUDENT ACTIVITIES

3.1 What type of business document would normally be used when goods are bought on credit

(a) to order the goods from the seller?

(b) to accompany goods sent from the seller?

(c) to record the receipt and any return of goods at the buyer's premises?

(d) to advise the seller of the amount of money being paid on account?

(e) to advise the buyer in the first instance of the amount of money due on an order?

(f) to accompany faulty goods sent back by the buyer?

3.2 An unsigned purchase order is sent out to a supplier. What is likely to happen to it, and why?

3.3 Which documents would normally be checked by the buyer against the purchase order? Answer (a) or (b) or (c) or (d).

(a) the delivery note and the returns note

(b) the invoice and the returns note

(c) the goods received note and the remittance advice

(d) the delivery note and the invoice

3.4 What is the difference between a returns note and a credit note?

3.5 What would be the problem if the seller of goods accidentally forgot to include the normal trade discount on an invoice to a regular customer? What should the customer do?

3.6 Eduservice, an educational consultancy, ordered some computer disks from Compusupply Limited on purchase order 53659 for courses it runs at Itec College in Broadfield. The goods were delivered to the Eduservice office at 45 The Ridings, Broadfield on 3 February.

You work in the Eduservice office as an administrative assistant. Part of your job is to deal with all the documents, including the accounting work.

You have today (February 4 1997) received an invoice from Compusupply. You are not happy with the service you are receiving from this company and are thinking of going elsewhere for a supplier.

Shown below and on the next page are:
- a list of Compusupply customer discounts (for information purposes)
- the original purchase order
- the invoice you receive

You are to write a letter to Compusupply setting out the errors that have been made. Address the letter to the Sales Manager and sign it with your own name as an administrative assistant. The date is 4 February 1997.

Compusupply – Customer discounts and credit limits (extracts)

Customer	Discount (%)	Credit limit (£)
Donmar Estates	15	12,000
Dugdale, E	10	5,000
Easifit Ltd	15	10,000
Eduservice	15	12,500
Estima Designs	10	5,000

EDUSERVICE

PURCHASE ORDER

45 The Ridings
Broadfield
BR2 3TR
Tel 01908 333691

TO

Compusupply Limited
Unit 17 Elgar Estate,
Broadfield, BR7 4ER

purchase order no   53659

date   27 January 1997

product code	quantity	description
4573	10	Zap 100MB Storage disks @ £95 per box of 10

Authorised   signature....*J Wales*...date.*27.1.97*..................

INVOICE

COMPUSUPPLY LIMITED
Unit 17 Elgar Estate, Broadfield, BR7 4ER
Tel 01908 765756 Fax 01908 765777 Email rob@compusupply.u-net.com
VAT Reg GB 0745 4689 13

invoice to

Eduservice
45 The Ridings
Broadfield
BR2 3TR

invoice no	20424
account	242
your reference	53659
date/tax point	30.01.1997

deliver to

J Wales
Itec College
Fairacre
Broadfield BR5 7YT

product code	description	quantity	price	unit	total	discount %	net
4574	Zap 200MB Storage disk	10	125.00	box (10)	125.00	10	112.50

terms
Net monthly
Carriage paid
E & OE

goods total	112.50
VAT	19.68
TOTAL	132.18

4 ACCOUNTING RECORDS

this chapter covers . . .

The previous two chapters have looked at the documents and procedures involved in selling on credit and buying on credit. In this chapter we examine the principles of the accounting system which is used to record the details of invoices and credit notes. In the two chapters which follow, we apply the accounting system to sales on credit and purchases on credit.

NVQ PERFORMANCE CRITERIA COVERED

unit 2: RECORDING AND ACCOUNTING FOR CREDIT TRANSACTIONS
element 1
process documents relating to goods and services supplied on credit
element 2
process documents relating to goods and services received on credit

KNOWLEDGE AND UNDERSTANDING – ACCOUNTING PRINCIPLES AND THEORY

❏ functions of a ledger account system and main types of account
❏ inter-relationship of accounts – double-entry principles
❏ function of primary records

THE ACCOUNTING SYSTEM

We have seen earlier in Chapter 1 (page 10) that the accounting system comprises a number of stages of recording and presenting financial transactions:

- documents
- primary accounting records (day books)
- double-entry book-keeping
- trial balance
- financial statements

In this chapter we look at the principles of recording documents relating to credit transactions in the primary accounting records and the double-entry accounts. Later in the book we will see how a list of the balances of every double-entry account is used to form the trial balance (Chapter 8). Financial statements – the profit and loss statement and balance sheet – are the end result of the accounting system; they are covered in later NVQ Accounting levels.

ACCOUNTING FOR CREDIT TRANSACTIONS

The accounting system starts its recording process from prime documents. For credit transactions the prime documents are:

- sales invoices
- purchases invoices
- credit notes issued
- credit notes received

The diagram on the next page shows the order in which the accounting records are prepared for credit transactions. You will see that the steps for recording credit transactions in the accounting system are:

- start with a *prime document* (the source document for the accounting records)
- enter it in the appropriate *primary accounting record* (the first accounting book – or book of original entry – in which the prime document is recorded and summarised)
- transfer the information from the prime document and the primary accounting record into the *double-entry accounts*

accounting for credit transactions

prime documents

- sales invoices

- purchases invoices

- credit notes issued

- credit notes received

primary accounting records

- sales day book

- purchases day book

- sales returns day book

- purchases returns day book

double-entry accounts

- sales ledger

- purchases ledger

- general ledger

- cash book

We will now look in more detail at the mechanics of the primary accounting records and the double-entry system. In the two chapters which follow we shall apply the accounting system to the recording of sales on credit and purchases on credit.

PRIMARY ACCOUNTING RECORDS

The primary accounting records comprise a number of *day books* which list money amounts and other details taken from the prime documents. The day books used for credit sales and purchases and returns are:

- sales day book
- purchases day book
- sales returns day book
- purchases returns day book

These day books, as well as being called primary accounting records, are also known as the books of original ('prime') entry. This is because they are the first place in the accounting system where prime documents are recorded.

DAY BOOKS

A day book is set out in the following way (the example shown is a sales day book, with sample entries shown):

Sales Day Book						
Date	Customer	Invoice No	Folio	Gross	VAT	Net
1997				£	£	£
3 Jan	Doyle & Co Ltd	901	SL 58	141.00	21.00	120.00
8 Jan	Sparkes & Sons Ltd	902	SL 127	188.00	28.00	160.00
13 Jan	T Young	903	SL 179	94.00	14.00	80.00
15 Jan	A-Z Supplies Ltd	904	SL 3	235.00	35.00	200.00
21 Jan	Sparkes & Sons Ltd	905	SL 127	141.00	21.00	120.00
31 Jan	Totals for month			799.00	119.00	680.00

Notes:

- The day book is prepared from prime documents – in this example from sales invoices (or copies of sales invoices).
- The *folio* column is used for cross-referencing to the book-keeping system: in this example, 'SL' refers to Sales Ledger, followed by the account number.
- The *gross* column records the amount of each prime document, ie after VAT has been included.
- The day book is totalled at intervals – daily, weekly, or monthly (as here) – the total of the *net* column tells the business the amount of sales (as here), purchases, sales returns, or purchases returns for the period.
- The amounts from the day books are recorded in the business' book-keeping system.
- When control accounts (see Chapter 10) are in use, the total of the gross column is entered into the sales ledger control account (for credit sales and sales returns), or the purchases ledger control account (for credit purchases and purchases returns).

We will look in more detail at sales day books in Chapter 5, and purchases day books in Chapter 6.

DAY BOOKS AND VALUE ADDED TAX

Many businesses and other organisations are registered for Value Added Tax (VAT). When a business is registered for VAT:

- VAT is charged on invoices issued to customers
- VAT charged on invoices received from VAT-registered suppliers is set off against VAT charged on invoices issued (any surplus which cannot be set off in this way can be reclaimed from HM Customs and Excise,(the VAT authority)
- an allowance for VAT is made on credit notes issued

When writing up day books from VAT invoices and credit notes:

- enter the total amount of the invoice or credit note in the gross column
- enter the VAT amount in the VAT column
- enter the total for goods or services before VAT in the net column

When a business is not registered for VAT, it cannot charge VAT on invoices issued and it cannot reclaim VAT charged on invoices received from suppliers. In such circumstances the total amount of the invoice is recorded in both the net and gross columns; a dash may be inserted in the VAT column. Likewise, VAT cannot be allowed on credit notes issued, nor recorded for credit notes received.

In Chapters 5 and 6 we shall see how the VAT columns from the day books are entered into the double-entry accounts.

DOUBLE-ENTRY ACCOUNTS

The accounting system is organised on the basis of a number of *accounts* which record the money amounts of financial transactions: collectively these accounts are known as 'the ledger'.

Accounts are kept in the names of customers and of suppliers of the business, and also for other transactions such as the receipt and payment of money for various purposes. Accounts can be kept in the form of:

- handwritten records
- computer records

In a handwritten system, accounts are maintained either in a bound book or a series of separate sheets of paper or card – each account occupying a separate page. The business can set up its own manual system, or can buy one ready-made from a business supplies shop.

In a computerised system each account is held as data in a computer file. Whether a handwritten or computerised system is being used, the principles remain the same. For the moment we will concentrate on handwritten accounts.

A handwritten system can either use specially ruled accounting paper – known as ledger paper – which can be purchased from a business supplies shop, or a suitable layout can be ruled as follows:

Debit | **Name of Account, eg Sales Account** | Credit

Date	Details	£ p	Date	Details	£ p
↑ of trans-action	↑ name of other account	↑ amount of trans-action			

Note the following points about the layout of this account:

- the name of the account is written at the top (often followed by the account number)

- the account is divided into two identical halves, separated by a central double vertical line

- the left-hand side is called the 'debit' side ('debit' is abbreviated to 'Dr' – short for DebitoR)

- the right-hand side is called the 'credit' (or 'Cr') side

- the date, details and amount of the transaction are entered in the account

- in the 'details' column is entered the name of the other account involved in the book-keeping transaction – this acts as a cross reference; as a further cross reference, a folio column is often incorporated on each side of an account – to the left of the money amounts columns

In practice, each account would occupy a whole page in a handwritten book-keeping system but, to save space when doing exercises, it is usual to put several accounts on a page. In future, in this book, the account layout will be simplified to give more clarity as follows (example transaction shown):

Dr		Sales Account		Cr
1997	£	1997		£
		31 Jan Sales Day Book		680

This layout is often known in accounting jargon as a 'T' account; it is used to illustrate accounts because it separates in a simple way the two sides – debit and credit – of the account. An alternative style of account has three money columns: debit, credit and balance. This type of account is commonly used for bank statements, building society passbooks and computer accounting statements. Because the balance of the account is calculated after every transaction, it is known as a *running balance account* (see page 106).

DEBITS AND CREDITS

The principle of double-entry book-keeping is that two entries are made, for every financial transaction, usually in different accounts:

- one account is *debited* with the money amount of the transaction, and
- one account is *credited* with the money amount of the transaction

The principle is often known as the *dual* aspect of book-keeping, ie each transaction has a dual effect on the accounts – one account gains, while another account gives value by recording a payment or a liability.

Debit entries are on the left-hand side of the appropriate account, while credit entries are on the right. The rules for debits and credits are:

- *debit entry* – the account which gains value, or records an asset, or an expense
- *credit entry* – the account which gives value, or records a liability, or an income item

Dr	First Account	Cr
Account which gains value or records an asset, or an expense		

Dr	Second Account	Cr
		Account which gives value or records a liability, or an income item

DIVISION OF THE LEDGER

Accounts, as mentioned above, are normally written on separate pages of a book known as 'the ledger'. In practice, several separate ledgers are kept, each containing different classes of accounts:

- sales ledger, containing the accounts of the firm's debtors (customers)
- purchases ledger, containing the accounts of the firm's creditors (suppliers)
- cash book, containing the bank account and cash account records of the business
- general ledger (often known as nominal ledger) containing all other accounts, such as income, expenses, fixed assets, owner's capital, etc.

PURCHASES AND SALES

In book-keeping the terms purchases and sales have specific meanings:

- *purchases* – the purchase of goods with the intention that they should be resold at a profit
- *sales* – the sale of goods in which the business or organisation trades

Thus an office stationery supplies business buying goods from a manufacturer records the transaction in purchases account. When office supplies are sold to customers, the transactions are recorded in sales account. Other items purchased in connection with the running of the business – eg buildings, equipment, vehicles – are recorded, not in purchases account, but in suitably named accounts, ie buildings account, equipment account, vehicles account, etc.

The following diagram shows how ledgers and accounts are used in connection with purchases and sales:

SALES LEDGER	**PURCHASES LEDGER**	**GENERAL (OR NOMINAL) LEDGER**
separate accounts for each *debtor*, ie customers who owe money to the business	separate accounts for each *creditor*, ie suppliers to whom the business owes money	• *purchases account* – to record the purchase of goods, whether bought on credit or for cash • *sales account* – to record the sale of goods, whether sold on credit or for cash • *Value Added Tax account* – to record the VAT amount of purchases and sales

METHODS OF CODING IN ACCOUNTING SYSTEMS

As a business grows, methods of coding need to be used in order to be able to trace transactions through the accounting system, ie:

- documents
- primary accounting records (day books)
- double-entry accounts system
- trial balance

Uses of coding in the stages of the accounting system are:

documents

- each document, eg invoice, credit note, is numbered
- goods listed on invoices have reference numbers, eg catalogue number, which, if a computer accounting system is used, will enable the business to analyse sales by product

primary accounting records (day books)

- the number of the document, eg invoice, credit note (see next chapter) is recorded
- the number of the debtors or creditors account is recorded in the folio column, eg 'SL' for sales ledger, followed by the account number (or short name – see below)

double-entry accounts system

- the accounts system is divided into sections, the division of the ledger (see page 98): sales ledger, purchases ledger, cash book, and general ledger
- each account is numbered (or some accounting systems use an abbreviated name, or short name, for debtors and creditors, eg the account of Peterhead Trading Company might be coded as 'PETER')
- general (or nominal ledger) accounts are numbered and are often arranged in a particular order, eg

0001 – 1299	Assets
2100 – 2399	Liabilities
3000 – 3099	Capital
4000 – 4999	Sales
5000 – 5299	Purchases
6000 – 8299	Expenses

trial balance

We shall see in Chapter 8 how the trial balance consists of a list of the balances of all the accounts within the accounting system. As well as the name of each account, it is quite usual to show the account number listed in a separate 'folio' column.

- The accounting system comprises a number of specific stages of recording and presenting financial transactions:
  - prime documents
  - primary accounting records (day books)
  - double-entry book-keeping
  - trial balance
  - financial statements

- The prime documents relating to credit sales are:
  - sales invoices
  - credit notes issued

- The prime documents relating to credit purchases are:
  - purchases invoices
  - credit notes received

- Day books are the primary accounting records (or books of original entry) for credit sales, credit purchases and returns

- The day books used for credit sales and purchases and returns are:
  - sales day book
  - purchases day book
  - sales returns day book
  - purchases returns day book

- Financial transactions are recorded in accounts using double-entry principles.

- The rules for debit and credit entries in accounts are:
  - debit entries, the account which gains value
  - credit entries, the account which gives value

KEY TERMS

- Division of the ledger divides the accounts contained in the accounting system between four sections:
    - sales ledger, containing the accounts of debtors
    - purchases ledger, containing the accounts of creditors
    - cash book, containing the bank account and cash account
    - general (or nominal) ledger, containing all other accounts

- Within an accounting system, use is made of coding to identify and cross-reference transactions and products.

prime documents	source documents for the accounting records
primary accounting records	the first accounting books in which transactions are recorded
books of original (prime) entry	another term for primary accounting records
folio	a form of cross-referencing used in the book-keeping system
accounts	records of the money amounts of financial transactions
ledger	collection of accounts; a sub-division of the accounting system
debit entry	records a gain in value, an asset, or an expense
credit entry	records the giving of value, a liability, or an income item
division of the ledger	separates the accounts into four main sections: – sales ledger – purchases ledger – cash book – general (or nominal) ledger
purchases	the purchase of goods with the intention that they should be resold at a profit
sales	the sale of goods in which the business or organisation trades
coding	methods used within the accounting system to identify and cross-reference transactions and products (see also 'folio', above)

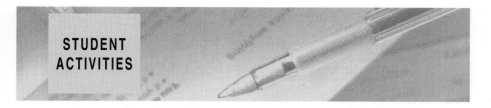

STUDENT ACTIVITIES

4.1   Which one of the following is a primary accounting record?

(a)   sales day book

(b)   sales account

(c)   account of T Smith, a debtor

(d)   profit and loss statement

Answer (a) or (b) or (c) or (d)

4.2   Which one of the following is in the right order?

(a)   double-entry accounts; primary accounting records; prime documents

(b)   primary accounting records; prime documents; double-entry accounts

(c)   prime documents; primary accounting records; double-entry accounts

(d)   double-entry accounts, prime documents, primary accounting records

Answer (a) or (b) or (c) or (d)

4.3   Explain in note format the principles for recording a credit transaction in the accounting system.

4.4   A person starting a new business is not clear about the meaning of 'double-entry book-keeping'. Explain what is meant by this system of accounting.

4.5   In which division of the ledger would you find the following accounts?

(a)   J Williams, a creditor

(b)   purchases account

(c)   H Wilson, a debtor

(d)   sales account

(e)   cash account

(f)   VAT account

4.6   Define the following:

- prime document
- primary accounting record
- double-entry book-keeping
- account
- ledger

5 ACCOUNTING FOR CREDIT SALES AND SALES RETURNS

this chapter covers . . .

This chapter applies the principles of the accounting system to credit sales and sales returns. We shall see how the prime documents for credit sales (sales invoices) are entered in the primary accounting record (the sales day book); then the information from the day book is transferred into the ledger accounts of the double-entry system. We will also examine the accounting for sales returns.

NVQ PERFORMANCE CRITERIA COVERED

unit 2: RECORDING AND ACCOUNTING FOR CREDIT TRANSACTIONS

element 1

process documents relating to goods and services supplied on credit

❏ invoices and credit notes are correctly entered as primary accounting records in a form acceptable to the organisation

❏ the analysis and totalling of the primary record is completed accurately

element 3

account for goods and services supplied on credit

❏ entries in the primary records are correctly transferred to the correct ledger accounts

ACCOUNTING SYSTEM FOR SALES

The accounting system for credit sales fits together in the following way:

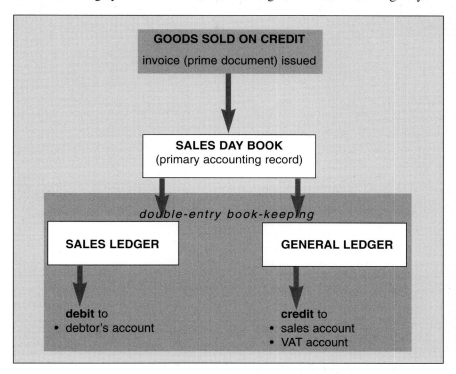

We shall now look in more detail at the sales day book and the double-entry accounts for credit sales. In the examples which follow (and also in the next chapter) we will assume that the business is registered for Value Added Tax and so:

- VAT is charged on invoices issued to customers
- VAT charged on invoices received from suppliers is either set off against VAT charged on invoices issued, or is reclaimed from HM Customs and Excise

SALES DAY BOOK

The sales day book lists the credit sales made by a business. Following the issue of an invoice for each transaction, the sales day book is prepared from the invoices. An example of a sales day book is shown on the next page (with sample entries made in the various columns).

Sales Day Book						
Date	Customer	Invoice No	Folio	Gross	VAT	Net
1997				£	£	£
3 Jan	Doyle & Co Ltd	901	SL 58	141.00	21.00	120.00
8 Jan	Sparkes & Sons Ltd	902	SL 127	188.00	28.00	160.00
13 Jan	T Young	903	SL 179	94.00	14.00	80.00
15 Jan	A-Z Supplies Ltd	904	SL 3	235.00	35.00	200.00
21 Jan	Sparkes & Sons	905	SL 127	141.00	21.00	120.00
31 Jan	Totals for month			799.00	119.00	680.00

Notes:

- The sales day book is prepared from invoices (or copy invoices) issued to customers.
- The *folio* column is used for cross-referencing to the book-keeping system: 'SL' refers to Sales Ledger, followed by the account number.
- The *gross* column records the amount of each invoice, ie after VAT has been added.
- The day book is totalled at appropriate intervals – daily, weekly, or monthly – and the total of the *net* column tells the business the amount of credit sales for the period.
- When control accounts (see Chapter 10) are in use, the total of the gross column from the sales day book is entered in the sales ledger control account.

Thus, to write up the sales day book, we take the sales invoices or copy invoices – that have been checked and authorised (see pages 33 and 34) – for the period and enter the details:

- date of invoice
- name of customer
- sales invoice number
- cross reference to the customer's account number in the sales ledger, eg 'SL 58'
- enter the gross amount of the invoice, being the final total

- enter the VAT amount shown on the invoice – don't be concerned with any adjustments to the VAT for the effect of any cash discounts (see page 28), simply record the VAT amount shown
- enter the net amount of the invoice (often described as 'goods total'), before VAT is added

DOUBLE-ENTRY BOOK-KEEPING FOR CREDIT SALES

After the sales day book has been written up and totalled, the information from it is transferred into the double-entry system. The accounts in the sales ledger and general ledger to record the transactions from the sales day book, seen earlier, are as follows:

SALES LEDGER

Dr			**A-Z Supplies Ltd** (account no 3)		Cr
1997		£	1997		£
15 Jan	Sales	235			

Dr			**Doyle & Co Ltd** (account no 58)		Cr
1997		£	1997		£
3 Jan	Sales	141			

Dr			**Sparkes & Sons Ltd** (account no 127)		Cr
1997		£	1997		£
8 Jan	Sales	188			
21 Jan	Sales	141			

Dr			**T Young** (account no 179)		Cr
1997		£	1997		£
13 Jan	Sales	94			

GENERAL LEDGER

Dr		**Sales Account**		Cr
1997	£	1997		£
		31 Jan	Sales Day Book	680

Dr			Value Added Tax Account		Cr
1997		£	1997		£
			31 Jan Sales Day Book		119

Note from the sales day book:

- the amounts from the gross column *for each separate sale* have been debited to the accounts of the customers, ie the business has a debtor for the amounts shown
- the total of the VAT column, £119, has been credited to VAT account (which has given value)
- the total of the net column, £680, has been credited to sales account (ie the account which has given value)
- the sales day book incorporates a folio column which cross-references each transaction to the personal account of each debtor in the sales ledger (SL); this enables a particular transaction to be traced from prime document (invoice issued), through the primary accounting record (sales day book), to the debtors' ledger account

RECORDING PAYMENTS FROM CUSTOMERS

When payment is received from customers, the method of payment is:

- either by cheque, or BACS (Bankers Automated Clearing Services – see page 196)
- or, less commonly, in cash

While separate accounts are kept for bank (ie cheque and BACS) transactions and cash transactions, most organisations bring these two accounts together in a division of the ledger called *cash book*. We shall be looking in detail at the use of the cash book in Chapter 15.

When customers (debtors) pay for goods that have been sold to them, the double-entry book-keeping entries are:

- payment received by cheque or BACS
  - *debit* bank account
  - *credit* debtor's account
- payment received in cash
  - *debit* cash account
  - *credit* debtor's account

ACCOUNTING SYSTEM FOR SALES RETURNS

A credit note (see page 24) is the document issued by a business when it makes a refund to a customer who has bought goods on credit. A credit note reduces the amount owed by the debtor. *Sales returns* (or returns in) are when goods previously sold on credit are returned to the business by its customers.

The accounting procedures for sales returns involve:

- prime documents – credit notes issued to customers
- primary accounting record – sales returns day book
- double-entry accounts – sales ledger (accounts for each debtor) and general ledger (sales returns account, which records the totals of credit notes issued, and Value Added Tax account, which records the VAT amount of sales returns)

The accounting system for sales returns is summarised as follows:

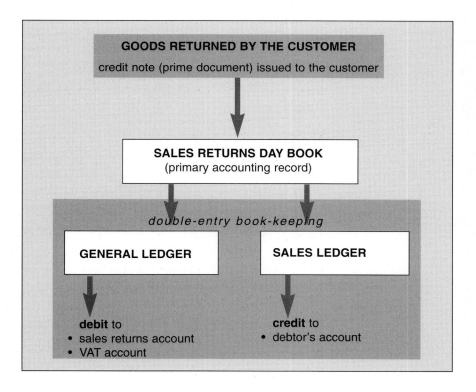

We shall now look in more detail at the sales returns day book and the double-entry accounts for sales returns.

SALES RETURNS DAY BOOK

The sales returns day book uses virtually the same layout as the sales day book seen earlier in this chapter. It operates in a similar way, storing up information about sales returns until such time as a transfer is made into the double-entry accounts system. The prime documents for sales returns day book are credit notes (or copies of credit notes) issued to customers.

example transactions

1997

15 Jan	T Young returns goods, £40 + VAT, credit note no CN702 issued
27 Jan	A-Z Supplies Ltd. returns goods, £120 + VAT, credit note no CN703 issued

The sales returns day book is written up as shown below:

		Sales Returns Day Book				
Date	Customer	Credit Note No	Folio	Gross	VAT	Net
1997				£	£	£
15 Jan	T Young	CN702	SL 179	47.00	7.00	40.00
27 Jan	A-Z Supplies Ltd	CN703	SL 3	141.00	21.00	120.00
31 Jan	Totals for month			188.00	28.00	160.00

Notes:

- The sales returns day book is prepared from credit notes (or copies of credit notes) issued to customers.
- The day book is totalled at appropriate intervals – weekly or monthly.
- The VAT-inclusive amounts from the gross column are credited to the debtors' personal accounts in the sales ledger.
- The total of the VAT column is transferred to the debit of the VAT account in the general ledger.

- The total of the net column tells the business the amount of sales returns for the period. This amount is transferred to the debit of sales returns account in the general ledger.
- The gross column records the amount of each credit note issued, ie after VAT has been included. When control accounts (see Chapter 10) are in use, the total of the gross column is entered into the sales ledger control account.

DOUBLE-ENTRY BOOK-KEEPING FOR SALES RETURNS

After the sales returns day book has been written up and totalled, the information from it is transferred into the double-entry system.

The accounts in the sales ledger and general ledger to record the transactions from the above sales returns day book (including any other transactions already recorded on these accounts) are:

SALES LEDGER

Dr			**A-Z Supplies Ltd** (account no 3)		Cr
1997		£	1997		£
15 Jan	Sales	235	27 Jan	Sales Returns	141

Dr			**T Young** (account no 179)		Cr
1997		£	1997		£
12 Jan	Sales	94	15 Jan	Sales Returns	47

GENERAL LEDGER

Dr			**Sales Returns Account**		Cr
1997		£	1997		£
31 Jan	Sales Returns Day Book	160			

Dr			**Value Added Tax Account**		Cr
1997		£	1997		£
31 Jan	Sales Returns Day Book	28	31 Jan	Sales Day Book	119

THE USE OF ANALYSED SALES DAY BOOKS

As well as the layout of the day books we have seen in this chapter, a business can use analysed day books whenever it needs to analyse its sales and sales returns between

- different departments, eg a store with departments for furniture, carpets and curtains, hardware
- different categories of goods sold, eg paint, wallpaper, brushes

For example, a wholesaler of decorators' supplies may decide to write up its sales day book as shown below.

sales day book								
Date	Customer	Invoice no	Folio	Gross	VAT	Paint	Wallpaper	Brushes
1997				£	£	£	£	£
8 Aug	DIY Sales Limited	1478	SL59	235.00	35.00	75.00	125.00	
12 Aug	T Lane Decorators	1479	SL108	141.00	21.00		100.00	20.00
15 Aug	Colour Painters Limited	1480	SL38	329.00	49.00	150.00	100.00	30.00
22 Aug	Southern Decorators	1481	SL211	188.00	28.00	100.00	60.00	
31 Aug	Totals for month			893.00	133.00	325.00	385.00	50.00

Notes:

- The references in the folio column are to 'SL' (Sales Ledger), followed by the customers account number.

- The analysis columns – here paint, wallpaper, brushes – show the amount of sales net of VAT (ie with VAT deducted).

- The analysis columns take the place of the net column used earlier; they analyse the net amounts between the categories of products sold.

In using analysed sales day books and sales returns day books, a business can adapt the accounting records to suit its own particular requirements for information. There is not a standard way in which to present the primary accounting records – the needs of the user of the information are all important. By using analysed day books, the owner of the business can see how much has been sold by departments, or categories of goods.

CHAPTER SUMMARY

- Sales day book is the primary accounting record for credit sales. It is prepared from sales invoices (or copy invoices) sent to customers.

- Sales returns day book is the primary accounting record for sales returns. It is prepared from credit notes (or copy credit notes) issued to customers.

- Analysed sales day books are used when a business wishes to analyse its sales between different departments (of the business) or different categories of goods sold.

- Recording credit sales in the double-entry system uses:
  - prime documents, sales invoices
  - primary accounting record, sales day book
  - double-entry accounts, sales ledger and general ledger

- Recording sales returns in the double-entry system uses:
  - prime documents, credit notes issued to customers
  - primary accounting record, sales returns day book
  - double-entry accounts, sales ledger and general ledger

KEY TERMS

sales day book	primary accounting record prepared from sales invoices (or copy invoices)
sales returns	goods sold on credit which are returned by customers
credit note	the prime document for returned goods – issued by the business allowing credit to the customer
sales returns day book	primary accounting record prepared from credit notes (or copy credit notes) issued to customers
analysed sales day book	day book which incorporates analysis columns, for example between – different departments – different categories of goods sold
sales ledger	division of the ledger which contains the accounts of the firm's debtors (customers)
cash book	division of the ledger which contains the bank account and cash account records of the business
general ledger	division of the ledger which includes – sales account – sales returns account – Value Added Tax account

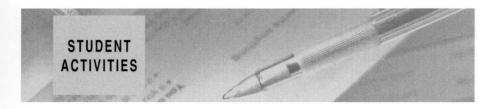

STUDENT
ACTIVITIES

5.1 Which one of the following is in the right order?

(a) sales invoice; sales day book; sales account; debtor's account

(b) sales day book; debtor's account; sales account; sales invoice

(c) sales day book; sales invoice; debtor's account; sales account

(d) sales account; debtor's account; sales invoice; sales day book

Answer (a) or (b) or (c) or (d)

5.2 Explain in note format:

(a) the principles for recording a credit sales transaction in the accounting system

(b) the principles for recording a sales returns transaction in the accounting system

---

In the activities which follow, the rate of Value Added Tax is to be calculated at the current rate (17.5% at the time of writing). When calculating VAT amounts, you should ignore fractions of a penny, ie round down to a whole penny.

Leave the folio column blank, and do not use account numbers, unless otherwise stated.

5.3 Wyvern Wholesalers sells office stationery mainly to other businesses in the area. During April 1997 the following credit transactions took place.

1997

2 Apr   Sold goods to Malvern Stores £55 + VAT, invoice no. 4578

4 Apr   Sold goods to Pershore Retailers £65 + VAT, invoice no. 4579

7 Apr   Sold goods to E Grainger £28 + VAT, invoice no. 4580

10 Apr   Sold goods to P Wilson £58 + VAT, invoice no. 4581

11 Apr   Sold goods to M Kershaw £76 + VAT, invoice no. 4582

14 Apr   Sold goods to D Lloyd £66 + VAT, invoice no. 4583

18 Apr   Sold goods to A Cox £33 + VAT, invoice no. 4584

22 Apr   Sold goods to Dines Stores £102 + VAT, invoice no. 4585

24 Apr   Sold goods to Malvern Stores £47 + VAT, invoice no. 4586

25 Apr   Sold goods to P Wilson £35 + VAT, invoice no. 4587

29 Apr   Sold goods to A Cox £82 + VAT, invoice no. 4588

You are to:

(a)   enter the above transactions in Wyvern Wholesaler's sales day book for April 1997

(b)   record the accounting entries in Wyvern Wholesaler's sales ledger and general ledger

5.4   The following details are the sales returns for Wyvern Wholesalers for April 1997. They are to be

(a)   entered in the sales returns day book for April 1997

(b)   recorded in the sales ledger and general ledger (use the ledgers already prepared in the answer to Activity 5.3)

1997

8 Apr   Pershore Retailers returns goods £20 + VAT, we issue credit note no. CN572

10 Apr   E Grainger returns goods £28 + VAT, we issue credit note no. CN573

16 Apr   D Lloyd returns goods £33 + VAT, we issue credit note no. CN574

28 Apr   Malvern Stores returns goods £20 + VAT, we issue credit note no. CN575

30 Apr   A Cox returns goods £40 + VAT, we issue credit note no. CN576

6 ACCOUNTING FOR CREDIT PURCHASES AND PURCHASES RETURNS

this chapter covers . . .

In this chapter we apply the principles of accounting, which were examined in Chapter 4, to credit purchases and purchases returns. We shall see how the prime documents for credit purchases (purchases invoices) are entered in the primary accounting record (purchases day book); then the information from the day book is transferred into the ledger accounts of the double-entry system. We will also examine the accounting for purchases returns.

At the end of the chapter is a Case Study which brings together all of the work covered in this chapter and Chapters 4 and 5.

NVQ PERFORMANCE CRITERIA COVERED

unit 2: RECORDING AND ACCOUNTING FOR CREDIT TRANSACTIONS

element 2
process documents relating to goods and services received on credit

❏   *documents are correctly entered as primary accounting records in a form acceptable to the organisation*

element 4
account for goods and services received on credit

❏   *entries in the primary records are correctly transferred to the correct ledger accounts*

ACCOUNTING SYSTEM FOR PURCHASES

The accounting system for credit purchases fits together in the following way:

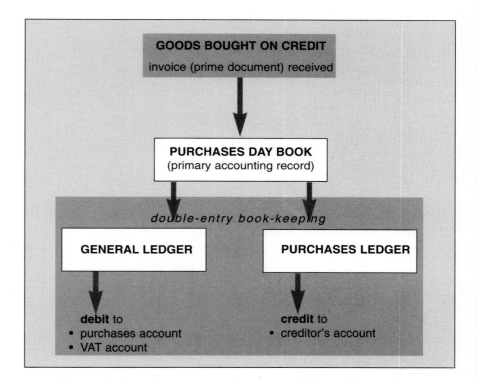

We shall now look in more detail at the purchases day book and the double-entry accounts for credit purchases. We will continue with the accounting system of the business used in the previous chapter, so some accounts may contain previous entries.

PURCHASES DAY BOOK

The purchases day book is a collection point for accounting information on the credit purchases of a business and may be set as shown on the next page(with sample entries shown):

Purchases Day Book						
Date	Supplier	Invoice No	Folio	Gross	VAT*	Net
1997				£	£	£
2 Jan	P Bond Ltd	1234	PL 125	94.00	14.00	80.00
10 Jan	D Webster	A373	PL 730	141.00	21.00	120.00
16 Jan	P Bond Ltd	1247	PL 125	47.00	7.00	40.00
20 Jan	Sanders & Sons	5691	PL 495	188.00	28.00	160.00
31 Jan	Totals for month			470.00	70.00	400.00

* VAT = 17.5 per cent

Notes:

- The purchases day book is prepared from purchases invoices received from suppliers.
- The folio column is used for cross-referencing to the book-keeping system: 'PL' refers to Purchases Ledger, followed by the account number.
- The gross column records the amount of each invoice, ie after VAT has been included.
- The day book is totalled at appropriate intervals – daily, weekly or monthly – and the total of the net column will tell the business the amount of credit purchases for the period.
- When control accounts (see Chapter 10) are in use, the total of the gross column from the purchases day book is entered into the purchases ledger control account.

Thus, to write up the purchases day book, we take the purchases invoices – that have been checked and authorised (see page 45) – for the period and enter the details:

- date of invoice
- name of supplier
- purchase invoice number
- cross-reference to the supplier's account number in the purchases ledger, eg 'PL 125'
- enter the gross amount of the invoice, being the final total
- enter the VAT amount shown on the invoice – don't be concerned with any adjustments to the VAT for the effect of any cash discounts (see page 28), simply record the VAT amount shown

- enter the net amount of the invoice (often described as 'goods total'), before VAT is added

DOUBLE-ENTRY BOOK-KEEPING FOR CREDIT PURCHASES

After the purchases day book has been written up and totalled, the information from it is transferred into the double-entry system.

The accounts in the purchases ledger and general ledger to record the transactions from the purchases day book seen earlier are as follows:

PURCHASES LEDGER

Dr			**P Bond Limited** (account no 125)		Cr
1997		£	1997		£
			2 Jan	Purchases	94
			16 Jan	Purchases	47

Dr			**Sanders & Sons** (account no 495)		Cr
1997		£	1997		£
			20 Jan	Purchases	188

Dr			**D Webster** (account no 730)		Cr
1997		£	1997		£
			10 Jan	Purchases	141

GENERAL LEDGER

Dr			**Purchases Account**		Cr
1997		£	1997		£
31 Jan	Purchases Day Book	400			

Dr			**Value Added Tax Account**		Cr
1997		£	1997		£
31 Jan	Sales Returns Day Book	*28	31 Jan	Sales Day Book	*119
31 Jan	Purchases Day Book	70			

* Amounts already entered from sales day book and sales returns day book (see Chapter 5)

Note that from the purchases day book:

- the amounts from the gross column *for each separate purchase* have been credited to the accounts of the suppliers, ie the business owes to each creditor the amounts shown

- the total of the VAT column, £70, has been debited to VAT account (which has gained value)

- the total of the net column, £400, has been debited to purchases account (ie the account which has gained value)

- the folio column in the day book gives a cross-reference to the creditors' accounts in the purchases ledger (PL)

RECORDING PAYMENTS TO SUPPLIERS

When payment is made to suppliers, the method of payment is:

- either by cheque, or BACS (Bankers Automated Clearing Services – see page 235)

- or, less commonly, in cash

Such payments are entered in the bank account or cash account. These two accounts are often brought together in the *cash book*, which we shall look at in detail in Chapter 15.

Payment to suppliers (creditors) is recorded by the following double-entry book-keeping entries:

- payment made by cheque or BACS
    - *debit* creditor's account
    - *credit* bank account
- payment made in cash
    - *debit* creditor's account
    - *credit* cash account

ACCOUNTING SYSTEM FOR PURCHASES RETURNS

Purchases returns (or returns out) are when goods previously bought on credit are returned by the business to its suppliers. A credit note (see page 24) is requested and, when received, it is entered in the accounting system to reduce the amount owing to the creditor.

The accounting procedures for purchases returns involve:

- *prime documents* – credit notes received from suppliers

- *primary accounting record* – purchases returns day book
- *double-entry accounts* – purchases ledger (accounts for each creditor) and general ledger (purchases returns account, which records the totals of credit notes received, and Value Added Tax account, which records the VAT amount of purchases returns)

The accounting system for purchases returns can be summarised as follows:

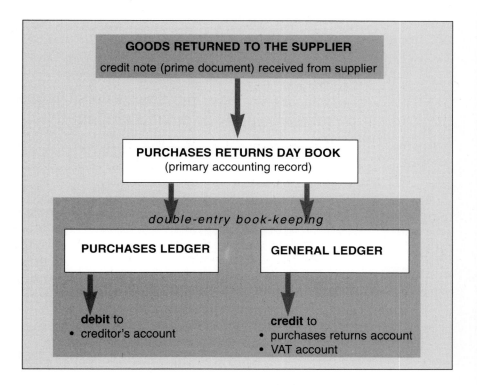

We shall now look in more detail at the purchases returns day book and the double-entry accounts for purchases returns.

PURCHASES RETURNS DAY BOOK

The purchases returns day book uses virtually the same layout as the purchases day book seen earlier in this chapter. It operates in a similar way, storing up information about purchases returns until such time as a transfer is made into the double-entry accounts system. The prime documents for purchases returns day book are credit notes received from suppliers.

The purchases returns day book is written up as follows:

Purchases Returns Day Book						
Date	Supplier	Credit Note No	Folio	Gross	VAT	Net
1997				£	£	£
20 Jan	D Webster	123	PL 730	47.00	7.00	40.00
27 Jan	Sanders & Sons	406	PL 495	94.00	14.00	80.00
31 Jan	Totals for month			141.00	21.00	120.00

Notes:
- The purchases returns day book is prepared from credit notes received from suppliers.
- The day book is totalled at appropriate intervals – weekly or monthly.
- The VAT-inclusive amounts from the gross column are debited to the creditors' personal accounts in the purchases ledger.
- The total of the VAT column is transferred to the credit of the VAT account in the general ledger.
- The total of the net column tells the business the amount of purchases returns for the period. This amount is transferred to the credit of purchases returns account in the general ledger (see below).
- The gross column records the amount of each credit note received, ie after VAT has been included. When control accounts (see Chapter 10) are in use, the total of the gross column is entered into the purchases ledger control account.

DOUBLE-ENTRY BOOK-KEEPING FOR PURCHASES RETURNS

After the purchases returns day book has been written up and totalled, the information from it is transferred into the double-entry system.

The accounts in the purchases ledger and general ledger to record the transactions from the above purchases returns day book (including any other transactions already recorded on these accounts) are:

PURCHASES LEDGER

Dr			Sanders & Sons (account no 495)		Cr
1997		£	1997		£
27 Jan	Purchases Returns	94	20 Jan	Purchases	188

Dr			D Webster (account no 730)		Cr
1997		£	1997		£
20 Jan	Purchases Returns	47	10 Jan	Purchases	141

GENERAL LEDGER

Dr			Purchases Returns Account		Cr
1997		£	1997		£
			31 Jan	Purchases Returns Day Book	120

Dr			Value Added Tax Account		Cr
1997		£	1997		£
31 Jan	Sales Returns Day Book	*28	31 Jan	Sales Day Book	*119
31 Jan	Purchases Day Book	70	31 Jan	Purchases Returns Day Book	21

* Amounts already entered from the sales day book and sales returns day book (see Chapter 5).

THE USE OF ANALYSED PURCHASES DAY BOOKS

Businesses use analysed day books whenever they wish to analyse purchases and purchases returns between different categories of purchases:

- goods for resale, perhaps split between types of goods, eg ladies' wear, men's wear

- other items, such as revenue expenditure and capital expenditure

An example of an analysed purchases day book is shown below

Analysed purchases day books and purchases returns day books can be adapted to suit the particular needs of a business. Thus there is not a standard way in which to present the primary accounting records – the needs of the user are all important. By using analysed day books, the owner of the business can see how much has been bought for each of the different categories of purchases.

purchases day book

Date	Supplier	Invoice no	Folio	Gross	VAT	Ladies wear	Mens wear	Other expenses
1997				£	£	£	£	£
2 Sep	Fashions Limited	1478	PL87	129.25	19.25	50.00	60.00	
4 Sep	Eastern Telephones	2479	PL61	175.66	26.16			149.50
8 Sep	Mercian Models	9799	PL102	301.74	44.94	256.80		
12 Sep	Media Advertising	2010	PL92	528.75	78.75			450.00
15 Sep	Style Limited	4621	PL379	432.87	64.47	218.20	150.20	
19 Sep	Wyvern Motors	7447	PL423	149.81	22.31			127.50
26 Sep	Denim Traders	3830	PL45	322.36	48.01	65.50	208.85	
30 Sep	Totals for month			2040.44	303.89	590.50	419.05	727.00

Notes:

- The references in the folio column are to the 'PL' (Purchase Ledger) and supplier's account number

- The analysis columns – here ladies wear, mens wear and other expenses – show the amount of purchases excluding VAT

- The analysis columns take the place of the net column used earlier and analyse each net amount by category of expenditure

CASE STUDY

WYVERN TRADERS

To bring together the material covered in this chapter and Chapters 4 and 5, we will look at a comprehensive worked example which makes use of

- *primary accounting records*
  - *purchases day book*
  - *sales day book*
  - *purchases returns day book*
  - *sales returns day book*
- *double-entry accounts*
  - *purchases ledger*
  - *sales ledger*
  - *general ledger*

situation

Wyvern Traders is a wholesaler of stationery and office equipment. The business is registered for VAT. The following are the credit transactions for April 1997:

1997	
1 Apr	Bought goods from Midland Supplies, £120.00 + VAT, their invoice no 12486
2 Apr	Sold goods to P Woodhouse, £200.00 + VAT, invoice no 2416
9 Apr	Returned goods to Midland Supplies, £20.00 + VAT, credit note no 104 received
10 Apr	P Woodhouse returns goods, £60.00 + VAT, we issue credit note no CN12
14 Apr	Bought goods from National Stationery, £60.00 + VAT, their invoice no A184
14 Apr	Sold goods to Blackheath Limited, £80.00 + VAT, invoice no 2417
21 Apr	Blackheath Limited returns goods, £10.00 + VAT, we issue credit note no CN13
25 Apr	Sold goods to Butterworth Limited, £160.00 + VAT, invoice no 2418
28 Apr	Bought goods from Swan Equipment, £160.00 + VAT, their invoice no P102
30 Apr	Returned goods to Swan Equipment, £40.00 + VAT, credit note no X102 received

The day books and double-entry accounts are illustrated on the next four pages: arrows indicate the transfers from the day books to the individual accounts. Note that some accounts have been repeated on different pages in order to show, on the same page, the accounts relating to a particular day book: in practice a business would keep all the transactions relating to an account together in one account.

Purchases Day Book

Date	Supplier	Invoice No	Folio	Gross		VAT		Net	
1997				£	p	£	p	£	p
1 Apr	Midland Supplies	12486	PL 45	141	00	21	00	120	00
14 Apr	National Stationery	A184	PL 67	70	50	10	50	60	00
28 Apr	Swan Equipment	P102	PL 112	188	00	28	00	160	00
30 Apr	Totals for month			399	50	59	50	340	00

PURCHASES LEDGER

Dr   **Midland Supplies** (account no 45)   Cr

Date	Details	£	p	Date	Details	£	p
				1997 1 Apr	Purchases	141	00

Dr   **National Stationery** (account no 67)   Cr

Date	Details	£	p	Date	Details	£	p
				1997 14 Apr	Purchases	70	50

Dr   **Swan Equipment** (account no 112)   Cr

Date	Details	£	p	Date	Details	£	p
				1997 28 Apr	Purchases	188	00

GENERAL LEDGER

Dr   **Value Added Tax Account**   Cr

Date	Details	£	p	Date	Details	£	p
1997 30 Apr	Purchases Day Book	59	50				

Dr   **Purchases Account**   Cr

Date	Details	£	p	Date	Details	£	p
1997 30 Apr	Purchases Day Book	340	00				

CASE STUDY: WYVERN TRADERS

Sales Day Book

Date	Customer	Invoice No	Folio	Gross	VAT	Net
1997				£ p	£ p	£ p
2 Apr	P Woodhouse	2416	SL 248	235 00	35 00	200 00
14 Apr	Blackheath Ltd	2417	SL 27	94 00	14 00	80 00
25 Apr	Butterworth Ltd	2418	SL 35	188 00	28 00	160 00
30 Apr	Totals for month			517 00	77 00	440 00

SALES LEDGER

Dr   **Blackheath Ltd** (account no 27)   Cr

Date	Details	£ p	Date	Details	£ p
1997 14 Apr	Sales	94 00			

Dr   **Butterworth Ltd** (account no 35)   Cr

Date	Details	£ p	Date	Details	£ p
1997 25 Apr	Sales	188 00			

Dr   **P Woodhouse** (account no 248)   Cr

Date	Details	£ p	Date	Details	£ p
1997 2 Apr	Sales	235 00			

GENERAL LEDGER

Dr   **Value Added Tax Account**   Cr

Date	Details	£ p	Date	Details	£ p
1997 30 Apr	Purchases Day Book*	59 50	1997 30 Apr	Sales Day Book	77 00

Dr   **Sales Account**   Cr

Date	Details	£ p	Date	Details	£ p
			1997 30 Apr	Sales Day Book	440 00

* transaction entered previously

Purchases Returns Day Book

Date	Supplier	Credit Note No	Folio	Gross	VAT	Net
1997				£ p	£ p	£ p
9 Apr	Midland Supplies	104	PL 45	23 50	3 50	20 00
30 Apr	Swan Equipment	X102	PL 112	47 00	7 00	40 00
30 Apr	Totals for month			70 50	10 50	60 00

PURCHASES LEDGER

Dr   **Midland Supplies** (account no 45)   Cr

Date	Details	£ p	Date	Details	£ p
1997 9 Apr	Purchases Returns	23 50	1997 1 Apr	Purchases	141 00*

Dr   **Swan Equipment** (account no 112)   Cr

Date	Details	£ p	Date	Details	£ p
1997 30 Apr	Purchases Returns	47 00	1997 28 Apr	Purchases	188 00*

GENERAL LEDGER

Dr   **Value Added Tax Account**   Cr

Date	Details	£ p	Date	Details	£ p
1997 30 Apr	Purchases Day Book	59 50*	1997 30 Apr	Sales Day Book	77 00*
			30 Apr	Purchases Returns Day Book	10 50

Dr   **Purchases Returns Account**   Cr

Date	Details	£ p	Date	Details	£ p
			1997 30 Apr	Purchases Returns Day Book	60 00

* transactions entered previously

Sales Returns Day Book

Date	Customer	Credit Note No	Folio	Gross		VAT		Net	
				£	p	£	p	£	p
1997									
10 Apr	P Woodhouse	CN 12	SL 248	70	50	10	50	60	00
21 Apr	Blackheath Ltd	CN 13	SL 27	11	75	1	75	10	00
30 Apr	Totals for month			82	25	12	25	70	00

SALES LEDGER

Dr   **Blackheath Ltd** (account no 27)   **Cr**

Date	Details	£	p	Date	Details	£	p
1997				1997			
14 Apr	Sales	94	00*	21 Apr	Sales Returns	11	75

Dr   **P Woodhouse** (account no 248)   **Cr**

Date	Details	£	p	Date	Details	£	p
1997				1997			
2 Apr	Sales	235	00*	10 Apr	Sales Returns	70	50

GENERAL LEDGER

Dr   **Value Added Tax Account**   **Cr**

Date	Details	£	p	Date	Details	£	p
1997				1997			
30 Apr	Purchases Day Book	59	50*	30 Apr	Sales Day Book	77	00*
30 Apr	Sales Returns Day Book	12	25	30 Apr	Purchases Returns Day Book	10	50*

Dr   **Sales Returns Account**   **Cr**

Date	Details	£	p	Date	Details	£	p
1997							
30 Apr	Sales Returns Day Book	70	00				

* transactions entered previously

The diagram below summarises the material we have studied in this and the previous two chapters. It shows the procedures for recording transactions in the accounting system for

• credit purchases and purchases returns
• credit sales and sales returns

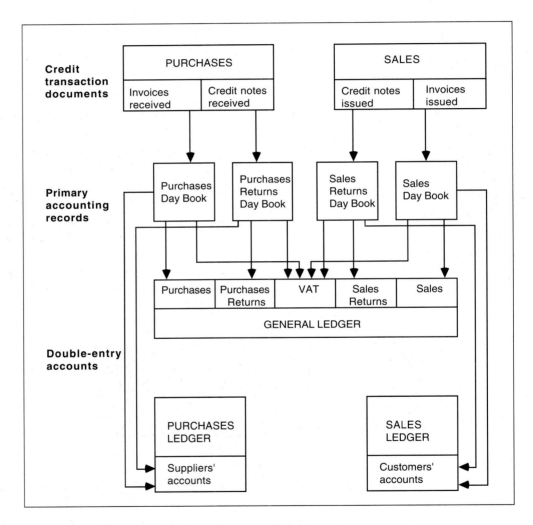

CHAPTER SUMMARY

• Purchases day book is the primary accounting record for credit purchases. It is prepared from purchases invoices received from suppliers.

• Purchases returns day book is the primary accounting record for purchases returns. It is prepared from credit notes received from suppliers.

• Analysed purchases day books are used when a business wishes to analyse its purchases between different categories of expenditure.

- Recording credit purchases in the double-entry system uses:
  - prime documents, purchases invoices
  - primary accounting record, purchases day book
  - double-entry accounts, purchases ledger and general ledger
- Recording purchases returns in the double-entry system uses:
  - prime documents, credit notes received from suppliers
  - primary accounting record, purchases returns day book
  - double-entry accounts, purchases ledger and general ledger

KEY TERMS

purchases day book	primary accounting record prepared from purchases invoices
purchases returns	goods purchased on credit which are returned to the supplier
purchases returns day book	primary accounting record prepared from credit notes received from suppliers
analysed purchases day book	day book which incorporates analysis columns between different categories of expenditure
purchases ledger	division of the ledger which contains the accounts of the firm's creditors (suppliers)

STUDENT ACTIVITIES

6.1 Which one of the following is in the right order?

(a) purchases returns day book; credit note issued; purchases returns account; creditor's account

(b) purchases returns account; creditor's account; purchases returns day book; credit note issued

(c) purchases returns day book; purchases returns account; creditor's account; credit note issued

(d) credit note issued; purchases returns day book; purchases returns account; creditor's account

Answer (a) or (b) or (c) or (d)

6.2   Which is the correct pairing?

   (a)   credit note issued; sales returns

   (b)   credit note received; sales returns

   (c)   invoice issued; purchases

   (d)   invoice received; sales

   Answer (a) or (b) or (c) or (d)

6.3   Explain in note format

   (a)   the principles for recording a credit purchases transaction in the accounting system

   (b)   the principles for recording a purchases returns transaction in the accounting system

---

In the activities which follow, the rate of Value Added Tax is to be calculated at the current rate (17.5% at the time of writing). When calculating VAT amounts, you should ignore fractions of a penny, ie round down to a whole penny.

Leave the folio column blank, and do not use account numbers, unless otherwise stated.

6.4   During April 1997, Wyvern Wholesalers had the following credit transactions:

   1997

   2 Apr   Bought goods from Severn Supplies £250 + VAT, their invoice no. 6789

   4 Apr   Bought goods from I Johnstone £210 + VAT, her invoice no. A241

   10 Apr   Bought goods from L Murphy £185 + VAT, his invoice no. 2456

   15 Apr   Bought goods from Mercia Manufacturing £180 + VAT, their invoice no. X457

   18 Apr   Bought goods from AMC Enterprises £345 + VAT, their invoice no. AMC 456

   24 Apr   Bought goods from S Green £395 + VAT, her invoice no. 2846

   You are to:

   (a)   enter the above transactions in Wyvern Wholesaler's purchases day book for April 1997

   (b)   record the accounting entries in Wyvern Wholesaler's purchases ledger and general ledger

6.5   The following are the purchases returns for Wyvern Wholesalers for April 1997. They are to be:

   (a)   entered in the purchases returns day book for April 1997

   (b)   recorded in the purchases ledger and general ledger (use the ledgers already prepared in the answer to Activity 6.4)

1997

7 Apr	Returned goods to Severn Supplies £50 + VAT, credit note no. CN225 received
14 Apr	Returned goods to L Murphy £80 + VAT, credit note no. X456 received
21 Apr	Returned goods to AMC Enterprises £125 + VAT, credit note no. C3921 received
29 Apr	Returned goods to S Green £68 + VAT, credit note no. CN/SG247 received

6.6 Jason Smythe owns a business selling furniture and carpets. During April 1997 he received the following invoices from his suppliers:

1997

2 Apr	Invoice no. 2790 for furniture from T Table Limited for £1,247.50 + VAT
7 Apr	Invoice no. 8461 for carpets from Eastern Imports for £796.80 + VAT
10 Apr	Invoice no. A2431 for carpets from Minster Carpets Limited for £1,875.24 + VAT
14 Apr	Invoice no. 27998 for furniture from Pegasus Limited for £498.13 + VAT
16 Apr	Invoice no. 98421 for carpets from United Carpets Limited for £476.22 + VAT
21 Apr	Invoice no. 47921 for furniture from Gerrard Furniture for £831.49 + VAT
23 Apr	Invoice no. 2934 for furniture from T Table Limited for £648.90 + VAT
28 Apr	Invoice no. 8991 for carpets from Eastern Imports for £1,297.31 + VAT

You are to:

(a) enter the above transactions into an *analysed* purchases day book including columns for VAT, furniture and carpets

(b) total the day book at 30 April

Note: entries in the purchases ledger and general ledger are *not* required.

7 FURTHER ASPECTS OF DOUBLE-ENTRY ACCOUNTS

this chapter covers . . .

So far we have studied the principles of double-entry book-keeping and applied them to transactions for credit sales, credit purchases, and returns. In this chapter, we see how accounts are used to record other types of transactions for:

- *capital*
- *fixed assets*
- *expenses*
- *income*
- *drawings*
- *loans*

Firstly though, we look in detail at the division of the ledger, and the types of accounts found in the book-keeping system.

NVQ PERFORMANCE CRITERIA COVERED

unit 2: RECORDING AND ACCOUNTING FOR CREDIT TRANSACTIONS

element 1

process documents relating to goods and services supplied on credit

element 2

process documents relating to goods and services received on credit

KNOWLEDGE AND UNDERSTANDING – ACCOUNTING PRINCIPLES AND THEORY

- ❏   *functions of a ledger system and main types of account*
- ❏   *inter-relationship of accounts – double-entry principles*
- ❏   *distinction between capital and revenue expenditure*
- ❏   *internal check, control and security principles*

DIVISION OF THE LEDGER

In the previous two chapters we have already made some use of the division of the ledger, whereby separate ledgers are kept, each containing different classes of account. The ledger of a business is usually divided into four sections:

- *sales ledger*, containing the accounts of the firm's debtors (customers)
- *purchases ledger*, containing the accounts of the firm's creditors (suppliers)
- *cash book*, containing bank account and cash account records of the business
- *general ledger* (often known as nominal ledger) containing all other accounts

When computers are used for accounting, the physical ledger books do not exist. However, the principles of manual and computerised accounting are the same, and the term 'ledgers' is used in computer accounting systems. Accounting software is available for each of the ledgers mentioned above, usually combined into one integrated computer program. The four divisions of the ledger are illustrated in full on the next page.

TYPES OF ACCOUNT

Within a book-keeping system there are different types of accounts: a distinction is made between personal and impersonal accounts. Personal accounts are in the names of people or businesses, eg the accounts for debtors and creditors. Impersonal accounts are non-personal accounts; these are usually divided between real accounts, which represent things such as cash, bank, computers, motor vehicles, machinery, etc, and nominal accounts, which record income and expenses such as sales, purchases, wages, etc. The diagram below distinguishes between the different types of account.

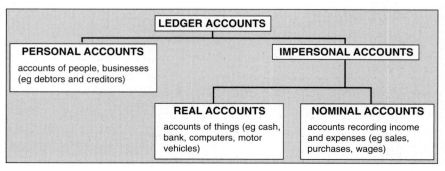

DIVISION OF THE LEDGER

sales ledger

Sales ledger contains the accounts of debtors, and records:
- sales made on credit to customers of the business
- sales returns by customers
- payments received from debtors
- cash discount allowed (see Chapter 9) for prompt settlement

Sales ledger does not record cash sales.

Sales ledger contains an account for each debtor and records the transactions with that debtor. The total of the sales ledger account balances is the debtors figure which appears in the trial balance (see Chapter 8).

purchases ledger

Purchases ledger contains the accounts of creditors, and records:
- purchases made on credit from suppliers of the business
- purchases returns made by the business
- payments made to creditors
- cash discount received (see Chapter 9) for prompt settlement

Purchases ledger does not record cash purchases.

Purchases ledger contains an account for each creditor and records the transactions with that creditor. The total of the purchases ledger account balances is the creditors figure which appears in the trial balance (see Chapter 8).

cash books

The cash books comprise:
- Cash Book (see Chapter 15)
  - records all transactions for bank account and cash account
  - cash book is also often used for listing the amounts of cash discount received and allowed and Value Added Tax

- Petty Cash Book (see Chapter 16)
  - records low value cash payments too small to be entered in the main cash book

general (nominal) ledger

The general (or nominal) ledger contains the other accounts of the business:
- Nominal Accounts
  - sales account (cash and credit sales)
  - purchases account (cash and credit purchases)
  - sales returns, purchases returns
  - expenses and income
  - loan
  - capital, drawings
  - Value Added Tax (where the business is VAT-registered)

- Real Accounts
  - fixed assets, eg premises, computers, motor vehicles

DOUBLE-ENTRY ACCOUNTS

In the previous two chapters we have used accounts to record transactions for purchases, sales, and returns. In order to see how accounts are used to record other types of transactions, we will look at a new business which has just been set up by Natasha Wilson:

1997	
1 Sep	Started in business with capital of £5,000, a cheque from Natasha Wilson paid into the bank account of the business
8 Sep	Bought office equipment for £2,500, paying by cheque
12 Sep	Paid rent for her office £500, by cheque
15 Sep	Received commission of £100, in cash
19 Sep	Withdrew £50 in cash for her own use (drawings)
26 Sep	Received a loan of £1,000 from James Herbertson by cheque

Note: the business is not registered for Value Added Tax

All of these transactions involve the firm's bank account or cash account. The rules of debit and credit for bank account and cash account transactions are:

- money in is recorded on the debit side (the account has gained value)
- money out is recorded on the credit side (the account has given value)

We will build up the entries in bank account and cash account by studying the transactions of Natasha Wilson's business listed above.

CAPITAL ACCOUNT

Capital is the amount of money invested in the business by the owner (or owners). The amount is owed by the business to the owner, although it is unlikely to be repaid immediately as then the business would be unable to operate. A capital account is used to record the amount(s) paid into the business; the book-keeping entries are:

- **capital introduced**

    – *debit* bank account or cash account

    – *credit* capital account

example transaction

1 September 1997
Started in business with capital of £5,000, a cheque from the owner paid into the bank account of the business.

Dr		Capital Account		Cr
1997		£	1997	£
			1 Sep Bank	5,000

Dr		Bank Account		Cr
1997		£	1997	£
1 Sep Capital		5,000		

The dual aspect (see page 60) of this transaction is that bank account has gained value and has been debited; capital account records a liability (to the owner) and is credited. Notice that book-keeping entries look at transactions from the point of view of the business or organisation.

The introduction of capital into a business is often the very first transaction to be entered into the accounts.

FIXED ASSETS

Fixed assets are items purchased by a business for use on a permanent or semi-permanent basis. Examples are buildings, machinery, motor vehicles and office equipment. All of these are bought by a business with the intention that they will be used for some time in the business. When a business buys fixed assets, the expenditure is referred to as *capital expenditure*. This means that items have been bought for use in the business for some years to come. By contrast, *revenue expenditure* is where the items bought will be used by the business quite quickly. For example, the purchase of a car is capital expenditure, while the cost of petrol for the car is revenue expenditure.

fixed assets and double-entry book-keeping

When fixed assets are bought, a separate account for each type of fixed asset is used, eg buildings account, machinery account, motor vehicles account, etc. The book-keeping entries are:

- **purchase of a fixed asset**
    - debit fixed asset account (using the appropriate account)
    - credit bank account or cash account

example transaction

8 September 1997 Natasha Wilson bought office equipment for £2,500, paying by cheque.

Dr		Office Equipment Account		Cr
1997		£	1997	£
8 Sep	Bank	2,500		

Dr		Bank Account		Cr
1997		£	1997	£
1 Sep	Capital	5,000	8 Sep Office equipment	2,500

Note: we have debited the account which has gained value – office equipment account. The account which has given value – bank – has been credited.

EXPENSES

Businesses and other organisations pay various running expenses, such as rent, wages, electricity, telephone, vehicle running expenses, etc. These day-to-day expenses are revenue expenditure. A separate account is used in the accounting system for each main class of revenue expenditure, eg rent account, wages account, etc.

The book-keeping entries are:

- **payment of an expense**
    - debit expense account (using the appropriate account)
    - credit bank account (or cash account)

example transaction

12 September 1997

Natasha Wilson paid rent for her office £500, by cheque.

Dr		Rent Paid Account			Cr
1997		£	1997		£
12 Sep	Bank	500			

Dr		Bank Account			Cr
1997		£	1997		£
1 Sep	Capital	5,000	8 Sep	Office equipment	2,500
			12 Sep	Rent paid	500

Note: we have debited the account which has gained value (rent paid – the business has had the use of the office for a certain time). The account which has given value (bank) has been credited.

INCOME

From time-to-time a business or organisation may receive amounts of income apart from its normal sales income, eg rent received, commission received, or fees received. These are recorded in separate accounts for each category of income, eg rent received account, commission received account. The book-keeping entries are:

- **receipt of income**

   – debit bank account or cash account

   – credit income account (using the appropriate account)

example transaction

15 September 1997   Natasha Wilson received commission of £100, in cash.

Dr		Cash Account		Cr
1997		£	1997	£
15 Sep	Commission received	100		

Dr		Commission Received Account		Cr
1997		£	1997	£
			15 Sep Cash	100

Note: We have debited the account which has gained value, ie cash, and credited the account which has given value, ie commission received.

OWNER'S DRAWINGS

Drawings is the term used when the owner takes money, in cash or by cheque (or sometimes goods), from the business for personal use. A drawings account is used to record such amounts; the book-keeping entries for withdrawal of money are:

- **owner's drawings**
  - debit drawings account
  - credit bank account or cash account

example transaction

19 September 1997   Natasha Wilson withdrew £50 in cash for her own use.

Dr		Drawings Account			Cr
1997		£	1997		£
19 Sep	Cash	50			

Dr		Cash Account			Cr
1997		£	1997		£
15 Sep	Commission received	100	19 Sep	Drawings	50

LOANS

When a business or organisation receives a loan, eg from a relative or the bank, it is the cash account or bank account which gains value, while a loan account (in the name of the lender) records the liability.

- loan received
  - debit bank account or cash account
  - credit loan account (in name of the lender)

example transaction

26 September 1997   Natasha Wilson received a loan of £1,000 from James Herbertson by cheque.

Dr		Bank Account			Cr
1997		£	1997		£
1 Sep	Capital	5,000	8 Sep	Office equipment	2,500
26 Sep	J Herbertson: Loan	1,000	12 Sep	Rent paid	500

Dr		James Herbertson: Loan Account			Cr
1997		£	1997		£
			26 Sep	Bank	1,000

FURTHER TRANSACTIONS

Using the accounts which we have seen already, here are some further transactions:

- **loan repayment**
  - debit loan account
  - credit bank account

- **sale of a fixed asset, or return of an unsuitable fixed asset**
  - debit bank account
  - credit fixed asset account

- **withdrawal of cash from the bank for use in the business**
  - debit cash account
  - credit bank account

- **payment of cash into the bank**
  - debit bank account
  - credit cash account

VAT AND DOUBLE-ENTRY ACCOUNTS

When a business is registered for Value Added Tax it is able to claim back VAT paid on purchases of goods, fixed assets, and expenses. At the same time it must charge VAT whenever it supplies goods and services (except for zero-rated and exempt goods and services).

We have already seen in the previous two chapters how VAT is dealt with for purchases, sales and returns. When a business buys, for example, fixed assets it will enter the amount of VAT direct to the debit side of VAT account.

example transaction

On 16 April 1997, XYZ Supplies Limited, a company which is registered for Value Added Tax, buys a new computer at a cost of £600 + VAT (at 17.5%) of £105, paying by cheque.

This is recorded in the double-entry accounts as:

Dr			Computer Account	Cr
1997		£	1997	£
16 Apr	Bank	600		

Dr			Value Added Tax Account	Cr
1997		£	1997	£
16 Apr	Bank	105		

Dr			Bank Account	Cr
1997		£	1997	£
			16 Apr Computer	705

The Value Added Tax account in the general ledger will record:

Value Added Tax Account	
Debits (input tax)	*Credits (output tax)*
VAT on purchases	VAT on sales and/or services
VAT on purchases of fixed assets (except cars)	VAT on the sale of fixed assets
VAT on expenses	VAT on purchases returns
VAT on sales returns	

Not all goods and services purchased can be assumed to include VAT: as well as zero-rated and exempt goods, the supplier might be a business which is not registered for VAT.

Where businesses and other organisations are not registered for Value Added Tax, they cannot reclaim VAT paid on purchases, fixed assets and expenses, nor can they charge VAT when they supply goods and services.

Likewise, for a non-registered business, expenses which include VAT are entered in the accounts at the full invoice value.

For further details of VAT and VAT calculations see pages 30 to 32.

RUNNING BALANCE ACCOUNTS

The layout of accounts that we have used has a debit side and a credit side. Whilst this layout is very useful when learning the principles of book-keeping, it is not always appropriate for practical business use. Most 'real-life' accounts have three money columns: debit transactions, credit transactions, and balance. A familiar example of this type of account is a bank statement. With a three-column account, the balance is calculated after each transaction has been entered – hence the name running balance accounts. For handwritten accounts, it can be rather tedious to calculate the balance after each transaction (and a potential source of errors) but, using computer accounting, the calculation is carried out automatically.

The bank account, used earlier in this chapter, is set out below in 'traditional' format:

Dr			**Bank Account**		Cr
1997		£	1997		£
1 Sep	Capital	5,000	8 Sep Office equipment	2,500	
26 Sep	J Herbertson: Loan	1,000	12 Sep Rent paid	500	

The account does not show the balance, and would need to be balanced (see next chapter).

In 'running balance' layout, the account appears as follows:

Bank Account

		Debit	Credit	Balance
1997		£	£	£
1 Sep	Capital	5,000		5,000 Dr
8 Sep	Office equipment		2,500	2,500 Dr
12 Sep	Rent paid		500	2,000 Dr
26 Sep	J Herbertson: loan	1,000		3,000 Dr

With a running balance account, it is necessary to state after each transaction whether the balance is debit (Dr) or credit (Cr). Note that the bank account in the books of this business has a *debit* balance, ie there is money in the bank – an asset of Natasha Wilson's business.

When looking at a bank account, do not get confused as to the meaning of the balance. In the example, above, the debit balance of £3,000 shows that *from the business' point of view* the business has an asset, ie there is £3,000 in the bank. However, the bank statement – which is *from the bank's point of view* will show a credit balance of £3,000, ie the bank owes the money back to the customer. To summarise:

- **money in the bank**

    - *debit* balance in firm's own accounts, ie an asset of the business

    - *credit* balance on bank statement, ie a liability of the bank

- **overdraft at the bank**

    - *credit* balance in firm's own accounts, a liability of the business

    - *debit* balance on bank statement, ie an asset of the bank

THE USE OF POSTING SHEETS

In a large business or organisation, the various aspects of the accounting function will be allocated to a number of staff. For example, to look more closely at the recording and payment of credit purchases:

- one person may be involved in checking invoices received
- another person may prepare the purchases day book
- another person may pass invoices or statements received for payment
- another person may prepare remittance advices and cheques for sending to creditors
- another person may keep the double-entry accounts up-to-date

These job allocations are given as an example only – as always, it is for the business to organise its accounting function to suit its needs. The essential point, though, is that in a larger business several people may be involved in just one area of record keeping, such as purchases, sales, etc. (In a small business, all of these tasks and more would, most likely, be carried out by just one person.)

One feature of a large business is that use may be made of a posting sheet. This lists transactions that are to be entered (or posted) into the double-entry accounts and will be prepared by a member of the accounts department. For example, a simple posting sheet for the transactions of Natasha Wilson in this chapter would be prepared as follows:

Posting Sheet			
Account	**Folio**	**Debit**	**Credit**
		£	£
Bank	CB	5,000	
Capital	GL		5,000
Office equipment	GL	2,500	
Bank	CB		2,500
Rent paid	GL	500	
Bank	CB		500
Cash	CB	100	
Commission received	GL		100
Drawings	GL	50	
Cash	CB		50
Bank	CB	1,000	
J. Herbertson: loan	GL		1,000
TOTALS		9,150	9,150

Prepared by _J. Jarvis_	Date _26 Sep 1997_
Checked by _N. Wilson_	Date _26 Sep 1997_
Posted by _S. Ahmed_	Date _26 Sep 1997_

Notes:

- The posting sheet can be designed in any format to suit the needs of the business.
- It can be used for one day's transactions, or for longer periods such as a week or a month – much depends on the number of transactions to be recorded.
- Essential information includes:
  - name of account
  - folio, usually together with the account number, eg PL 253
  - amount of debit entry
  - amount of credit entry
- The posting sheet is totalled – this shows that the money amounts of debit entries are equal to credit entries.
- The name of the person preparing the posting sheet is stated with the date, together with the person checking it and the date.
- The name of the person posting the transactions to the firm's double-entry accounts, together with the date, is given.

batched data entry

A variation on the posting sheet is often used – particularly with computer accounting programs. Here it is usual to batch a series of transactions, eg to deal with a number of sales ledger transactions, or purchases ledger transactions. By batching, there is less need to keep changing from one area of the program to another. Before entering a batch of transactions, it is usual to pre-list them on a separate form such as that shown below for a batch of sales invoices:

Sales Invoice Batch

Customer		Invoice		Gross	VAT	Net
Account No	Name	Date	No	£	£	£
Check list totals						

The sales invoice batch form will be completed from invoices which have been prepared separately. The transactions will then be entered from the invoices into the computer. The computer screen will show the total money amount of invoices and this is compared with the check list total from the sales invoice batch form; if there is a discrepancy, the error must be located and corrected.

CHAPTER SUMMARY

- • Ledger accounts are classified between:
  - – personal accounts
  - – impersonal accounts (which are further classified between real accounts and nominal accounts)
- • Entries in the bank account and cash account are:
  - – debit money in
  - – credit money out
- • Other accounts are opened in the book-keeping system for:
  - – capital
  - – fixed assets
  - – expenses
  - – income

    – drawings

    – loans

- Posting sheets are used to list transactions to be entered in the double-entry accounts.

- Batched data entry is used when entering the same type of transactions – such as sales invoices – into the double-entry accounts; particularly used for inputting data to computer accounting systems.

KEY TERMS

personal accounts	accounts in the names of people or businesses, eg the accounts for debtors and creditors
impersonal accounts	non-personal accounts, usually divided between real accounts and nominal accounts
real accounts	accounts which represent things, such as cash, bank, computers, motor vehicles, machinery
nominal accounts	accounts which record income and expenses, such as sales, purchases, wages
capital account	records the amount of money invested in the business by the owner (or owners)
fixed assets	items purchased by a business for use on a permanent or semi-permanent basis, such as buildings, machinery, motor vehicles, office equipment – the capital expenditure of a business
expenses	the running expenses (or revenue expenditure) of a business, such as rent, wages, electricity, telephone, vehicle running expenses
drawings	amount of money taken by the owner in cash, or by cheque (or sometimes goods), from the business for personal use
running balance accounts	accounts which show the balance after each transaction has been entered; consist of three money columns: debit, credit and balance
posting sheets	a list of transactions to be entered in the double-entry accounts
batched data entry	a batch of the same type of transactions to be entered into the double-entry accounts

STUDENT ACTIVITIES

7.1 Sales ledger contains:

(a)   creditors' accounts

(b)   sales account

(c)   debtors' accounts

(d)   sales returns account

Answer (a) or (b) or (c) or (d)

7.2 Which one of the following is not a division of the ledger?

(a)   general ledger

(b)   sales account

(c)   sales ledger

(d)   cash book

Answer (a) or (b) or (c) or (d)

7.3 A friend has recently set up in business. To help him, you have written up the first month's double-entry accounts. Your friend comments:

- "I bought a computer, but you've shown it on the debit side. Surely it must go on the credit side? You must be wrong."

- "Why is the transaction for my capital on the credit side of capital account. I've paid in capital, so surely this is the account which has gained value?"

7.4 Debits and credit entries to a bank account means different things to businesses and to banks. Complete the two columns below with either 'debit or credit'.

Transaction	how the bank sees it	how the business sees it
(a) a cheque is paid into the bank		
(b) bank charges		
(c) a loan taken out from the bank		
(d) cash is paid into the bank		
(e) the business buys an asset, paying by cheque		

7.5 James Anderson has kept his bank account up-to-date, but has not got around to the other double-entry book-keeping entries. Rule up the other accounts for him, and make the appropriate entries.

Dr			**Bank Account**			Cr
1997		£	1997			£
3 Feb	Capital	7,500	6 Feb	Computer		2,000
14 Feb	Bank Loan	2,500	7 Feb	Rent paid		750
20 Feb	Commission received	145	12 Feb	Wages		425
			24 Feb	Drawings		200
			25 Feb	Wages		380
			28 Feb	Van		6,000

Note: James Anderson is not registered for Value Added Tax.

7.6 The following are the business transactions of Tony Long for the month of May 1997:

1 May	Started a business with capital of £6,000 in the bank
5 May	Bought a machine for £3,500, paying by cheque
6 May	Bought office equipment for £2,000, paying by cheque
9 May	Paid rent £350, by cheque
12 May	Obtained a loan of £1,000 from a friend, Lucy Warner, and paid her cheque into the bank
15 May	Paid wages £250, by cheque
19 May	Commission received £150, by cheque
20 May	Drawings £85, by cheque
26 May	Paid wages £135, by cheque

You are to:

(a) Write up Tony Long's bank account

(b) Complete the double-entry book-keeping transactions

Note: Tony Long is not registered for Value Added Tax.

7.7   Enter the following transactions into the double-entry book-keeping accounts of Jean Lacey, who is registered for Value Added Tax:

1997

1 Aug	Started in business with capital of £5,000 in the bank
4 Aug	Bought a computer for £1,800 + VAT, paying by cheque
7 Aug	Paid rent £100, by cheque
10 Aug	Received commission £200 + VAT, in cash
12 Aug	Bought office fittings £2,000 + VAT, paying by cheque
15 Aug	Received a loan, £1,000 by cheque, from a friend, Sally Orton
17 Aug	Drawings £100, in cash
20 Aug	Returned some of the office fittings (unsuitable) and received a refund cheque of £240 + VAT
25 Aug	Received commission £160 + VAT, by cheque
27 Aug	Made a loan repayment to Sally Orton of £150, by cheque

Note: use the current rate of Value Added Tax (17.5% at the time of writing).

8 BALANCING ACCOUNTS AND THE TRIAL BALANCE

this chapter covers . . .

With the 'traditional' form of account (the 'T' account), it is necessary to calculate the balance of each account from time-to-time, according to the needs of the business, and at the end of each financial year. The balance of an account is the running total of that account to date, eg the amount of wages paid, the amount of sales made, the amount of money in the bank. In this chapter we shall see how this balancing of accounts is carried out.

We shall then use the balances from each account in order to check the double-entry book-keeping by extracting a trial balance, which is a list of the balances of ledger accounts.

NVQ PERFORMANCE CRITERIA COVERED

unit 2 RECORDING AND ACCOUNTING FOR CREDIT TRANSACTIONS

KNOWLEDGE AND UNDERSTANDING – ACCOUNTING TECHNIQUES
❏   operation of manual and computerised accounting systems

KNOWLEDGE AND UNDERSTANDING – ACCOUNTING PRINCIPLES AND THEORY
❏   inter-relationship of accounts – double-entry principles
❏   internal check, control and security principles

BALANCING THE ACCOUNTS

At regular intervals, often at the end of each month, accounts are balanced in order to show the amounts, for example:

* owing to each creditor
* owing by each debtor
* of sales
* of purchases
* of sales returns (returns in)
* of purchases returns (returns out)
* of expenses incurred by the business
* of fixed assets, eg premises, machinery, etc owned by the business
* of capital and drawings of the owner of the business
* of other liabilities, eg loans

We have already noted earlier that, where running balance accounts (see page 106) are used, there is no need to balance each account, because the balance is already calculated – either manually or by computer – after each transaction.

METHOD OF BALANCING ACCOUNTS

Set out below is an example of an account which has been balanced at the month-end:

Dr			**Bank Account**			Cr
1997		£	1997			£
1 Sep	Capital	5,000	2 Sep	Computer		1,800
5 Sep	J Jackson: loan	2,500	8 Sep	Purchases		500
10 Sep	Sales	750	12 Sep	Drawings		100
			15 Sep	Wages		200
			30 Sep	Balance c/d		5,650
		8,250				8,250
1 Oct	Balance b/d	5,650				

The steps involved in balancing accounts are set out on the next page.

Step 1

The entries in the debit and credit money columns are totalled; these totals are not recorded in ink on the account at this stage, but can be recorded either as sub-totals in pencil on the account, or noted on a separate piece of paper. In the example above, the debit side totals £8,250, while the credit side is £2,600.

Step 2

The difference between the two totals is the balance of the account and this is entered on the account:

- on the side of the smaller total
- on the next available line
- with the date of balancing (often the last day of the month)
- with the description 'balance c/d', or 'balance carried down'

In the bank account above, the balance carried down is £8,260 − £2,600 = £5,650, entered in the credit column.

Step 3

Both sides of the account are now totalled, including the balance which has just been entered, and the totals (the same on both sides) are entered on the same line in the appropriate column, and double underlined. The double underline indicates that the account has been balanced at this point using the figures above the total: the figures above the underline should not be added in to anything below the underline.

In the bank account on the previous page the totals on each side of the account are £8,250.

Step 4

As we are using double-entry book-keeping, there must be an opposite entry to the 'balance c/d' calculated in Step 2. The same money amount is entered on the other side of the account below the double-underlined totals entered in Step 3. We have now completed both the debit and credit entry. The date is usually recorded as the next day after 'balance c/d', ie often the first day of the following month, and the description can be 'balance b/d' or 'balance brought down'.

In the example above, the balance brought down on the bank account on 1 October 1997 is £5,650 debit; this means that, according to the firm's accounting records, there is £5,650 in the bank.

A practical point:

When balancing accounts, use a pen and not a pencil (except for Step 1). If any errors are made, cross them through neatly with a single line, and write the corrected version on the line below. Do not use correcting fluid: at best it conceals errors, at worst it conceals fraudulent transactions.

FURTHER EXAMPLES OF BALANCING ACCOUNTS

Dr		**Wages account**			Cr
1997		£	1997		£
9 Apr	Bank	750	30 Apr	Balance c/d	2,250
16 Apr	Bank	800			
23 Apr	Bank	700			
		2,250			2,250
1 May	Balance b/d	2,250			

The above wages account has transactions on one side only, but is still balanced in the same way. This account shows that the total amount paid for wages is £2,250.

Dr		**B Lewis Limited**			Cr
1997		£	1997		£
10 Apr	Purchases returns	30	7 Apr	Purchases	280
25 Apr	Bank	250			
		280			280

This account in the name of a creditor has a 'nil' balance after the transactions for April have taken place. The two sides of the account are totalled and, as both debit and credit side are the same amount, there is nothing further to do, apart from entering the double-underlined total.

Dr		A Holmes			Cr
1997		£	1997		£
1 Apr	Balance b/d	105	10 Apr	Bank	105
11 Apr	Sales	125	11 Apr	Sales returns	25
			30 Apr	Balance c/d	100
		230			230
1 May	Balance b/d	100			

This is the account of a debtor and, at the start of the month, there was a debit balance of £105 brought down from March. After the various transactions for April, there remains a debit balance of £100 owing at 1 May.

Dr		Office Equipment account		Cr
1997		£	1997	£
14 Apr	Bank	2,000		

This account has just the one transaction and, in practice, there is no need to balance it. It should be clear that the account has a debit balance of £2,000, which is represented by the asset of office equipment.

Dr		Malvern Manufacturing Company			Cr
1997		£	1997		£
29 Apr	Bank	250	18 Apr	Purchases	250

This creditor's account has a 'nil' balance, with just one transaction on each side. All that is needed here is to double underline the amount on both sides.

EXTRACTING A TRIAL BALANCE

The book-keeper extracts a trial balance from the accounting records in order to check the arithmetical accuracy of the double-entry book-keeping, ie that the debit entries equal the credit entries.

A trial balance is a list of the balances of every account forming the ledger, distinguishing between those accounts which have debit balances and those which have credit balances.

A trial balance is extracted at regular intervals – often at the end of each month. Now study the example on the next page.

Trial balance of A-Z Suppliers as at 31 January 1997

Name of account	Dr £	Cr £
Purchases	7,500	
Sales		16,000
Sales returns	250	
Purchases returns		500
J Brown (debtor)	1,550	
T Sweet (creditor)		1,100
Rent paid	1,000	
Wages	1,500	
Heating and lighting	1,250	
Office equipment	5,000	
Machinery	10,000	
Cash	500	
Bank	4,550	
J Williams: loan		8,000
Capital		10,000
Drawings	2,500	
	35,600	35,600

Notes:

- The debit and credit columns have been totalled and are the same amount. Thus the trial balance proves that the accounting records are arithmetically correct. (A trial balance does not prove the complete accuracy of the accounting records – see below.)

- The balance for each account listed in the trial balance is the figure brought down after the accounts have been balanced.

- As well as the name of each account, it is quite usual to show in the trial balance the account number. Most accounting systems give numbers to accounts and these can be listed in a separate 'folio' or 'reference' column.

DEBIT AND CREDIT BALANCES – GUIDELINES

Certain accounts always have a debit balance, while others always have a credit balance. You should already know these, but the lists set out below will act as a revision guide, and will also help in your understanding of trial balances.

Debit balances include:

- cash account

- purchases account

- sales returns account (returns in)

- fixed asset accounts, eg premises, motor vehicles, machinery, office equipment, etc

- expenses accounts, eg wages, telephone, rent paid, etc

- drawings account

- debtors' accounts (many businesses use a sales ledger control account – see Chapter 10 – the balance of which gives the total of debtors: this balance is entered in the trial balance as 'debtors')

Credit balances include:

- sales account

- purchases returns account (returns out)

- income accounts, eg rent received, commission received, fees received

- capital account

- loan account

- creditors' accounts (many businesses use a purchases ledger control account – see Chapter 10 – the balance of which gives the total of creditors: this balance is entered in the trial balance as 'creditors')

Notes:

- Bank account can be either debit or credit – it will be debit when the business has money in the bank, and credit when it is overdrawn.
- Value Added Tax account can be either debit or credit – it will be debit when VAT is due to the business and credit when the business owes VAT to HM Customs & Excise.

IF THE TRIAL BALANCE DOESN'T BALANCE . . .

If the trial balance fails to balance, ie the two totals are different, there is an error (or errors):

- *either* in the addition of the trial balance
- *and/or* in the double-entry book-keeping

The procedure for finding the error(s) is as follows:

- check the addition of the trial balance
- check that the balance of each account has been correctly entered in the trial balance, and under the correct heading, ie debit or credit
- check that the balance of every account in the ledger has been included in the trial balance
- check the calculation of the balance on each account
- calculate the amount that the trial balance is wrong, and then look in the accounts for a transaction for this amount: if one is found, check that the double-entry book-keeping has been carried out correctly
- halve the amount by which the trial balance is wrong, and look for a transaction for this amount: if it is found, check the double-entry book-keeping
- if the amount by which the trial balance is wrong is divisible by nine, then the error may be a reversal of figures, eg £65 entered as £56, or £45 entered as £54
- if the trial balance is wrong by a round amount, eg £10, £100, £1,000, the error is likely to be in the calculation of the account balances
- if the error(s) is still not found, it is necessary to check the book-keeping transactions since the date of the last trial balance, by going back to the prime documents and books of primary accounting records

ERRORS NOT SHOWN BY A TRIAL BALANCE

As mentioned earlier, a trial balance does not prove the complete accuracy of the accounting records. There are six types of errors that are not shown by a trial balance.

1. Error of omission

Here a business transaction has been completely omitted from the accounting records, ie both the debit and credit entries have not been made.

2. Reversal of entries

With this error, the debit and credit entries have been made in the accounts but on the wrong side of the two accounts concerned. For example, a cash sale has been entered wrongly as debit sales account, credit cash account. (This should have been entered as a debit to cash account, and a credit to sales account.)

3. Mispost/error of commission

Here, a transaction is entered to the wrong person's account. For example, a sale of goods on credit to A T Hughes has been entered as debit to A J Hughes' account, credit sales account. Double-entry book-keeping has been completed, but when A J Hughes receives a statement of account, he or she will soon complain about being debited with goods not ordered or received.

4. Error of principle

This is when a transaction has been entered in the wrong type of account. For example, the cost of petrol for vehicles has been entered as debit motor vehicles account, credit bank account. The error is that motor vehicles account represents fixed assets, and the transaction should have been debited to the expense account for motor vehicle running expenses.

5. Error of original entry (or transcription)

Here, the correct accounts have been used, and the correct sides: what is wrong is that the amount has been entered incorrectly in both accounts. This could be caused by a 'bad figure' on an invoice or a cheque, or it could be caused by a 'reversal of figures', eg an amount of £45 being entered in both accounts as £54. Note that both debit and credit entries need to be made incorrectly for the trial balance still to balance; if one entry has been made incorrectly and the other is correct, then the error will be shown.

6. Compensating error

This is where two errors cancel each other out. For example, if the balance of purchases account is calculated wrongly at £10 too much, and a similar error has occurred in calculating the balance of sales account, then the two errors will compensate each other, and the trial balance will not show the errors.

Correction of errors is covered fully in Chapter 11.

IMPORTANCE OF THE TRIAL BALANCE

A business will extract a trial balance on a regular basis to check the arithmetic accuracy of the book-keeping. However, the trial balance is also used as the starting point in the production of the final accounts of a business. These final accounts, which are produced once a year (often more frequently) comprise:

- profit and loss statement
- balance sheet

The final accounts show the owner(s) how profitable the business has been, what the business owns, and how the business is financed. The preparation of final accounts is an important aspect of accountancy. Final accounts are covered in later NVQ levels. For the moment, we can say that extraction of a trial balance is an important exercise in the business accounts process: it proves the book-keeper's accuracy, and also lists the account balances which form the basis for the final accounts of a business.

CHAPTER SUMMARY

- The traditional 'T' account needs to be balanced at regular intervals – often at the month-end.

- When balancing accounts, the book-keeper must adhere strictly to the rules of double-entry book-keeping.

- When each account in the ledger has been balanced, a trial balance can be extracted.

- A trial balance does not prove the complete accuracy of the accounting records; errors not shown by a trial balance are:

  – error of omission

  – reversal of entries

  – mispost/error of commission

  – error of principle

  – error of original entry

  – compensating error

- The trial balance is used as the starting point for the preparation of a business' final accounts.

KEY TERMS

balance of account	the total of the account to date
trial balance	list of the balances of every account forming the ledger, distinguishing between those accounts which have debit balances and those which have credit balances
error of omission	business transaction completely omitted from the accounting records
reversal of entries	debit and credit entries made on the wrong side of the accounts
mispost/error of commission	transaction entered to the wrong person's account
error of principle	transaction entered in the wrong type of account
error of original entry	wrong amount entered incorrectly in accounts
compensating error	where two errors cancel each other out

STUDENT ACTIVITIES

8.1 Which one of the following accounts always has a debit balance?

(a) capital account

(b) purchases account

(c) sales account

(d) purchases returns account

Answer (a) or (b) or (c) or (d)

8.2 Which one of the following accounts always has a credit balance?

(a) sales returns account

(b) premises account

(c) capital account

(d) wages account

Answer (a) or (b) or (c) or (d)

8.3 An amount has been entered into the book-keeping system as £65 instead of £56. The error is called:

(a) compensating error

(b) mispost

(c) error of principle

(d) error of original entry

Answer (a) or (b) or (c) or (d)

8.4 Balance the following accounts at 30 April 1997:

Dr			**Sales Account**		Cr
1997		£	1997		£
			1 Apr	Balance b/d	12,550
			30 Apr	Sales Day Book	4,620

Dr		**Wages Account**			Cr
1997		£	1997		£
1 Apr	Balance b/d	3,710			
11 Apr	Bank	780			
25 Apr	Bank	690			

Dr		**Wyvern Traders**			Cr
1997		£	1997		£
1 Apr	Balance b/d	375	24 Apr	Bank	375

Dr		**T Johnson**			Cr
1997		£	1997		£
15 Apr	Bank	240	1 Apr	Balance b/d	240
18 Apr	Purchases Returns	45	10 Apr	Purchases	180
			29 Apr	Purchases	215

8.5 Andrew Jarvis started in business on 1 April 1997.

During the month he had the following transactions:

1997

1 Apr	Paid £1,000 into business bank account as opening capital
2 Apr	Bought goods for resale, paying by cheque, £255
4 Apr	Paid for advertising by cheque, £60
7 Apr	Sold goods, £195, a cheque being received
8 Apr	Paid rent by cheque, £125
10 Apr	Sold goods, £248, a cheque being received
11 Apr	Drawings £100 by cheque
14 Apr	Bought goods for resale, paying by cheque, £240
16 Apr	Received a loan from J Couchman, £1,000 by cheque
18 Apr	Sold goods, £220, a cheque being received
21 Apr	Bought shop fittings, £1,250, paying by cheque
23 Apr	Bought goods for resale, paying by cheque, £180
24 Apr	Paid for advertising by cheque, £90
25 Apr	Sold goods, £312, a cheque being received
28 Apr	Paid rent by cheque, £125
30 Apr	Drawings £125 by cheque

You are to:

(a) Record the transactions in his bank account

(b) Record the transactions in his other double-entry accounts

(c) Balance all the accounts that have more than one transaction at 30 April 1997

(d) Draw up a trial balance at 30 April 1997

Notes:

• *day books are not required*

• *Andrew Jarvis is not registered for VAT*

8.6   Produce the trial balance of Jane Greenwell as at 28 February 1997. She has omitted to open a capital account. You are to fill in the missing figure in order to balance the trial balance.

	£
Bank overdraft	1,250
Purchases	850
Cash	48
Sales	730
Purchases returns	144
Creditors	1,442
Equipment	2,704
Van	3,200
Sales returns	90
Debtors	1,174
Wages	1,500
Capital	?

9 DEBTORS AND CREDITORS

this chapter covers . . .

Having studied accounting for credit sales (Chapter 5) and credit purchases (Chapter 6), in this chapter we focus on further aspects of debtors and creditors. In particular, we will look at:

- control of debtors

- the problem of bad debts

- recording bad debts in the accounting system

- how bad debts can be minimised

- aspects of creditors, including reconciliation of creditors' statements

- recording cash discount in debtors' and creditors' accounts

NVQ PERFORMANCE CRITERIA COVERED

element 3

account for goods and services supplied on credit

❏ adjustments involving debtors' accounts are properly authorised and documented, and are correctly transferred to the correct ledger accounts

❏ where required, statements of account are sent to debtors promptly

❏ the organisation's procedures and timescales are observed

❏ discrepancies, unusual features or queries are identified and either resolved or referred to the appropriate person

❏ communications with debtors regarding accounts are handled promptly, courteously and effectively

element 4

account for goods and services received on credit

❏ the organisation's procedures and timescales are observed

❏ discrepancies, unusual features or queries are identified and either resolved or referred to the appropriate person

❏ communications with creditors regarding accounts are handled promptly, courteously and effectively

CONTROL OF DEBTORS

So far in this book we have taken for granted that a supplier will sell goods on credit terms (ie allow the buyer to pay later), and also that the buyer will pay up on receipt of the statement of account. Unfortunately these are assumptions which, in reality, cannot be taken for granted. When selling on credit the seller must:

- investigate a new buyer to ensure that he or she is creditworthy – ie has the financial resources to pay on the due date
- monitor existing buyers to ensure that they do pay up on time
- chase up debts which are overdue

This overall process is known as *credit control*. It is a sign of a well-run business that credit control is tight, and the debtors are chased up, and even taken to court for non-payment if the amount and the circumstances are appropriate.

We will now look at credit control through two Case Studies: the first looks at a person 'vetting' the creditworthiness of a potential buyer; the second looks at a supplier chasing up overdue debts.

CASE STUDY

SELLING ON CREDIT

situation

Matthew has recently started up in business with a fruit and vegetable stall in the local market. Up until now all his sales have been paid for by his customers in cash or by cheque (collectively known as 'cash sales'). He has today been approached by Goodfood, a firm of caterers who operate a number of works canteens in the locality, to quote for all their fruit and vegetable supplies. The value of this potential contract is sales of about £300 each week; Goodfood require an invoice at the end of each week listing Matthew's sales to them for the week, and they agree to make payment not later than 30 days after the date of the invoice. What should Matthew do?

solution

The steps that need to be taken by Matthew are:

- When approached by a previously unknown organisation wishing to buy goods on credit, the seller should ask for two references. One of these should be the buyer's bank, and the other a trader with whom the buyer has previously done business.
- The seller, Matthew, before supplying goods on credit, must take up both references and obtain satisfactory replies.

- Once satisfactory replies have been received, a credit limit for the customer should be established. The actual amount of the credit limit will depend very much on the expected amount of future business – perhaps £1,500 in this example. The credit limit should not normally be exceeded.

- Matthew should ensure that invoices and monthly statements are sent out promptly.

- If a customer does not pay within a reasonable time, procedures should be followed to chase up the debt promptly and efficiently; these include letters, telephone calls and even court action.

CASE STUDY

CHASING DEBTS

situation

Matthew has found that Goodfood, despite the good references received, are not paying up, and he is owed a total of £450 which should have been paid three months ago. What should he do? He has various courses of action available to him; what he does will depend on how reluctant Goodfood are to pay.

solution

A typical procedure used by an organisation chasing up debts, which Matthew could adopt, would be:

- Write a courteous letter along the lines of:

> *"Dear Sir,*
>
> <u>*Overdue Account*</u>
>
> *We do not appear to have received settlement of your account with us, the balance. of which is £450. We enclose an up-to-date statement and shall be grateful if you settle this overdue amount by return of post."*

- If nothing is heard within seven days, then telephone and ask to speak to their Accounts Department, Purchases Ledger Section. Ask about the overdue payment. You may be told "the cheque is in the post" (it rarely is!) or "can we have a copy of the last invoice – we don't seem to have received it?" These replies can be stalling tactics to buy time; on the other hand, the telephone call may produce results and a payment in the post.

- If payment is not received as a result of the telephone call, Matthew has a number of options open to him:

  – to employ a solicitor to send Goodfood a formal demand for the money and possibly to take Goodfood to court (this is an expensive option)

      –   to employ the services of a debt-collecting agency

      –   to take Goodfood to the Small Claims Court (used for claims under £3,000), a time-consuming process with no guarantee of success

Matthew should realise that taking Goodfood to court and obtaining judgement against them still does not mean he will get his money back. It is often thought that going to court will solve all problems; it often results in a large solicitor's bill and nothing from the debtor. Goodfood may not have the money, and may even be bankrupt, which means that their liabilities exceed their assets. An unsecured creditor like Matthew is unlikely to be repaid anything at all. At a time like this Matthew will probably want to cut his losses and write off the £450 as a 'bad debt' – an expense to his business.

BAD DEBTS

A bad debt is a debt owing to a business or organisation which it considers will never be paid.

Bad debts are written off when they become uncollectable. This means that all reasonable efforts to recover the amount owing have been exhausted, ie statements and letters have been sent to the debtor requesting payment and legal action, where appropriate, or the threat of legal action has failed to obtain payment.

In writing off a debtor's account as bad, the business is bearing the cost of the amount due. The debtor's account is closed and the amount (or amounts, where a number of accounts are dealt with in this way) is debited to bad debts written off account. This account stores up the amounts of account balances written off during the year (in much the same way as an expense account).

The book-keeping transactions to write off a bad debt are:

– *debit* bad debts written off account

– *credit* debtor's account

VAT relief on bad debts

A VAT-registered business can reclaim VAT originally charged on debts which are now being written off. However, in order to claim relief, *the debt must be more than six months overdue*, ie more than six months from the date the payment was originally due. Thus a sale made on 30 day terms on 1 January would be due for payment on 31 January; if this sale is written off as a bad debt, VAT relief would be available after 31 July.

We will now look at a Case Study which shows how a bad debt is written off by a VAT-registered business.

CASE STUDY

WRITING OFF A BAD DEBT – DON'S DINER

situation

You work as a sales ledger clerk in the accounts department of Severn Catering Supplies Limited. The company, which is VAT-registered, sells kitchen equipment to hotels and restaurants throughout the country. The company's terms of trade are for payment within 30 days of invoice date.

It is December 1997 and the accounts supervisor, Sue Robinson, has been reviewing the debtors' accounts in the sales ledger before the end of the financial year on 31 December. She has been looking at the following account:

Dr		Don's Diner		Cr
1997	£	1997		£
6 Jan Sales	47			

Monthly statements and 'chaser' letters have been sent to this debtor – the last letter was dated 30 September and was returned marked 'gone away, not known at this address'.

Solution

The accounts supervisor has decided that it is time to write off the account of Don's Diner as a bad debt. The debt outstanding is £47 and it is not worthwhile taking legal action for such an amount. You are sent the following memo which authorises you to go ahead with the write off:

MEMORANDUM

TO: Sales Ledger Accounts Clerk

FROM: Accounts Supervisor

DATE: 10 December 1997

SUBJECT: DON'S DINER

Please write off the balance of this account as a bad debt – we have done all we can to collect the amount. As we charged VAT on the original invoice, do not forget to reclaim VAT when writing off the balance.

Thanks

Sue

Sue Robinson

prime document

The memo acts as the prime document for this accounting transaction.

primary accounting record

The primary accounting record for non-regular transactions – such as writing off a bad debt – is called the journal. Like the day books that we have seen earlier, it is used to list transactions before they are recorded in the double-entry accounts. The journal entry to write off the account of Don's Diner is as follows:

Date	Details	Folio	Dr	Cr
1997			£	£
15 Dec	Bad debts written off	GL	40	
	Value Added Tax	GL	7	
	Don's Diner	SL		47
	Bad debt written off as per memo from		47	47
	accounts supervisor dated 10 December 1997			

notes on the journal entries

- The names of the accounts to be debited and credited in the book-keeping system are written in the details column. In a journal entry, it is customary to show debit transactions first.

- The money amounts of the debit and credit entries are stated in the columns. A journal entry always balances, ie the debit entry is equal to the credit entry.

- It is usual to include a brief narrative explaining why the transaction is being carried out.

- Each journal entry is complete in itself and is ruled off to separate it from the next entry.

- Journal entries are dealt with in more detail in Chapter 11.

double-entry accounts

The account of Don's Diner is closed off as follows:

SALES LEDGER

Dr		Don's Diner		Cr
1997	£	1997		£
6 Jan Sales	47	10 Dec Bad debts written off		40
		10 Dec Value Added Tax		7
	47			47

The balance net of VAT, ie £40, is transferred to the debit of Bad debts written off account, (together with any other accounts being written off). The VAT amount, ie £7, (VAT at 17.5%) is transferred to the debit of VAT account.

GENERAL LEDGER

Dr		Bad Debts Written Off Account		Cr
1997	£	1997		£
10 Dec Don's Diner	40			

Dr		Value Added Tax Account		Cr
1997	£	1997		£
10 Dec Don's Diner	7			

Thus the account of Don's Diner is now closed and no further goods will be supplied to this customer on credit terms. To summarise writing off a bad debt:

- *prime document* – memo or other authority from accounts supervisor
- *primary accounting record* – the journal
- *double-entry accounts* (for a VAT-registered business claiming VAT relief)
    - *debit* bad debts written off account with the amount of the bad debt, net of VAT
    - *debit* Value Added Tax account with the VAT part of the debt
    - *credit* debtor's account with the amount of the bad debt (including the VAT)

Remember that the debt must be more than six months overdue before VAT relief can be claimed.

MINIMISING THE RISK OF BAD DEBTS

The following are some of the procedures that can be followed:

- When first approached by an unknown business or organisation wishing to buy goods on credit, the seller should ask for two references. One of these should be the buyer's bank, and the other a trader with whom the buyer has previously done business. The seller, before supplying goods on credit, should take up both references and obtain satisfactory replies.

- Once satisfactory replies have been received, a credit limit for the customer should be established, and an account opened in the sales ledger. The amount of the credit limit will depend very much on the expected amount of future business – eg £1,000 might be appropriate. The credit limit should not normally be exceeded – the firm's accounts supervisor or accountant will approve any transactions above the limit.

- Larger businesses sometimes require their customers to sign a *credit agreement*, which sets out the terms of payment.

- Invoices and month-end statements of account should be sent out promptly; invoices should state the terms of trade (see Chapter 2), and statements should analyse the balance to show how long it has been outstanding, eg 'current, 30 days, 60 days, older' – computer-produced statements can show this automatically.

- If a customer does not pay within a reasonable time, the firm should follow established procedures in order to chase up the debt promptly. As well as telephone calls, these procedures are likely to include 'chaser' letters, the first of which points out that the account is overdue, with a later letter threatening legal action. Whether or not legal action is taken will depend on the size of the debt – for a small amount the costs and time involved in taking legal action may outweigh the benefits of recovering the money.

The key to effective credit control is:

- promptness – in sending out invoices, statements, and follow-up procedures
- courtesy – when communicating with debtors, polite letters and telephone calls

These, together with well set-out procedures for dealing with debtors at all stages of the account should ensure that bad debts are kept to a minimum.

AGED SCHEDULE OF DEBTORS

To help with credit control, many firms produce an aged schedule of debtors at the end of each month. This analyses individual debtor balances into the time that the amount has been owing. Thus it shows the long outstanding debts that are, potentially, bad debts, against whom early action is necessary. An aged schedule is easily produced using a computer accounting system – an example is shown below from the sales ledger of Computer Shop Limited.

COMPUTER SHOP LTD   Sales Ledger - Account Balances (Aged)   Date: 310397

A/C	Account Name	Credit Limit	Balance	Current	30 Days	60 Days	Older
201	Able, Baker & Clark	1000.00	164.50	164.50	0.00	0.00	0.00
202	Hitech Trading Co	750.00	376.00	376.00	0.00	0.00	0.00
204	Sixth Form College *	1000.00	1632.75	799.00	833.75	0.00	0.00
205	Teleservice *	1500.00	1926.88	1880.00	46.88	0.00	0.00
208	Stone, Wall Ltd	750.00	499.38	499.38	0.00	0.00	0.00
	Totals :	5000.00	4599.51	3718.88	880.63	0.00	0.00

an asterisk indicates debtors whose balances are above the credit limit

The aged debtors' schedule shown here indicates problems with two accounts:

- Sixth Form College is over the credit limit and, also, £833.75 has been owing for more than 30 days. Computer Shop Limited should seek an immediate payment of the overdue amount; pending receipt of this, it would seem inadvisable to supply further goods to this customer.

- Teleservice is also over the credit limit; most of the balance due is for the current month and a payment should be watched for. The possibility should be considered of not supplying further goods until a payment is received. It may be appropriate to consider increasing the credit limit from £1,500 to, perhaps, £2,000.

- The other accounts are in order.

CREDITORS

Creditors are people or organisations to whom the business owes money. Creditors are normally the suppliers of a business.

The overall objectives of the creditor management are to ensure that:

- creditors are paid within the timescales of company policy

- where cash discounts are offered, payment is made within the period covered by the cash discount *where it is financially attractive to do so*

- continuity of supplies to the business is not jeopardised by late payment to creditors

aged creditors' schedule

An aged creditors' schedule is used by many businesses. This analyses individual creditor balances into the time that the amount has been owing; thus the business can decide in which order creditors should be paid.

An example of an aged creditors' schedule is shown below.

```
COMPUTER SHOP LTD        Purchases Ledger - Account Balances (Aged)          Date: 310397
 A/C    Account  Name       Credit Limit  Balance   Current   30 Days   60 Days    Older
-----   ---------------------   ----------------  -----------  ----------  -----------  -----------  -------
 101    Axis Supplies Ltd          5000.00   3250.25   1830.41    752.93    666.91     0.00
 102    Bell Computers Ltd         4000.00   1876.39   1876.39      0.00      0.00     0.00
 104    Granta Trading Co          2500.00   1741.84   1233.61    508.23      0.00     0.00
 105    Kingsway Technical  *      1000.00   1175.38    560.19    331.97    283.22     0.00
 106    Pratt & Co Ltd             2000.00    681.83    681.83      0.00      0.00     0.00
                                ------------  ----------  -----------  ----------  ----------  ------
              Totals : 14500.00   8725.69   6182.43   1593.13    950.13     0.00

         *an asterisk indicates where balances are above the credit limit
```

This aged creditors' schedule, taken from the purchases ledger of Computer Shop Limited, shows potential problems with two creditors:

- The analysis of the account of Axis Supplies Limited shows that £752.93 has been outstanding for between 30 and 60 days, while £666.91 has been outstanding for 60 days or more. Computer Shop Limited should ensure that these amounts are paid as quickly as possible, otherwise the creditor may decide not to supply further goods.

- The account of Kingsway Technical is over the credit limit; the analysis of the balance shows that £283.22 has been outstanding for 60 days or more. To ensure continuity of purchases, Computer Shop Limited should certainly pay £283.22 quickly; it should then seek to clear the amount of £331.97 which has been outstanding for between 30 and 60 days. Once the account has been brought down to within the credit limit, it might be appropriate for Computer Supplies to ask Kingsway Technical for an increase in the credit limit from £1,000 to, perhaps, £1,500.

- The other accounts are in order, although payment should be made soon to Granta Trading for the amount of £508.23 which has been outstanding for more than 30 days.

reconciliation of creditors' statements

When a statement of account (see Chapter 2) is received from a supplier, it is often necessary to reconcile, or agree, the statement balance with the creditor's account in the book-keeping records. This reconciliation can be summarised as follows:

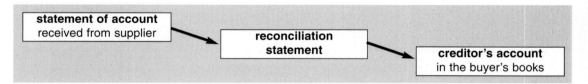

Assuming that there are no errors either on the statement of account or in the creditor's account, the discrepancies are caused by:

- items in transit, which have been invoiced by the supplier, but the invoice is not yet recorded by the buyer

- payments in the post or banking system, recorded by the buyer, but not yet received and recorded on the supplier's statement

- purchases returns, for which a credit note has been issued by the supplier, but is not yet recorded by the buyer

These three discrepancies are all caused by timing differences, ie the business document – invoice, payment, credit note – has not yet been recorded in the accounts of both buyer and seller. The reconciliation statement must take note of these.

CASE STUDY

RECONCILIATION OF A CREDITOR'S STATEMENT

situation

The following creditor's account appears in the purchases ledger of A Jarvis:

Dr			£				£
1997				1997			
10 Jan	Bank		200	1 Jan	Balance b/d		200
30 Jan	Bank		150	13 Jan	Purchases		150
31 Jan	Balance c/d		125	24 Jan	Purchases		125
			475				475
				1 Feb	Balance b/d		125

Centre heading: **T Smith** — Cr

Note: The credit balance of £125 on T Smith's account, in the books of A Jarvis at 1 February, indicates that Jarvis owes Smith £125.

The following statement of account is received from T Smith on 2 February:

Statement of Account: A Jarvis		Dr	Cr	Balance	
1997		£	£	£	
1 Jan	Balance b/d	200		200	Dr
9 Jan	Invoice no. 374	150		350	Dr
14 Jan	Payment received		200	150	Dr
20 Jan	Invoice no. 382	125		275	Dr
29 Jan	Invoice no. 413	100		375	Dr
31 Jan	Credit note CN24		25	350	Dr

Note: The debit balance of £350 on the statement from T Smith indicates that, in Smith's books, A Jarvis owes £350.

How will the creditor's account balance be reconciled with that of the statement received by A Jarvis?

solution

Reconciliation of T Smith's statement of account as at 31 January 1997

	£
Balance of account at 31 January 1997	125
Add: payment sent on 30 January, not yet appearing on statement	150
	275
Add: invoice no 413 sent by T Smith on 29 January, not yet received	100
	375
Less: credit note CN24 sent by T Smith on 31 January, not yet received	25
Balance of statement at 31 January 1997	350

As each of these items are timing differences, they will correct themselves within a few days as they are entered into the accounts of buyer and seller.

CASH DISCOUNT IN DEBTORS' AND CREDITORS' ACCOUNTS

We saw earlier (in Chapters 2 and 3) that cash discount is an allowance off the invoice amount for quick settlement, eg 2% cash discount for settlement within seven days. A business can be involved with cash discount in two ways:

- discount allowed to debtors
- discount received from creditors

(Note that, although the terms discount allowed and discount received do not use the word 'cash', they do in fact refer to cash discount.)

discount allowed

When cash discount is taken by a debtor it is entered into the accounts as shown by the following transactions:

10 Oct 1997   Sold goods, £100, on credit to P Henry, allowing her a cash discount of 2% for settlement within seven days (note: the seller of the goods is not registered for VAT)

15 Oct 1997   P Henry pays £98 by cheque

Dr		Sales Account		Cr
1997	£	1997		£
		10 Oct	P Henry	100

Dr		P Henry		Cr
1997	£	1997		£
10 Oct Sales	100	15 Oct	Bank	98
		15 Oct	Discount allowed	2
	100			100

Dr		Bank Account		Cr
1997	£	1997		£
15 Oct P Henry	98			

Dr		Discount Allowed Account		Cr
1997	£	1997		£
15 Oct P Henry	2			

Notes:

- The amount of the payment received from the debtor is entered in the bank account.
- The amount of discount allowed is entered in both the debtor's account and discount allowed account:
  – debit discount allowed account
  – credit debtor's account
- Discount allowed is an expense of the business, because it represents the cost of collecting payments more speedily from the debtors.
- The account of P Henry has been totalled to show that both the debit and credit money columns are the same – her account now has a nil balance.

discount received

With cash discount received, a business is offered cash discount for quick settlement by its creditors. The following transactions are an example:

20 Oct 1997   Bought goods, £200, on credit from B Lewis Limited; 2.5% cash discount is offered for settlement by the end of October (note: the seller of the goods is not registered for VAT)

30 Oct 1997   Paid B Lewis Ltd £195 by cheque

Dr			**Purchases Account**		Cr
1997		£	1997		£
20 Oct	B Lewis Limited	200			

Dr			**B Lewis Limited**		Cr
1997		£	1997		£
30 Oct	Bank	195	20 Oct	Purchases	200
30 Oct	Discount received	5			
		200			200

Dr			**Bank Account**		Cr
1997		£	1997		£
			30 Oct	B Lewis Limited	195

Dr			**Discount Received Account**		Cr
1997		£	1997		£
			30 Oct	B Lewis Limited	5

Notes:

- The business is receiving cash discount from its creditor, and the amount is entered as: *debit* creditor's account, *credit* discount received account
- Discount received account is an income account.
- The money columns of the account of B Lewis Limited have been totalled to show that the account now has a nil balance.

summary

- Cash discount – when taken – is recorded in the debtors' and creditors' accounts.
- Discount allowed account (expenses) and discount received account (income) record the amounts of cash discount.
- The cash book (see Chapter 15) is usually used for listing the amounts of discount received and allowed – transfers are then made at the end of each month to the respective discount accounts.
- Trade discount is never recorded in the double-entry accounts; only the net amount of an invoice, after trade discount has been deducted, is entered in the accounts.

CHAPTER SUMMARY

- Before goods are sold on credit to a new customer, steps should be taken to check the customer's creditworthiness

- When payment is not received from customers, procedures should be followed to chase up debts.

- If a debt remains unpaid despite 'chaser' procedures then it may well be written off as a bad debt.

- Bad debts written off during the year are held in bad debts written off account.

- The journal book is used to list non-regular transactions, such as bad debts written off.

- Bad debts represent a cost. Businesses that sell their goods on credit should take steps to minimise the possibility of bad debts.

- Information about overdue debtors is often presented in the form of an aged debtors' schedule which lists the accounts, amounts and the periods the debts have been outstanding.

- An aged creditors' schedule is used to ensure that payment is made to creditors within the timescales of company policy.

- Statements of account received from creditors may need to be reconciled with the creditor's account; discrepancies are caused by:
  - items in transit
  - payments in the post or banking system
  - purchases returns

- Cash discount is an allowance off the invoice amount for quick settlement.

KEY TERMS

bad debt	a debt owing to a business or organisation which it considers will never be paid
bad debts written off account	the account to which the amounts of account balances written off as bad are transferred
journal	primary accounting record for non-regular transactions
aged debtors' schedule	analysis of individual debtor balances into the time that the amount has been owing
aged creditors' schedule	analysis of individual creditor balances into the time that the amount has been owing
cash discount	an allowance off the invoice amount for quick settlement
discount allowed	cash discount allowed to debtors
discount received	cash discount received from creditors

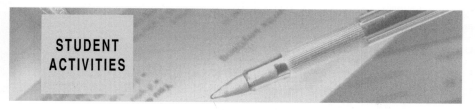

STUDENT ACTIVITIES

9.1   Ken Shah, a debtor, is unable to pay the amount owing and the accounts supervisor has decided to write off his account as a bad debt. This is recorded in the double-entry accounts by:

	Debit	*Credit*
(a)	bad debts written off	K Shah's account
(b)	K Shah's account	bad debts written off
(c)	cash account	K Shah's account
(d)	journal	K Shah's account

Answer (a) or (b) or (c) or (d)

(Ignore VAT relief on bad debt write-off)

9.2   A friend has recently set up in business. You have been helping with setting up the book-keeping system.

Today your friend has received an order from a customer who wishes to buy on credit terms. As your friend does not know the buyer, give advice as to the steps that should be taken:

•   before the goods are supplied

•   in any subsequent dealings with the customer

9.3   James Roberts is a debtor of your business. The balance of his account on 1 January 1997 is £70. On 17 February he pays you £40 by cheque; on 20 March he pays you £10 in cash. All further requests for payment are ignored. Your business is not VAT registered.

On 10 July your business is notified that he has been made a bankrupt. On 20 October a payment of 10% of the amount owing is paid to you by cheque by his trustee in bankruptcy. After receiving this amount, the accounts supervisor sends you a memorandum (dated 21 October) telling you to write off the balance of his account as a bad debt.

You are to show:

•   the journal entry made on 21 October

•   the transactions on James Roberts' account in the firm's sales ledger

•   the bad debts written off account in the firm's general ledger

9.4   During November and December 1997 the following transactions took place on Natalie Watson's account in your firm's sales ledger:

1997

1 Nov   Balance brought down, Natalie Watson owes your firm £320

3 Nov	Natalie Watson pays the balance of her account by cheque, being allowed a cash discount of 2.5%
10 Nov	Natalie Watson buys goods on credit from your firm for £200 (including VAT)
15 Nov	Natalie Watson returns goods £50 (including VAT) – a credit note is issued by you
20 Nov	A cheque is received from Natalie Watson for £100
3 Dec	Cash is received from Natalie Watson for £25
22 Dec	The accounts supervisor advises you by memorandum that Natalie Watson has gone out of business and that the balance on her account is to be written off as bad (VAT relief does not apply).

You are to show:

* the journal entry made on 22 December

* the transactions on Natalie Watson's account in the firm's sales ledger

* the bad debts written off account in the firm's general ledger

9.5 You work in the accounts department of Electralarm Limited, a company which installs electronic alarm systems. The company address is 67 Newtown Road, West Roxton, WR6 6YP. Three months ago the company installed a domestic alarm system for Mr Tom Gunsmith, at 8 Tresham Close, West Roxton, WR3 5FG. He was sent:

* an invoice for £785.00 three months ago

* a statement of account at the end of month one

* a statement of account at the end of month two

No money has been received from Mr Gunsmith.

(a) Using today's date and assuming that the item for £785 was the only one on the statement, write an appropriate letter to Mr Gunsmith chasing up this debt.

(b) If you do not receive a reply to this letter, what courses of action are open to Electralarm Limited? What would you choose to do?

9.6 The following account appears in your firm's purchases ledger:

Dr			£		Apple Supplies Limited	Cr	£
1997				1997			
6 May	Bank		780	1 May	Balance b/d		800
6 May	Discount		20	5 May	Purchases		255
12 May	Purchases returns		55	26 May	Purchases		150
30 May	Bank		195				
30 May	Discount		5				

During the first week of June, the following statement of account was received from Apple Supplies Ltd:

		Dr	Cr	Balance
1997		£	£	£
1 May	Balance b/d			800 Dr
2 May	Invoice 678	255		1,055 Dr
9 May	Payment received		780	
9 May	Discount allowed		20	255 Dr
14 May	Credit note 413		55	200 Dr
23 May	Invoice 721	150		350 DR

You are to:

*   Balance the account of Apple Supplies Limited in your purchases ledger at 31 May 1997

*   Reconcile the balance on your purchases ledger account at 31 May 1997 with that shown on the statement

9.7   Enter the following transactions into the double-entry accounts of Sonya Smith:

1997

2 Feb	Bought goods £200, on credit from G Lewis
4 Feb	Sold goods £150, on credit to L Jarvis
7 Feb	Sold goods £240, on credit to G Patel
10 Feb	Paid G Lewis the amount owing by cheque after deducting a cash discount of 5%
12 Feb	L Jarvis pays the amount owing by cheque after deducting a cash discount of 2%
17 Feb	Bought goods £160, on credit from G Lewis
20 Feb	G Patel pays the amount owing by cheque after deducting a cash discount of 2.5%
24 Feb	Paid G Lewis the amount owing by cheque after deducting a cash discount of 5%

Notes:

*   *Sonya Smith is not registered for VAT*

*   *day books are not required*

10 CONTROL ACCOUNTS

this chapter covers . . .

Control accounts are 'master' accounts which record by means of totals the transactions passing through the accounts that they control. In this chapter we will look at:

- the concept of control accounts
- the layout of sales ledger and purchases ledger control accounts
- the use of control accounts as an aid to the management of a business
- control accounts and book-keeping

NVQ PERFORMANCE CRITERIA COVERED

unit 2 RECORDING AND ACCOUNTING FOR CREDIT TRANSACTIONS

element 3

account for goods and services supplied on credit

❏ the control account in the general ledger is reconciled with the total of balances in the sales (debtors) ledger

element 4

account for goods and services received on credit

❏ the control account in the general ledger is reconciled with the total of balances in the purchases (creditors) ledger

THE CONCEPT OF CONTROL ACCOUNTS

Control accounts are 'master' accounts which control a number of subsidiary ledger accounts. Control accounts work in the following way:

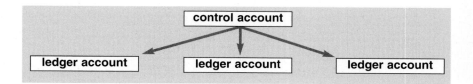

The control account (also known as a *totals account*) is used to record the totals of transactions passing through the subsidiary accounts. In this way, the balance of the control account will always be equal to the total balances of the subsidiary accounts, unless an error has occurred. Two commonly-used control accounts are:

- sales ledger control account – the total of the debtors
- purchases ledger control account – the total of the creditors

In the illustration above we have seen how a control account acts as a master account for a number of subsidiary accounts. The principle is that, if the total of the opening balances for subsidiary accounts is known, together with the total of amounts increasing these balances, and the total of amounts decreasing these balances, then the total of the closing balances for the subsidiary accounts can be calculated.

For example:

		£
Total of opening balances		50,000
Add increases		10,000
		60,000
Less decreases		12,000
Total of closing balances		48,000

The total of the closing balances can now be checked against a separate listing of the balances of the subsidiary accounts to ensure that the two figures agree. If so, it proves that the ledgers within the section are correct (subject to any errors such as misposts and compensating errors). Let us now apply this concept to one of the divisions of the ledger – sales ledger.

The diagram on page 149 shows the personal accounts which form the entire sales ledger of a particular business (in practice there would, of course, be more than four accounts involved). The sales ledger control account acts as a totals account, which records totals of the transactions passing through the individual accounts which it controls. Notice that transactions appear in the control account *on the same side* as they appear in the individual accounts. The sales ledger control account can be reconciled with the balances of the individual accounts which it controls (see below). Thus, control accounts act as an aid to locating errors: if the control account and subsidiary accounts agree, then the error is likely to lie elsewhere. In this way the control account acts as an intermediate checking device – proving the arithmetical accuracy of the ledger section.

Normally the whole of a ledger section is controlled by one control account, eg sales ledger control account or purchases ledger control account. However, it is also possible to have a number of separate control accounts for subdivisions of the sales ledger and purchases ledger, eg sales ledger control account A-K, purchases ledger control account S-Z, etc. It is for a business – the user of the accounting system – to decide what is most suitable, taking into account the number of accounts in the sales and purchases ledger, together with the type of book-keeping system – manual or computerised.

In the diagram on the next page the sales ledger control account and subsidiary accounts are agreed at the beginning and end of the month, as follows:

Reconciliation of sales ledger control account with debtor balances

	1 January 1997	31 January 1997
	£	£
A Ackroyd	100	150
B Barnes	200	200
C Cox	50	180
D Douglas	150	150
Sales ledger control account	500	680

Note: The business will decide how often to reconcile the control account with the subsidiary accounts – weekly, monthly, quarterly or annually.

SALES LEDGER CONTROL ACCOUNT

The set-out of a sales ledger control account (or debtors' control account) is shown on the next page. Study the layout carefully and read the text which explains the additional items.

Dr	**SALES LEDGER CONTROL ACCOUNT**				Cr
1997		£	1997		£
1 Jan	Balances b/d	500	31 Jan	Bank	443
31 Jan	Sales	700	31 Jan	Discount allowed	7
			31 Jan	Sales returns	70
			31 Jan	Balances c/d	680
		1,200			1,200
1 Feb	Balances b/d	680			

Dr	**A Ackroyd**				Cr
1997		£	1997		£
1 Jan	Balance b/d	100	10 Jan	Bank	98
6 Jan	Sales	150	10 Jan	Discount allowed	2
			31 Jan	Balance c/d	150
		250			250
1 Feb	Balance b/d	150			

Dr	**B Barnes**				Cr
1997		£	1997		£
1 Jan	Balance b/d	200	13 Jan	Bank	195
6 Jan	Sales	250	13 Jan	Discount allowed	5
			27 Jan	Sales returns	50
			31 Jan	Balance c/d	200
		450			450
1 Feb	Balance b/d	200			

Dr	**C Cox**				Cr
1997		£	1997		£
1 Jan	Balance b/d	50	20 Jan	Bank	50
15 Jan	Sales	200	29 Jan	Sales returns	20
			31 Jan	Balance c/d	180
		250			250
1 Feb	Balance b/d	180			

Dr	**D Douglas**				Cr
1997		£	1997		£
1 Jan	Balance b/d	150	30 Jan	Bank	100
20 Jan	Sales	100	31 Jan	Balance c/d	150
		250			250
1 Feb	Balance b/d	150			

relationship of the sales ledger control account to the individual sales ledger accounts

Dr		Sales Ledger Control Account		Cr
	£			£
Balances b/d (large amount)		Balances b/d (small amount)		
Credit sales		Cash/cheques received from debtors		
Returned cheques		Cash discount allowed		
Interest charged to debtors		Sales returns		
Balances c/d (small amount)		Bad debts written off		
		Set-off/contra entries		
		Balances c/d (large amount)		
Balances b/d (large amount)		Balances b/d (small amount)		

balances b/d

In the layout above there is a figure for balances b/d on both the debit side and the credit side of the control account. The usual balance on a debtor's account is debit and so this will form the large balance on the debit side. However, from time-to-time, it is possible for some debtors to have a credit balance on their accounts. This may come about, for example, because they have paid for goods, and then returned them, or because they have overpaid in error: the business owes them the amount due, ie they have a credit balance for the time being. Such credit balances are always going to be in the minority and so they will be for the smaller amount. Clearly, if there are small credit balances at the beginning of the month, there are likely to be credit balances at the month-end, and these need to be recorded separately as balances carried down – do not 'net off' the two types of balances. In a balance sheet, the small credit balances should be included with creditors.

credit sales

Only credit sales – and not cash sales – are entered in the control account because only credit sales are recorded in the debtors' accounts. The total sales of the business will comprise both credit and cash sales.

returned cheques

If a debtor's cheque is returned unpaid by the bank, ie the cheque has 'bounced', then entries have to be made in the book-keeping system to record this. These entries are:

– *debit* debtor's account

– *credit* cash book (bank columns)

As a transaction has been made in a debtor's account, then the amount must also be recorded in the sales ledger control account – on the debit side.

interest charged to debtors

Sometimes a business will charge a debtor for slow payment of an account. The accounting entries are:

– *debit* debtor's account

– *credit* interest received account

As a debit transaction has been made in the debtor's account, so a debit entry must be recorded in the control account.

bad debts written off

The book-keeping entries for writing off a bad debt (see Chapter 9) are:

– *debit* bad debts written off account

– *credit* debtor's account

A credit transaction is entered in a debtor's account. This is because the control account 'masters' the sales ledger and so the transaction must also be recorded as a credit transaction in the control account.

set-off/contra entries

See page 154.

PURCHASES LEDGER CONTROL ACCOUNT

The specimen layout for the purchases ledger control account (or creditors' control account) is shown below.

The layout is explained on the next page.

Dr	Purchases Ledger Control Account		Cr
	£		£
Balances b/d small amount)		Balances b/d (large amount)	
Cash/cheques paid to creditors		Credit purchases	
Cash discount received		Interest charged by creditors	
Purchases returns		Balances c/d (small amount)	
Set-off/contra entries			
Balances c/d (large amount)			
Balances b/d (small amount)		Balances b/d (large amount)	

balances b/d

As with sales ledger control account, it is possible to have balances on both sides of the account. For purchases ledger, containing the accounts of creditors, the large balance b/d is always on the credit side. However, if a creditor has been overpaid, the result may be a small debit balance b/d. It may also be that there are closing balances on both sides of the account at the end of the period. In the balance sheet, any small debit balances should be included with debtors.

credit purchases

Only credit purchases – and not cash purchases – are entered in the control account. However, the total purchases of the business will comprise both credit and cash purchases.

interest charged by creditors

If creditors charge interest because of slow payment, this must be recorded on both the creditor's account and the control account.

set-off/contra entries

See page 154.

reconciliation of purchases ledger control account

The diagram on page 153 shows how a purchases ledger control account acts as a totals account for the creditors of a business. Reconciliation of the balances on the purchases ledger control account and subsidiary accounts is made as follows:

Reconciliation of purchases ledger control account with creditor balances

	1 January 1997	31 January 1997
	£	£
F Francis	100	200
G Gold	200	350
H Harris	300	500
I Ingram	400	900
Purchases ledger control account	1,000	1,950

Dr	PURCHASES LEDGER CONTROL ACCOUNT			Cr
1997		£	1997	£
31 Jan	Purchases returns	150	1 Jan Balances b/d	1,000
31 Jan	Bank	594	31 Jan Purchases	1,700
31 Jan	Discount received	6		
31 Jan	Balances c/d	1,950		
		2,700		2,700
			1 Feb Balances b/d	1,950

Dr	F Francis			Cr
1997		£	1997	£
17 Jan	Bank	98	1Jan Balance b/d	100
17 Jan	Discount received	2	3 Jan Purchases	200
31 Jan	Balance c/d	200		
		300		300
			1 Feb Balance b/d	200

Dr	G Gold			Cr
1997		£	1997	£
15 Jan	Purchases returns	50	1 Jan Balance b/d	200
28 Jan	Bank	100	9 Jan Purchases	300
31 Jan	Balance c/d	350		
		500		500
			1 Feb Balance b/d	350

Dr	H Harris			Cr
1997		£	1997	£
28 Jan	Purchases returns	100	1 Jan Balance b/d	300
30 Jan	Bank	200	17 Jan Purchases	500
31 Jan	Balance c/d	500		
		800		800
			1 Feb Balance b/d	500

Dr	I Ingram			Cr
1997		£	1997	£
22 Jan	Bank	196	1 Jan Balance b/d	400
22 Jan	Discount received	4	27 Jan Purchases	700
31 Jan	Balance c/d	900		
		1,100		1,100
			1 Feb Balance b/d	900

relationship of the purchases ledger control account to the individual purchase ledger accounts

SET-OFF/CONTRA ENTRIES

These entries occur when the same person or business has an account in both sales ledger and purchases ledger, ie they are both buying from, and selling to, the business whose accounts we are preparing. For example, M Patel Limited has the following accounts in the sales and purchases ledgers:

SALES LEDGER

Dr		A Smith		Cr
		£		£
Balance b/d		200		

PURCHASES LEDGER

Dr		A Smith		Cr
		£		£
			Balance b/d	300

From these accounts we can see that:

• A Smith owes M Patel Limited £200 (sales ledger)

• M Patel Limited owes A Smith £300 (purchases ledger)

To save each having to write out a cheque to send to the other, it is possible (with A Smith's agreement) to set-off one account against the other, so that they can settle their net indebtedness with one cheque. The book-keeping entries in M Patel's books will be:

– *debit* A Smith (purchases ledger) £200

– *credit* A Smith (sales ledger) £200

The accounts will now appear as:

SALES LEDGER

Dr		A Smith		Cr
		£		£
Balance b/d		200	Set-off purchases ledger	200

PURCHASES LEDGER

Dr		A Smith		Cr
		£		£
Set-off purchases ledger		200	Balance b/d	300

The net result is that M Patel Limited owes A Smith £100. The important point to note is that, because transactions have been recorded in the personal accounts, an entry needs to be made in the two control accounts:

– *debit* purchases ledger control account

– *credit* sales ledger control account

SOURCES OF INFORMATION FOR CONTROL ACCOUNTS

Control accounts use totals (remember that their other name is totals accounts) for the week, month, quarter or year – depending on what time period is decided upon by the business. The totals come from a number of sources in the accounting system:

sales ledger control account

- total credit sales (including VAT) – from the 'gross' column of the sales day book
- total sales returns (including VAT) – from the 'gross' column of the sales returns day book
- total cash/cheques received from debtors – from the cash book (see Chapter 15)
- total discount allowed – from the discount allowed column of the cash book (see Chapter 15), or from discount allowed account
- bad debts – from the journal, or bad debts written off account

purchases ledger control account

- total credit purchases (including VAT) – from the 'gross' column of the purchases day book
- total purchases returns (including VAT) – from the 'gross' column of the purchases returns day book
- total cash/cheques paid to creditors – from the cash book (see Chapter 15)
- total discount received – from the discount received column of the cash book (see Chapter 15), or from discount received account

CONTROL ACCOUNTS AS AN AID TO MANAGEMENT

When the manager of a business needs to know the figure for debtors or creditors – important information for the manager – the balance of the appropriate control account will give the information immediately: there is no need to add up the balances of all the individual debtors' or creditors' accounts. With a computer accounting system, control accounts can be printed at any time.

The use of control accounts makes fraud more difficult – particularly in a manual accounting system. If a fraudulent transaction is to be recorded on a personal account, the transaction must also be entered in the control account. As the control account will be either maintained by a supervisor, or checked regularly by the manager, the control accounts add another level of security within the accounting system.

We have already seen in this chapter how control accounts can help in locating errors. Remember, though, that a control account only proves the arithmetical accuracy of the accounts which it controls – there could still be errors, such as misposts and compensating errors, within the ledger section.

CONTROL ACCOUNTS AND BOOK-KEEPING

A business must decide how to use control accounts in its book-keeping system. There are two possible ways of doing this:

1   incorporate the control accounts into double-entry book-keeping

This method uses the control accounts as the double-entry system, ie the balances of the sales ledger control account and the purchases ledger control account are recorded in the trial balance as the figures for debtors and creditors respectively. This means that the personal accounts of debtors and creditors are not part of double-entry, but are *memorandum accounts* which record how much each debtor owes, and how much is owed to each creditor.

From time-to-time, the balances of the memorandum accounts are agreed with the balance of the appropriate control account.

The use of this approach is consistent with the way in which computerised accounts are prepared and presented – the control account gives the total and there are separate memorandum accounts for individual debtors and creditors.

2 the control accounts are used as memorandum accounts

This second method uses the opposite approach: here the personal accounts of debtors and creditors are *included* in the double-entry book-keeping system, while the control accounts are *memorandum accounts* used as checking devices.

Now look at the diagrams on the next four pages which show these two different methods of using control accounts in the book-keeping system.

diagram 1

The first diagram (on the next page) gives an example of the sales ledger control account incorporated into the double-entry book-keeping system, while the individual debtors' accounts are kept in the form of memorandum accounts.

diagram 2

The second diagram (on page 159) shows the situation where the sales ledger control account is a memorandum account and the debtors' accounts are part of the double-entry book-keeping system.

diagram 3

The third diagram (on page 160) gives an example of the purchases ledger control account incorporated into the double-entry book-keeping system, while the individual creditors' accounts are kept in the form of memorandum accounts.

diagram 4

The fourth diagram (on page 161) shows the situation where the purchases ledger control account is a memorandum account and the creditors' accounts are part of the double-entry book-keeping system .

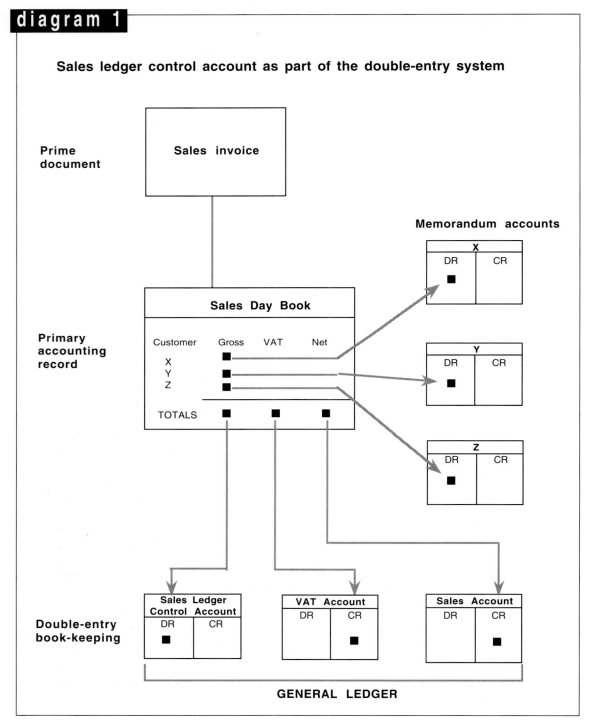

Sales ledger control account incorporated into the double-entry book-keeping system; the debtors' accounts are memorandum accounts

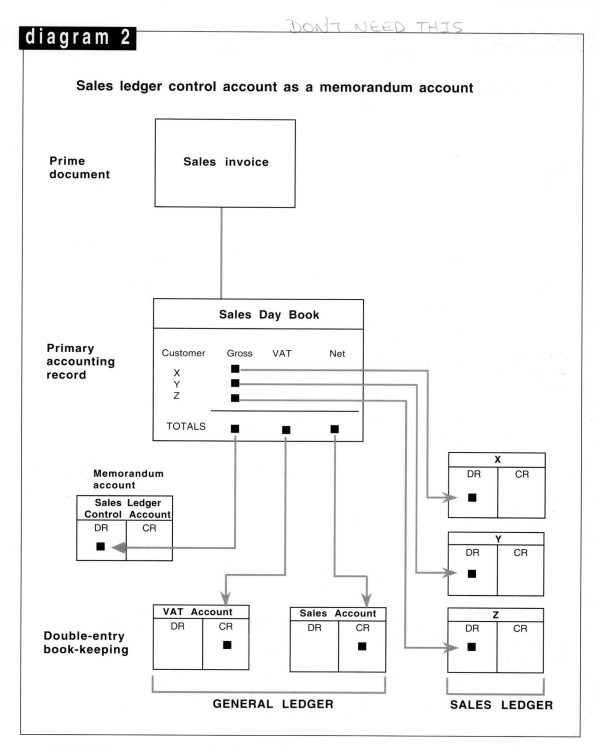

Sales ledger control account is a memorandum account; the debtors' accounts are incorporated into the double-entry book-keeping system.

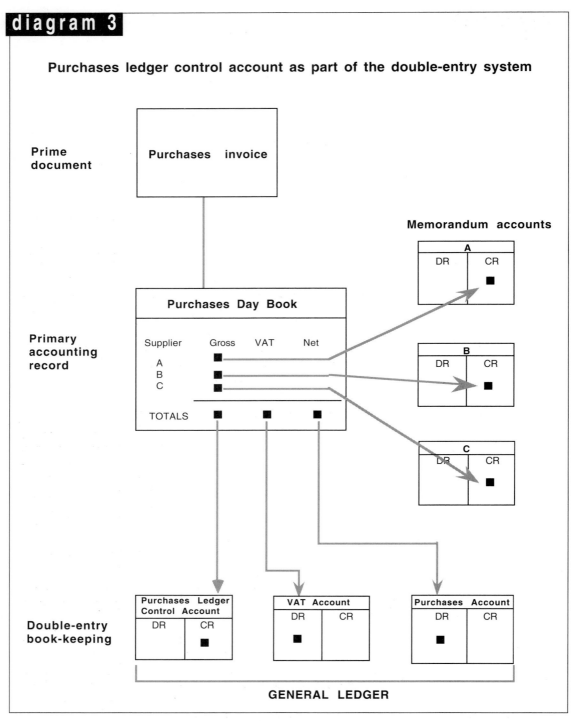

Purchases ledger control account incorporated into the double-entry book-keeping system; the creditors' accounts are memorandum accounts.

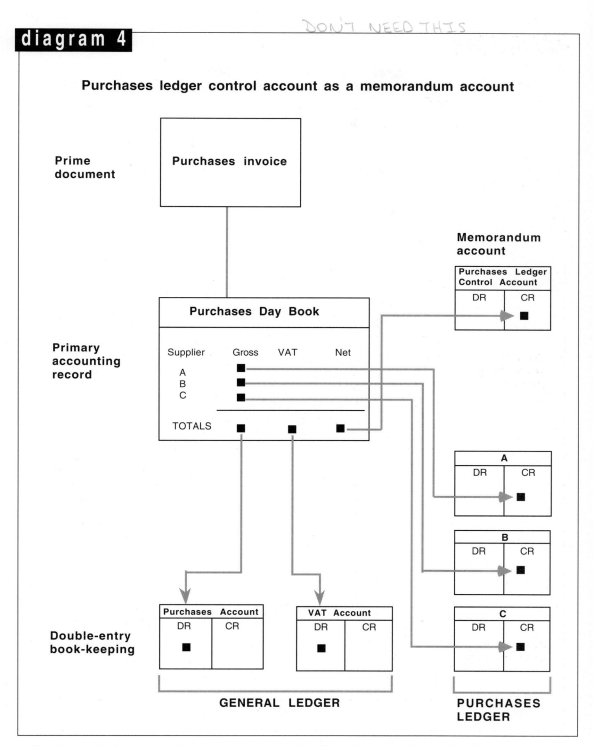

diagram 4

DON'T NEED THIS

Purchases ledger control account as a memorandum account

Prime document → Purchases invoice

Memorandum account → Purchases Ledger Control Account (DR | CR)

Primary accounting record → Purchases Day Book

Supplier	Gross	VAT	Net
A	■		
B	■		
C	■		
TOTALS	■	■	■

A (DR | CR)

B (DR | CR)

C (DR | CR)

Double-entry book-keeping → Purchases Account (DR | CR), VAT Account (DR | CR)

GENERAL LEDGER

PURCHASES LEDGER

Purchases ledger control account is a memorandum account; the creditors' accounts are incorporated into the double-entry book-keeping system.

CHAPTER SUMMARY

- Control accounts (or totals accounts) are 'master' accounts, which control a number of subsidiary accounts.

- Two commonly used control accounts are:
  - sales ledger control account
  - purchases ledger control account

- Transactions are recorded on the same side of the control account as on the subsidiary accounts.

- Set-off/contra entries occur when one person has an account in both sales and purchases ledger, and it is agreed to set-off one balance against the other to leave a net balance. This usually results in the following control account entries:
  - debit purchases ledger control account
  - credit sales ledger control account

- Control accounts are an aid to management:
  - they give up-to-date information on the total of debtors or creditors
  - by making fraud more difficult
  - in helping to locate errors

- Control accounts can be either:
  - incorporated into the double-entry book-keeping system
  - used as separate memorandum accounts

KEY TERMS

control account	a 'master' account which controls a number of subsidiary accounts
sales ledger control account	a 'master' account which controls debtors' accounts (or a section of the sales ledger)
purchases ledger control account	'master' account which controls creditors' accounts (or a section of the purchases ledger)
set-off/contra entries	where balances in sales ledger and purchases ledger are to be set-off against one another
memorandum account	an account which is not part of the double-entry system

STUDENT ACTIVITIES

10.1 You have the following information:

- opening creditor balances at start of month   £18,600
- cash/cheques paid to creditors during month   £9,400
- purchases for month   £9,100
- purchases returns for month   £800

What is the figure for closing creditor balances at the end of the month?

(a)   £18,100

(b)   £19,100

(c)   £36,300

(d)   £17,500

Answer (a) or (b) or (c) or (d)

10.2 Which one of the following does not appear in sales ledger control account?

(a)   bad debts written off

(b)   discount received

(c)   sales returns

(d)   cash/cheques received from debtors

Answer (a) or (b) or (c) or (d)

10.3 A friend has recently started work as an accounts clerk for a large electrical wholesalers. He asks you the following questions about control accounts:

- "What are the principles of control accounts?"
- "I've heard it said that control accounts help the management of the business. How is this?"
- "In our business we treat the control accounts as being part of the double-entry accounts, with 'memorandum' accounts kept for each debtor and creditor. I thought you told me earlier that debtors' and creditors' accounts were always part of double-entry ..."

Write answers to your friend.

10.4 Prepare a sales ledger control account for the month of June 1997 from the following information:

1997		£
1 Jun	Sales ledger balances	17,491
30 Jun	Credit sales for month	42,591
	Sales returns	1,045
	Payments received from debtors	39,024
	Cash discount allowed	593
	Bad debts written off	296

The debtors figure at 30 June is to be entered as the balancing figure.

10.5 Prepare a purchases ledger control account for the month of April 1997 from the following information:

1997		£
1 Apr	Purchases ledger balances	14,275
30 Apr	Credit purchases for month	36,592
	Purchases returns	653
	Payments made to creditors	31,074
	Cash discount received	1,048
	Transfer of credit balances to sales ledger	597

The creditors figure at 30 April is to be entered as the balancing figure.

10.6 The sales ledger of Rowcester Traders contains the following accounts on 1 February 1997:

> Arrow Valley Retailers, balance £826.40 debit
> B Brick (Builders) Limited, balance £59.28 debit
> Mereford Manufacturing Company, balance £293.49 debit
> Redgrove Restorations, balance £724.86 debit
> Wyvern Warehouse Limited, balance £108.40 debit

The following transactions took place during February:

3 Feb	Sold goods on credit to Arrow Valley Retailers £338.59, and to Mereford Manufacturing Company £127.48
7 Feb	Redgrove Restorations returned goods £165.38
15 Feb	Received a cheque from Wyvern Warehouse Limited for the balance of the account after deduction of 2.5% cash discount
17 Feb	Sold goods on credit to Redgrove Restorations £394.78, and to Wyvern Warehouse Limited £427.91
20 Feb	Arrow Valley Retailers settled an invoice for £826.40 by cheque after deducting 2.5% cash discount
24 Feb	Mereford Manufacturing Company returned goods £56.29
28 Feb	Transferred the balance of Mereford Manufacturing Company's account to the company's account in the purchases ledger
28 Feb	Wrote off the account of B Brick (Builders) Limited as a bad debt

contra

You are to:

(a) write up the personal accounts in the sales ledger of Rowcester Traders for February 1997, balancing them at the end of the month

(b) prepare a sales ledger control account for February 1997, balancing it at the end of the month

(c) reconcile the control account balance with the debtors' accounts at 1 February and 28 February 1997.

Note: VAT is to be ignored on all transactions and day books are not required.

10.7 The purchases ledger of Rowcester Traders contains the following accounts on 1 February 1997:

Apple Supplies Limited, balance £1,843.22 credit

Beatty Brothers, £51.47 debit

J Johnson, £675.38 credit

Mereford Manufacturing Company, balance £478.29 credit

Newtown Equipment Limited, balance £684.86 credit

W Wright, balance £987.20 credit

The following transactions took place during February:

3 Feb	Bought goods on credit from Apple Supplies Limited, £1,027.98, and from Beatty Brothers £150.68
6 Feb	Paid W Wright a cheque for the balance of her account after deducting 2.5% cash discount
10 Feb	Bought goods on credit from J Johnson £328.22, and from W Wright £476.38
11 Feb	Paid Newtown Equipment Limited a cheque for the balance of the account
14 Feb	Returned goods to Apple Supplies Limited for £157.20
17 Feb	Paid Apple Supplies a cheque for the balance of the account, after deducting 2.5% cash discount
18 Feb	Returned goods to Newtown Equipment Limited for £105.68
24 Feb	Paid J Johnson the amount owing by cheque, after deducting 2.5% cash discount
27 Feb	Bought goods on credit from Apple Supplies Limited £849.36
28 Feb	Transfer of debit balance of £364.68 in the sales ledger to Mereford Manufacturing Company's account in the purchases ledger

You are to:

(a) write up the personal accounts in the purchases ledger of Rowcester Traders for February 1997, balancing them at the end of the month

(b) prepare a purchases ledger control account for February 1997, balancing it at the end of the month

(c) reconcile the control account balance with the creditors' accounts at 1 February and 28 February 1997

Note: VAT is to be ignored on all transactions and day books are not required.

11 THE JOURNAL

this chapter covers . . .

The journal is the primary accounting record for non-regular transactions, eg correction of errors and other transfers. The journal – like the day books (or journals) that we have seen in Chapters 4 to 6 – is used to list transactions before they are entered into the double-entry system.

The main uses of the journal are for transactions such as:

- *opening entries*
- *purchase and sale of fixed assets on credit*
- *correction of errors*
- *other transfers*

NVQ PERFORMANCE CRITERIA COVERED

unit 2 RECORDING AND ACCOUNTING FOR CREDIT TRANSACTIONS

element 3
account for goods and services supplied on credit

❏ *adjustments involving debtors' accounts are properly authorised and documented, and are correctly transferred to the correct ledger accounts*

element 4
account for goods and services received on credit

❏ *adjustments involving creditors' accounts are properly authorised and documented, and are correctly transferred to the correct ledger accounts*

USES OF THE JOURNAL

The journal is used for listing transactions which are not recorded in any other primary accounting record. The categories of such transactions include:

- opening entries
- purchase and sale of fixed assets on credit
- correction of errors
- other transfers

The reasons for using a journal are:

- to eliminate the need for remembering why non-regular transactions were put through the accounts – the journal acts as a notebook
- to reduce the risk of fraud, by making it difficult for unauthorised transactions to be entered in the accounting system
- to reduce the risk of errors, by listing the transactions that are to be put into the double-entry accounts
- to ensure that entries can be traced back to a prime document, thus providing an audit trail for non-regular transactions

THE JOURNAL – A PRIMARY ACCOUNTING RECORD

The journal is a primary accounting record; it is not, therefore, part of the double-entry book-keeping system. The journal is used to list the transactions that are to be put through the accounts. The accounting system for non-regular transactions is as follows:

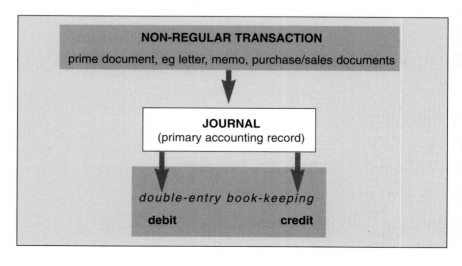

An entry in the journal is recorded in the following way (with an example transaction shown):

Date	Details	Folio	Dr	Cr
1997			£	£
1 Jan	Bank account	CB	10,000	
	Capital account	GL		10,000
	Opening capital introduced			

Notes:

- the names of the accounts to be debited and credited in the book-keeping system are written in the details column; it is customary to show the debit transaction first
- the money amounts of each debit and credit are stated in the appropriate columns
- the folio column cross-references to the division of the ledger where each account is found – here 'CB' to Cash Book and 'GL' to General Ledger
- a journal entry always balances
- it is usual to include a brief narrative explaining why the transaction is being carried out, and making reference to the prime document whenever possible (in assessments and examinations you should always include a narrative unless specifically told otherwise)
- each journal entry is complete in itself and is ruled off to separate it from the next entry

OPENING ENTRIES

These are the transactions which open the accounts of a new business. For example, a first business transaction is:

1 Jan 1997   Started in business with £10,000 in the bank

This non-regular transaction is entered in the journal as follows:

Date	Details	Folio	Dr	Cr
1997			£	£
1 Jan	Bank account	CB	10,000	
	Capital account	GL		10,000
	Opening capital introduced			

After the journal entry has been made, the transaction can be recorded in the double-entry accounts.

Here is another opening entries transaction to be recorded in the journal:

1 Feb 1997   *Started in business with cash £100, bank £5,000, stock £1,000, machinery £2,500, creditors £850*

The journal entry is:

Date	Details	Folio	Dr	Cr
1997			£	£
1 Feb	Cash account	CB	100	
	Bank account	CB	5,000	
	Stock account	GL	1,000	
	Machinery account	GL	2,500	
	Creditors accounts	PL		850
	Capital account*	GL		7,750
			8,600	8,600
	Assets and liabilities at the start of business			

* Note that capital is the balancing figure, ie assets minus liabilities. The amounts will now need to be recorded in the double-entry accounts.

PURCHASE AND SALE OF FIXED ASSETS ON CREDIT

The purchase and sale of fixed assets are non-regular business transactions which are recorded in the journal as the primary accounting record. Strictly, only *credit* transactions are entered in the journal (because cash/bank transactions are recorded in the cash book as the primary accounting record). However, a business (or an assessment/examination question) may choose to journalise cash entries: strictly, though, this is incorrect as two primary accounting records are being used.

15 Apr 1997   *Bought a machine for £1,000 plus VAT (at 17.5%) on credit from Machinery Supplies Limited, purchase order no. 2341.*

Date	Details	Folio	Dr	Cr
1997			£	£
15 Apr	Machinery account	GL	1,000	
	VAT account	GL	175	
	Machinery Supplies Limited*	GL		1,175
			1,175	1,175
	Purchase of machine: order 2341			

* see next page

20 May 1997   *Car sold for £2,500 on credit to Wyvern Motors Limited (no VAT chargeable).*

Date	Details	Folio	Dr	Cr
1997			£	£
20 May	Wyvern Motors Limited*	GL	2,500	
	Car account	GL		2,500
	Sale of car, registration L201 HAB			

* A general ledger account has been opened for the creditor (Machinery Supplies Limited) and the debtor (Wyvern Motors Limited). This has been done to avoid confusion with trade creditors (in the purchases ledger) and trade debtors (in the sales ledger).

CORRECTION OF ERRORS

In any book-keeping system there is always the possibility of an error. Ways to avoid errors, or ways to reveal them sooner, include:

- division of the accounting function between a number of people, so that no one person is responsible for all aspects of a business transaction

- regular circulation of statements to debtors, who will check the transactions on their accounts and advise any discrepancies

- checking of statements received from creditors

- extraction of a trial balance at regular intervals

- the preparation of bank reconciliation statements (see Chapter 17)

- checking cash and petty cash balances (see Chapters 15 and 16) against cash held

- the use of control accounts (see Chapter 10)

- the use of a dedicated computer accounting program

Despite all of these, errors will still occur from time-to-time and, in this section, we will look at:
- correction of errors not shown by a trial balance
- correction of errors shown by a trial balance, using a suspense account

ERRORS NOT SHOWN BY A TRIAL BALANCE

In Chapter 8 we have already seen that some types of errors in a book-keeping system are not revealed by a trial balance. These are:

- error of omission
- reversal of entries
- mispost/error of commission
- error of principle
- error of original entry (or transcription)
- compensating error

Although these errors are not shown by a trial balance, they are likely to come to light if the procedures suggested on the previous page are followed. For example, a debtor will soon let you know if his/her account has been debited with goods he/she did not buy. When an error is found, it needs to be corrected by means of a journal entry which shows the book-keeping entries that have been made.

We will now look at an example of each of the errors not shown by a trial balance, and will see how it is corrected by means of a journal entry.
(A practical hint which may help in correcting errors is to write out the 'T' accounts as they appear with the error. Then write in the correcting entries and see if the result has achieved what was intended.)

error of omission

Credit sale of goods, £100 (invoice 4967) to H Jarvis completely omitted from the accounting system; the error is corrected on 12 May 1997

Date	Details	Folio	Dr	Cr
1997			£	£
12 May	H Jarvis	SL	100	
	Sales account	GL		100
	Invoice 4967 omitted from accounts			

This type of error can happen in a very small business – often where the book-keeping is done by one person. For example, an invoice, when typed out, is 'lost' down the back of a filing cabinet. In a large business, particularly one using a computer accounting system, it should be impossible for this error to occur. Also, if documents are numbered in sequence, then none should be mislaid.

reversal of entries

A payment, on 2 May 1997 by cheque of £50 to a creditor, S Wright (receipt no. 93459) has been debited in the cash book and credited to Wright's account; the error is corrected on 12 May 1997.

Date	Details	Folio	Dr	Cr
1997			£	£
12 May	S Wright	PL	50	
	Bank account	CB		50
	S Wright	PL	50	
	Bank account	CB		50
	Correction of £50 reversal of entries:		100	100
	receipt 93459			

To correct this type of error it is best to reverse the entries that have been made incorrectly (the first two journal entries), and then to put through the correct entries. Although it will correct the error, it is wrong to debit Wright £100 and credit bank £100; this is because there was never a transaction for this amount – the original transaction was for £50.

As noted earlier, it is often an idea to write out the 'T' accounts, complete with the error, and then to write in the correcting entries. As an example, the two accounts involved in this last error are shown with the error made on 2 May, and the corrections made on 12 May indicated by the shading (the opening credit balance of S Wright's account is shown as £50):

Dr			S Wright			Cr
1997		£	1997			£
12 May	Bank	50	1 May	Balance b/d		50
12 May	Bank	50	2 May	Bank		50
		100				100

Dr			Bank Account			Cr
1997		£	1997			£
2 May	S Wright	50	12 May	S Wright		50
			12 May	S Wright		50

The accounts now show a net debit transaction of £50 on S Wright's account, and a net credit transaction of £50 on bank account, which is how this payment to a creditor should have been recorded in order to clear the balance on the account.

mispost/error of commission

Credit sales of £40 (invoice no 321) have been debited to the account of J Adams, instead of J Adams Limited; the error is corrected on 15 May 1997.

Date	Details	Folio	Dr	Cr
1997			£	£
15 May	J Adams Limited	SL	40	
	J Adams	SL		40
	Correction of mispost (invoice 321)			

This type of error can be avoided, to some extent, by the use of account numbers, and by persuading the customer to quote the account number or reference on each transaction. All computer accounting systems use numbers/references to identify accounts, but it is still possible to post a transaction to the wrong account.

error of principle

The cost of petrol, £15 (receipt no 34535), has been debited to vehicles account; the error is corrected on 20 May 1997.

Date	Details	Folio	Dr	Cr
1997			£	£
20 May	Vehicle running expenses account	GL	15	
	Vehicles account	GL		15
	Correction of error: receipt 34535			

This type of error is similar to a mispost except that, instead of the wrong person's account being used, it is the wrong class of account. In this example, the vehicle running costs must be kept separate from the cost of the asset (the vehicle), otherwise the expense and asset accounts will be incorrect.

error of original entry

Credit sale of goods, £45 (invoice no. 3668) to J Lamb entered in the accounts as £54; the error is corrected on 27 May 1997.

Date	Details	Folio	Dr	Cr
1997			£	£
27 May	Sales account	GL	54	
	J Lamb	SL		54
	J Lamb	SL	45	
	Sales account	GL		45
	Correction of error: invoice 3668		99	99
	entered into the accounts wrongly			

This error could have been corrected by debiting sales account and crediting J Lamb with £9, being the difference between the two amounts. However, there was no original transaction for this amount, and it is better to reverse the wrong transaction and put through the correct one. A reversal of figures, as above, either has a difference of nine, or an amount divisible by nine. An error of original entry can also be a 'bad' figure on a cheque or an invoice, which is entered wrongly into both accounts.

compensating error

Rates account is over-cast (over-added) by £100; sales account is also over-cast by the same amount; the error is corrected on 30 May 1997.

Date	Details	Folio	Dr	Cr
1997			£	£
30 May	Sales account	GL	100	
	Rates account	GL		100
	Correction of over-cast on rates account and sales account			

Here, an account with a debit balance – rates – has been over-cast; this is compensated by an over-cast on an account with a credit balance – sales. There are several variations on this theme, eg two debit balances, one over-cast, one under-cast; a debit balance under-cast, a credit balance under-cast.

important notes

- The journal is the primary accounting record for non-regular transactions. The journal entries must then be recorded in the book-keeping system.
- For journal entries which include transactions on debtors' and creditors' accounts, remember that where sales ledger and purchases ledger control accounts are in use, the book-keeping entry must be recorded in both the personal account and the control account.

TRIAL BALANCE ERRORS: USE OF SUSPENSE ACCOUNT

There are many types of errors that cause an imbalance in the trial balance. Included amongst these are:

- omission of one part of the double-entry transaction
- recording two debits or two credits for a transaction
- recording a different amount for a transaction on the debit side from the credit side

- errors in the calculation of balances (not compensated by other errors)
- error in transferring the balance of an account to the trial balance
- error of addition in the trial balance

When errors are shown, the trial balance is 'balanced' by recording the difference in a suspense account. For example, on 30 June 1997 the trial balance totals are:

	Dr £	Cr £
Trial balance totals	100,000	99,850
Suspense account		150
	100,000	100,000

A suspense account is opened in the general ledger with, in this case, a credit balance of £150:

Dr		Suspense Account		Cr
1997	£	1997		£
		30 Jun Trial balance difference		150

A detailed examination of the book-keeping system is now made in order to find the errors. As errors are found, they are corrected by means of a journal entry. The journal entries will balance, with one part of the entry being either a debit or a credit to suspense account. In this way, the balance on suspense account is eliminated by book-keeping transactions. Taking the above suspense account, the following errors are found and corrected on 15 July 1997:

- sales account is under-cast by £100

- a payment to a creditor, A Wilson, for £65, has been recorded in the bank as £56

- telephone expenses of £55 have not been entered in the expenses account

- stationery expenses £48 have been debited to both the stationery account and the bank account

These errors are corrected by the journal entries shown on the next page. Note that the journal narrative includes details of cheque numbers and dates taken from the records of the business.

Date	Details	Folio	Dr	Cr
1997			£	£
15 Jul	Suspense account	GL	100	
	Sales account	GL		100
	Under-cast on 27/5/97 now corrected			
15 Jul	Bank account	CB	56	
	Suspense account	GL		56
	Suspense account	GL	65	
	Bank account	CB		65
	Payment to A Wilson for £65 (cheque no. 783726) on 30/5/97 entered in bank as £56 in error		121	121
15 Jul	Telephone expenses account	GL	55	
	Suspense account	GL		55
	Omission of entry in expenses account paid by cheque no. 783734			
15 Jul	Suspense account	GL	48	
	Bank account	CB		48
	Suspense account	GL	48	
	Bank account	CB		48
	Correction of error: payment by cheque 783736 debited in error to bank account		96	96

After these journal entries have been recorded in the accounts, the suspense account appears as:

Dr			**Suspense Account**		Cr
1997		£	1997		£
15 Jul	Sales	100	30 Jun	Trial balance difference	150
15 Jul	Bank	65	15 Jul	Bank	56
15 Jul	Bank	48	15 Jul	Telephone expenses	55
15 Jul	Bank	48			
		261			261

All the errors have now been found, and suspense account has a nil balance.

OTHER TRANSFERS

Any other non-regular transactions need to be recorded in the journal. Examples of such transactions include:

- bad debts written off
- expenses charged to owner's drawings
- goods for the owner's use

bad debts written off

We have already seen, in Chapter 9, the double-entry book-keeping entries to write off a debtor's account as bad:

- *debit* bad debts written off account
- *credit* debtor's account

15 Dec 1997   *Write off the account of Don's Diner which has a balance of £47, as a bad debt*

The journal entry is:

Refer to Page 132 for memo

Date	Details	Folio	Dr	Cr
1997			£	£
15 Dec	Bad debts written off*	GL	47	
	T Hughes	SL		47
	Bad debt written off as per memo from accounts supervisor 10/12/97			

* Note that if VAT relief is available, £7 of the £47 will be debited to VAT account.

expenses charged to the owner's drawings

Sometimes the owner of a business uses business facilities for private use, eg telephone, or car. The owner will agree that part of the expense shall be charged to him or her as drawings, while the other part represents a business expense. The book-keeping entry to record the adjustment is:

- *debit* drawings account
- *credit* expense account, eg telephone

31 Dec 1997   *The balance of telephone account is £600; of this, one-quarter is the estimated cost of the owner's private usage*

The journal entry is:

Date	Details	Folio	Dr	Cr
1997			£	£
31 Dec	Drawings account	GL	150	
	Telephone account	GL		150
	Transfer of private use to drawings account			

goods for the owner's use

When the owner of a business takes some of the goods in which the business trades for his or her own use, the double-entry book-keeping is:

– *debit* drawings account

– *credit* purchases account

15 Oct 1997: Owner of the business takes goods for own use, £105

The journal entry is:

Date	Details	Folio	Dr	Cr
1997			£	£
15 Oct	Drawings account	GL	105	
	Purchases account	GL		105
	Goods taken for owner's use			

Note: where a business is VAT-registered, VAT must be accounted for on goods taken by the owner.

CHAPTER SUMMARY

- The journal is used to list non-regular transactions.
- The journal is a book of prime entry – it is not a double-entry account.
- The journal is used for:
  - opening entries
  - purchase and sale of fixed assets on credit
  - correction of errors
  - other transfers
- Correction of errors is always a difficult topic to put into practice: it tests knowledge of book-keeping procedures and it is all too easy to make the error worse than it was in the first place! The secret of dealing with this topic well is to write down – in account format – what has gone wrong. It should then be relatively easy to see what has to be done to put the error right.
- Errors not shown by a trial balance include: error of omission, reversal of entries, mispost/error of commission, error of principle, error of original entry (or transcription), compensating error.

- Errors shown by a trial balance include: omission of one part of the book-keeping transaction, recording two debits/credits for a transaction, recording different amounts in the two accounts, calculating balances incorrectly, transferring wrong balances to the trial balance.

- All errors are non-regular transactions and need to be corrected by means of a journal entry: the book-keeper then records the correcting transactions in the accounts.

- When error(s) are shown by a trial balance, the amount of the error is placed in a suspense account. As the errors are found, journal entries are made which 'clear out' the suspense account.

KEY TERMS

journal	the primary accounting record for non-regular transactions
opening entries	the transactions which open the accounts of a new business
suspense account	account used to place an error in the trial balance, pending further investigation
goods for the owner's use	goods taken by the owner of a business for personal use

STUDENT ACTIVITIES

11.1 Which one of the following will not be recorded in the journal?

   (a)   credit purchase of a fixed asset

   (b)   cash sale of goods

   (c)   write-off of a bad debt

   (d)   correction of an error not shown by the trial balance

   Answer (a) or (b) or (c) or (d)

11.2 Which business transaction goes with which primary accounting record?

business transaction	*primary accounting record*
• credit sale of a fixed asset	• sales day book
• credit purchase of goods from a supplier	• purchases day book
• returned credit purchases to the supplier	• sales returns day book
• customer returns goods sold on credit	• purchases returns day book
• cheque received from a debtor	• journal
• credit sale of goods to a customer	• cash book

11.3 A trial balance fails to agree by £75 and the difference is placed to a suspense account. Later it is found that a credit sale for this amount has not been entered in the sales account. Which one of the following journal entries is correct?

(a) debit suspense account £75; credit sales account £75

(b) debit suspense account £150; credit sales account £150

(c) debit sales account £75; credit suspense account £75

(d) credit sales account £75

Answer (a) or (b) or (c) or (d)

11.4 Henry Lewis is setting up the book-keeping system for his new business, which sells office stationery. He decides to use the following primary accounting records:

- Journal

- Sales Day Book

- Purchases Day Book

- Sales Returns Day Book

- Purchases Returns Day Book

- Cash Book

The following business transactions take place:

(a) He receives an invoice from Temeside Traders for £956 for goods supplied on credit

(b) He issues an invoice to Malvern Models for £176 of goods

(c) He buys a computer for use in his business for £2,000 on credit from A-Z Computers Limited

(d) He issues a credit note to Johnson Brothers for £55 of goods

(e) A debtor, Melanie Fisher, settles the balance of her account, £107, by cheque

(f) He makes cash sales of £25

(g) Henry Lewis withdraws cash £100 for his own use

(h) He pays a creditor, Stationery Supplies Limited, the balance of the account, £298, by cheque

(i) A debtor, Jim Bowen, with an account balance of £35 is to be written off as a bad debt

(j) A credit note for £80 is received from a creditor, Ian Johnson

You are to take each business transaction in turn and state:

- the name of the primary accounting record

- the name of the account to be debited

- the name of the account to be credited

Note: VAT is to be ignored.

11.5 The trial balance of Thomas Wilson balanced. However, a number of errors have been found in the book-keeping system:

(a) Credit sale of £150 to J Rigby has not been entered in the accounts

(b) A payment by cheque for £125 to H Price Limited, a creditor, has been recorded in the account of H Prince

(c) The cost of a new delivery van, £10,000, has been entered to vehicle expenses account

(d) Purchases returns of £55 to S Mortimer, a creditor, have been entered on the wrong sides of both accounts

(e) The totals of the purchases day book and the purchases returns day book have been under-cast by £100

(f) A payment for £89 from L Johnson, a debtor, has been entered in the accounts as £98

You are to take each error in turn and:

* state the type of error

* show the correcting journal entry

Notes:

* *VAT is to be ignored*

* *Thomas Wilson does not use control accounts in his book-keeping system*

11.6 Jeremy Johnson extracts a trial balance from his book-keeping records on 30 September 1997. Unfortunately the trial balance fails to balance and the difference, £19 debit, is placed to a suspense account pending further investigation.

The following errors are later found:

(a) A payment of £85 to Wyvern Supplies, a creditor, has been entered in the cash book but no entry has been made in the personal account.

(b) A purchases invoice for £78 has been correctly entered in the purchases day book but in the creditor's account of Henry Barton it is recorded as £87.

(c) The sales returns day book has been over-cast by £100.

(d) A credit note for £25 issued to Teresa Jarvis has been entered twice in her account.

You are to:

* make journal entries to correct the errors

* show the suspense account after the errors have been corrected

Note: Jeremy Johnson does not use control accounts in his book-keeping system.

12 RECEIVING AND RECORDING PAYMENTS

This chapter explains the different ways in which money is received by an organisation and then sets out the procedures it follows in recording those payments. It covers:

- receiving money in the form of cash, cheques and similar items, inter-bank transfers and payment by debit and credit card

- the legal meaning of cheque crossings and endorsements

- checking of the money against covering documentation where appropriate

- checking cash, giving change and issuing receipts

- recording incoming payments on remittance lists, cash books and cash registers

- dealing with problem payments – incorrect cheques, suspicious cards, situations where the money received does not tally with the accompanying documentation

NVQ PERFORMANCE CRITERIA COVERED

unit 1: RECORDING AND ACCOUNTING FOR CASH TRANSACTIONS
element 1
record and bank monies received

- ❏ incoming monies are checked against relevant supporting documentation
- ❏ cash is correctly counted and correct change given where applicable
- ❏ monies received are correctly and legibly recorded
- ❏ written receipts are correctly issued where required
- ❏ totals and balances are correctly calculated
- ❏ documentation is correctly filed
- ❏ cash handling, security and confidentiality procedures are followed
- ❏ discrepancies, unusual features or queries are identified and either resolved or referred to the appropriate person

INCOMING PAYMENTS

Payments can be received by an organisation in a variety of ways:

- cash
- cheque
- credit card and debit card transactions
- direct to the bank by inter-bank transfer

It clearly depends on the nature and the size of the organisation how the payments are made and processed. In the retail sector, for example, a newsagent will depend to a great extent on cash transactions and the cash register, a large supermarket on the other hand will use electronic tills and accept cash, cheques, and credit and debit card payments.

CASH

Cash is still used for most small transactions, and we are still nowhere near the 'cashless society' which is often talked about. For the purchaser, cash is a convenient and fast method of paying small money amounts but, for larger amounts, it is unsuitable because it is bulky to carry and can be lostor stolen. As far as the organisation accepting payments in cash is concerned, the main disadvantage of cash is the security problem, and there is a risk of receiving forged notes.

receiving payment in cash

For a business receiving sums of money in the form of cash it is necessary for a member of staff to count the cash received and check it against the amount due. Notes should be checked for forgeries (held against the light or viewed on special machines). Change will need to be given when the exact amount is not tendered (given). For example:

Sale	£3.64
Amount tendered (given) by customer	£10.00
Change to be given	£6.36

The amount of change is the difference between the amount tendered and the amount of the sale. When a cash till is in use, modern types of till will indicate the amount of change to be given after the amount tendered has been entered through the keypad. You will know, from having bought items in shops, that many cashiers count out the change starting with the amount of the sale and working to the amount tendered. From the above example this would be done as follows:

Sale		£3.64
Change given:	1p coin	£3.65
	5p coin	£3.70
	10p coin	£3.80
	20p coin	£4.00
	£1 coin	£5.00
	£5 note	£10.00 (amount tendered)
	£6.36	

Often when payment is made in cash, a receipt is given: this can take the form of a machine-produced receipt, such as is given in a shop, or a handwritten receipt (examples of each are shown below).

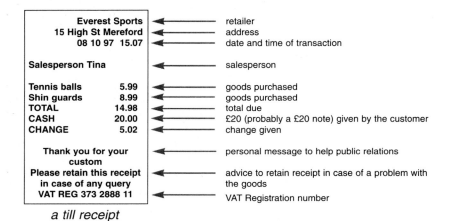

```
        Everest Sports      ◄──────────  retailer
   15 High St Mereford       ◄──────────  address
        08 10 97  15.07      ◄──────────  date and time of transaction

Salesperson Tina             ◄──────────  salesperson

Tennis balls      5.99       ◄──────────  goods purchased
Shin guards       8.99       ◄──────────  goods purchased
TOTAL            14.98       ◄──────────  total due
CASH             20.00       ◄──────────  £20 (probably a £20 note) given by the customer
CHANGE            5.02       ◄──────────  change given

  Thank you for your         ◄──────────  personal message to help public relations
       custom
Please retain this receipt   ◄──────────  advice to retain receipt in case of a problem with
  in case of any query                    the goods
  VAT REG 373 2888 11        ◄──────────  VAT Registration number
```

a till receipt

ENIGMA MUSIC LIMITED   *receipt*   **958**

13 High Street, Mereford MR1 2TF
VAT Reg 343 7645 23

Customer .... *R V Williams* .... **date** .. *9 Oct 1997* ..

'Golden Oldies' by J Moore	£20.00
	£20.00
VAT @ 17.5%	£3.50
Total	£23.50

a hand-written receipt

Those who handle cash in an organisation are responsible for its safekeeping: it should be kept in a cash till or in a cash box. When not being used, these should be kept locked and the key retained under the control of the cashier.

a modern electronic till

tills and cash floats

At the end of the day it will be necessary to 'cash up' by balancing the amount of cash held. As most cash tills start each day with a float of cash (to enable change to be given, if necessary, to the first customers), the amount in the till at the end of the day will be:

cash float at start

plus sales made during the day (listed on the till roll)

equals amount of cash held at end of day

A cash float will be kept back for the next day, and the surplus will be transferred to the safe for paying into the bank next day. Alternatively, a bank paying-in slip (see the next chapter) might be made out, and the cash, together with the paying-in slip and any cheques received placed in a 'wallet' to be deposited in the bank's night safe (see the next chapter).

For example:

cash float at start	£150.00
plus sales made during the day (listed on the till roll)	£2608.50
equals amount of cash held at end of day	£2758.50
less cash float retained for next day	£150.00
amount transferred to safe or bank's night safe	£2608.50

If the cash in the till does not agree with the total on the till roll, the discrepancy needs investigation. Regular discrepancies for significant amounts, eg £5 or £10, will lead to urgent investigations – there could be pilfering taking place if the till is often short at the end of the day, or it could be caused by poor cashiering – giving the wrong change.

CHEQUES

Cheques are issued by banks to their personal and business account customers. Building societies also issue cheques on current accounts – their customers are mainly personal. Payment by cheque is one of the most common methods of payment for all but the smallest amounts. A specimen cheque is shown below (there is more on how to write out a cheque in Chapter 14).

what is a cheque?

A cheque, as used in normal business practice, may be defined as

a written order to the bank (known as the 'drawee') signed by its customer (known as the 'drawer') to pay a specified amount to a specified person (known as the 'payee')

Some organisations – large retail stores, for example – have machines which print out their customers' cheques on the till. A large number of cheques, however, are still written by hand, and great care must be taken both when writing out cheques and also when receiving cheques in payment. The cheques must be examined to ensure that all the details and signatures are correct. The vast majority of cheques are 'crossed' – they have two parallel lines on the front of the cheque.

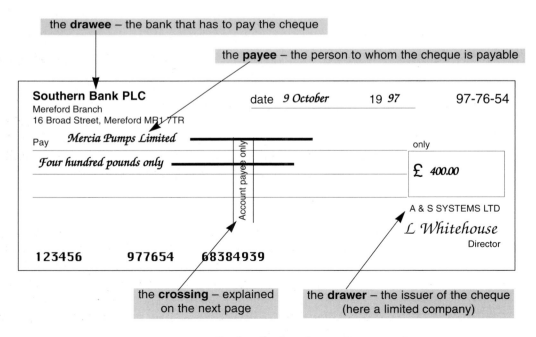

the 'parties' and crossing on a cheque

examining the cheque

If you are receiving payment by cheque, whether it is direct from the customer over the counter or through the post on a remittance advice, there are a number of basic checks to carry out:

- is the cheque signed? – it is invalid if it is not

- is the payee's name correct? – it should be changed and initialled by the drawer (issuer) if it is not

- is the cheque in date? – a cheque becomes out of date ('stale') and invalid after six months; note that if the date is missing, it may be written in

- do the words and figures agree? – the cheque may be returned by the bank if they do not

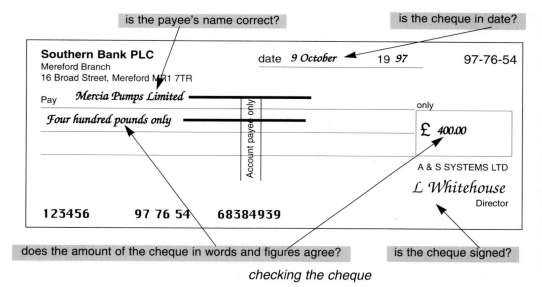

checking the cheque

If the organisation accepting payment by cheque is inefficient and does not carry out these precautions, the cheque concerened may be returned to the organisation's bank after it has been paid in, and the amount of the cheque deducted from the organisation's bank account. If the cheque is issued with a guarantee card, different conditions apply (see page 190).

crossings

Cheques may, as in the example shown above, be *crossed,* that is, they are printed with two parallel lines across the face of the cheque. Often there are words printed or written in the crossing. If a cheque is not crossed, it is an *open* cheque. *A crossed cheque may only be paid into a bank account*; it cannot be cashed (ie exchanged for cash) by the payee (the person to whom the cheque is made payable) unless the person writing out the cheque makes it payable to him/herself.

endorsements

In law the payee of a cheque is entitled to sign it on the back – *endorse* it – so that it can be passed on to another person who can pay it into a bank account and receive payment. This signature on the back – the *endorsement* – should read as follows:

> *Pay Ivor Brown*
> *James Smith*

Here James Smith, the payee, is endorsing the cheque over to Ivor Brown who will pay it into his bank account. He has actually written 'Pay Ivor Brown' above his signature.

It is very important to make sure that if you are endorsing a cheque you write above your signature the name of the person or organisation into whose account the cheque is being paid. If you merely sign the back of the cheque without adding the name of the other person or organisation it technically becomes a 'bearer' cheque which can be paid into a bank account by anyone who finds or steals the cheque. You will see that banknotes have 'pay bearer' written on the front. A bearer cheque is as good as cash!

when endorsements are *not* possible

Endorsement and passing on of a cheque is *not* possible if

- the word 'only' appears after the payee's name on the front of the cheque
- the words 'account payee' or 'account payee only' appear in the crossing on the front of the cheque (see below)

As these words are more and more frequently being printed on cheques, endorsements are becoming much less common. As these cheques cannot be endorsed over to another person, they can only be paid into the payee's account.

types of crossing

If you are receiving cheques you will need to know the different types of crossing, as the nature of crossing will affect whether or not the cheque can be paid into the organisation's bank account. These are the basic types:

crossing		*effect*
& co and		A *general* crossing – no effect – the cheque can be paid into the bank
Midland Bank Pershore		This crossing is known as a *special* crossing – the cheque can *only* be paid into Midland Bank in Pershore

crossing	*effect*
not negotiable	This cheque *can* be endorsed and passed on to someone other than the payee – but in practice this is *not* recommended. It should be paid into the payee's account.
account payee	This cheque should only be paid into the account of the payee of the cheque. It should not be endorsed over to anyone else.

BANK GUARANTEE CARDS

In order to encourage shops and other businesses to accept cheques more readily, banks and some building societies issue guarantee cards to suitable personal and business customers. This plastic 'card' acts as a guarantee that cheques up to and including a stated limit(normally £50, sometimes £100 or £200) will be paid as long as certain conditions are fulfilled. Many banks now issue 'payment cards' which combine the functions of

- cheque guarantee – guaranteeing single cheques up to a set limit
- cash card – enabling the holder to withdraw cash from cash machines – ATMs (automated teller machines)
- debit card – enabling the holder to make payment for goods and services from a bank account without writing out a cheque – examples include Switch cards and Barclay's Connect card

a Barclays Connect payment card

guarantee card conditions

The rules for the use of a cheque guarantee card are normally set out in the agreement form signed when the card is issued. The following is an example of some of the conditions:

XYZ Bank plc guarantees in any single transaction the payment of one cheque taken from one of its own cheque books for up to £100 provided the cheque is not drawn on the account of a Limited Company, and

(1)   The cheque bears the same name and code number as this card.

(2)   It is signed, before the expiry of the card, in the United Kingdom of Great Britain and Northern Ireland, the Channel Islands or the Isle of Man in the presence of the payee by the person whose signature appears on this card.

(3)   The card number is written on the back of the cheque by the payee.

(4)   The card has not been altered or defaced.

receiving payment by cheque and guarantee card

If you have read the guarantee card conditions set out above you will appreciate that when you accept payment by cheque and cheque guarantee card you must take great care that all the conditions are met. If you do not, the purchaser's bank may not 'honour' (pay) the cheque, and your organisation stands to lose the money. Also, because of the large number of stolen and fraudulent cards in circulation, you must be on your guard against suspicious-looking cards and customers. The procedure is therefore as follows:

- examine the card to make sure it is not defaced – rub your finger along the signature strip, does it feel normal? – a stolen card may have been tampered with and a new signature added

- if the card is handed to you in a plastic wallet, take the card out, as it may be a forgery

- examine the card for

  - expiry date

  - amount of the guarantee

  - name agreeing with the name on the cheque

  - bank details agreeing with those on the cheque

- examine the cheque for

  - signature (this should agree with the signature on the card)

  - date

  - payee's name

  - amount in words and figures (they should agree)

- write the card number on the back of the cheque – an essential procedure, adding any other details which your organisation requires (some businesses use a rubber stamp on the back of the cheque to list the required details)

cheque card limits – a common mistake

Bank customers sometimes think that if the cost of the item being purchased is above the cheque guarantee limit, then a number of cheques may be issued and payment is guaranteed. This is not correct – the cheque card guarantee covers only *one cheque per transaction*.

CREDIT CARDS

Credit cards provide a means of obtaining goods and services immediately, but paying for them later. The commonest credit cards used in the UK use the names Visa and Mastercard.

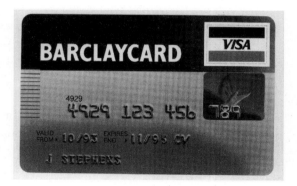

a Barclaycard credit card

Credit cards are issued, upon application, to customers of banks, building societies, and retail groups. A credit limit is set on each cardholder's credit card account (which is entirely separate from his or her normal bank account). Goods and services can be obtained at shops and other outlets having computer terminals or the special machine (imprinter) for preparing sales vouchers to record the transaction. Credit cards can also be used for mail order and telephone order sales. Retailers pay to the credit card company a set percentage (up to 5%) of each transaction amount for the use of the credit card facility.

Each month a cardholder is sent a statement of the purchases made and can choose to pay off the balance of the account, or to pay part only (subject to a certain minimum amount), carrying forward the remaining balance to next month. Interest is charged on balances owing to the credit card company. An annual flat fee is normally charged to the cardholder for the use of the card.

credit card – 'over the counter' sales

A business will have one of two methods of receiving payment by credit card by a customer who calls in person:

- a mechanical imprinter machine, which imprints the embossed details from the credit card onto the sales voucher
- a 'swipe' machine – as seen on electronic tills – which is able to read the details from a credit card as it is passed through the card 'reader'

mechanical imprinter machine

The procedure is as follows:

- check that the card has not been defaced or tampered with – check the signature strip carefully
- check that the card has not expired
- imprint the sales voucher (see illustration on the next page)
- complete the sales voucher with date, details of goods, and total money amount
- the customer signs the imprinted sales voucher, and the signature should be compared with that on the card
- the list of stolen cards is checked
- if the payment is above a certain amount – the *floor limit* (which varies according to the type of business) it will be necessary to telephone the credit card company to obtain an authorisation code allowing the transaction to go ahead (the authorisation code is recorded on the sales voucher)
- the top copy of the sales voucher is handed to the customer, and the other three copies are retained
- of the three copies of the sales voucher which are retained, the white copy is treated in the same way as a cheque, and is kept in the till and added to the cheques and cash received to give the total sales figure; the other two copies (yellow and blue) are kept in the event of a query in the future
- the white copy of the sales voucher kept in the till is then banked along with the cash and cheques

National Bank PLC

7654 654 356 356

R J OSBORNE

987 8765 67

TUSCANY WINE STORE

MEREFORD

VISA   DELTA

Date	Send?	Take?
28.03.98	–	✓

Dept	Sales No	Initials
02	176	JP

Description

Goods

Retailer – Please retain this copy for a minimum of 6 months as your own proof of the transaction.

Sale Confirmed – Cardholder's Signature	Authorisation Code	Total £
Robert Osborne		3 0 0 0

Cardholder's Declaration: The issuer of the card identified on this item is authorised to pay the amount shown as **Total** upon proper presentation. I promise to pay such **Total** (together with any other charges due thereon) subject to and in accordance with the agreement governing the use of such card.

MasterCard   EUROCARD

a credit card sales voucher

credit card sales with an electronic 'swipe' machine

A 'swipe' machine is so-called because the cashier accepting the payment 'swipes' it through an electronic reader on either a 'standalone' machine (used by smaller organisations) or connected to an electronic till (as in the big supermarkets – see the photograph on page 185).

The cashier or clerk should:

- 'swipe' the card through the card reader - this 'captures' the details encoded in the magnetic stripe on the reverse of the card
- having captured the data, the system checks automatically that the card number is valid
- the amount of the transaction is keyed into the electronic till, and the system (if the till is on-line) checks the cardholder's credit limit and authorises the transaction
- a telephone call to the card company may be necessary to authorise the transaction if the till is not on-line
- the till prints a two-part receipt which includes space for the cardholder's signature
- the customer signs, and the signature is compared with that on the card
- the customer is handed the top-copy of the receipt, and the other copy is kept in the event of a query in the future
- the amount of the transaction is automatically debited to the cardholder's credit card account, while the bank account of the business is credited

credit card – telephone and mail order sales

Buying goods and services by credit card over the telephone or by mail order is becoming increasingly common. When accepting payment by this means, the organisation must exercise the same degree of care as a shop accepting an 'over the counter' transaction. Some organisations will complete the same type of sales voucher used for an 'over the counter' transaction and send the top copy to the customer as a receipt; some organisations will use a 'swipe' machine, and send a copy of the receipt to the customer. Organisations which have a large volume of transactions will not use vouchers but instead record the details of sales on a Mail Order Schedule, a form which will provide space for recording ten transactions or more.

When accepting payment by credit card by telephone or mail order, the following details must be obtained:

- the card number
- the expiry date of the card
- the name and initials of the cardholder as shown on the card
- the cardholder's address
- the cardholder's signature (mail order only)
- authorisation of amounts over the 'floor limit' must be carried out in the normal way

DEBIT CARDS

Debit cards are issued to personal customers by banks and building societies to enable their customers to make payments from their bank accounts by Electronic Funds Transfer (see below). *No cheque is written out.* Debit cards are issued to selected customers of the bank; they enable a payment to be made from the person's bank account electronically. A debit card has the obvious advantages of being quicker to use and more convenient. Examples of debit cards are Barclays' Visa 'Delta' and Midland's 'Switch' cards.

From a seller's point of view, when a customer wishes to pay by debit card in person, the transaction is handled in a similar way to a credit card, using either

- a manually completed sales voucher on an imprinter, or, more commonly
- an electronic swipe machine, either 'standalone' (used by smaller organisations) or connected to an electronic till (as in the big supermarkets)

As noted earlier, some card issuers have combined the functions of a debit card with that of cheque guarantee card and cash card (ATM card).

ELECTRONIC FUNDS TRANSFER AT POINT OF SALE (EFTPOS)

Credit cards and debit cards can be used to make electronic payments by means of a system called *Electronic Funds Transfer at Point Of Sale* (EFTPOS). This is a system which allows a retail outlet to debit the bank account or credit card account of the purchaser at the point of sale and, at the same time, to credit the retailer's bank account. Besides removing the need to carry a lot of cash, the system reduces the paperwork of writing out cheques or filling in credit card vouchers.

EFTPOS is operated by means of plastic cards – either debit cards issued by banks/building societies, or by credit cards. As we have seen, when goods are to be paid for using this method, the retailer 'swipes' the card through a card reader and the total amount is entered into an electronic checkout till. The till prints a sales slip which is signed by the customer to authenticate the transaction. The retailer checks that the signature on the sales slip is the same as that shown on the card. Details of the transaction are transmitted electronically by means of a computer link to a central computer either immediately, or later in the day. Sometimes a telephone call has to be made to authorise the transaction. The cost of the goods being purchased is checked against the amount available in the card holder's bank or building society account, or the available credit in the credit card account. If everything is in order, the customer's account is debited and the retailer's account is credited with the appropriate amount. The benefits of EFTPOS to a retail business are:

- greater efficiency, with less time taken by customers to make payment

- reduced queuing time

- less cash to handle (giving fewer security risks)

- guaranteed payment once acceptance has been made

PAYABLE ORDERS

Sometimes a business will receive documents similar to cheques as a a means of payment. These *payable orders* include

- *Postal orders* – money orders purchased from the Post Office, often used by people who do not have bank accounts and who wish to send money through the post.

- *Bank drafts* – these are cheques issued by a *bank* and are as good as cash. The bank is both drawer (issuer) and drawee (the organisation who has to make payment), so the cheque is not going to 'bounce'. They are often used by people wanting to pay large amounts, eg for a house or car purchase. If you need a bank draft you have to order it in advance; you will be charged for the service.

- *Building society cheques* – these work on the same principle as bank drafts, except that the drawer (issuer) is a building society and the drawee (the organisation who has to make payment) is a bank. Like bank drafts, they are considered to be as good as cash payments.

If you receive payment in the form of a postal order, bank draft or building society cheque, it can be paid into the bank account like a cheque.

CHECKING PAYMENTS AGAINST DOCUMENTATION

It is important that incoming payments received from customers are checked against any documentation that the supplier receives. This is to ensure that the correct amount is received and that no future disputes can arise – for example "We sent you £450, that's what it says on our advice" … "No you didn't, you only sent us £405, that's what it shows on your account."

The most common type of document which advises the amount of a payment is a *remittance advice*. Payments from customers can be received either through the post, or through the bank as inter-bank transfers. A remittance advice will be issued in both instances by the person paying.

postal payments

Any cheque received through the post should be checked carefully against the accompanying remittance advice, which can be

- a special form prepared by the person paying, setting out the amount of the cheque, the date and the item(s) the cheque is covering, or
- a tear-off slip sent with the statement of account by the seller; often the items being paid are ticked off by the buyer, but the amount of the cheque may not be written down

In both cases (and particularly the second) the organisation receiving payment *must* check that the total of the items being paid less any credit due equals the amount of the cheque. Failure to carry out this simple check could cause problems later on if there is a discrepancy. Any differences should be marked on the remittance advice which is then normally queried with the customer by telephone.

inter-bank transfers

An increasing number of payments are now made automatically from bank account to bank account on the instructions of the payer through the BACS system (BACS stands for Bankers Automated Clearing Services). As no cheque is issued, payment is made more quickly and more cheaply. The problem of how the seller is to *know* that payment is made is solved by the buyer sending a BACS advice – essentially a remittance advice for a BACS payment. The organisation receiving payment will have to check each advice carefully against the bank statement when it arrives to ensure that the correct amount has been received.

Examples of remittance advices are shown below.

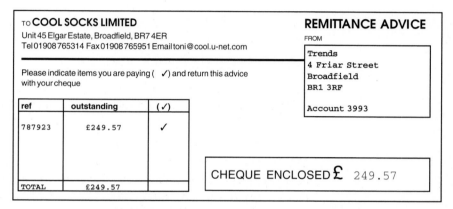

remittance advice sent with a cheque payment

remittance advice sent to advise of a BACS payment

RECORDING MONEY RECEIVED

The individual amounts of money received should be recorded by the organisation. The *way* in which they are recorded will depend on the way in which they are received. The fact that the amounts are recorded will help security by discouraging employees from being tempted to raid the till and steal money.

cash registers

Money received over a counter is likely to be recorded on a cash register tally roll or electronic till memory – the totals on the till roll or memory can then be checked with the actual money received, ready for paying into the bank. The more modern cash registers (supermarket tills, for example) are linked to a central computer and automatically change the stock level records as items are sold. The security of cash registers is tightly controlled: they are operated by a security key and any transfer of change is recorded.

remittance lists (postal items)

Cheques and other money received may be recorded manually on a *remittance list*. 'Remittance list' just means a list of what you have been sent. It can record items received through the post by a business, or it can be used at the counter of old-fashioned shops (eg old bookshops) instead of a cash register. A remittance list for items received through the post is likely to include columns for the date, the sender, the nature of the 'remittance,' the amount, and, as a security measure, the signature of the person opening the post.

date	sender	remittance	amount	signature
12.3.98	Travers Toys Ltd	cheque	234.50	G.Palmer
12.3.98	Grampian Traders	bank draft	10,500.00	G Palmer
12.3.98	Mrs D Dodds	cash	14.50	R Patel
12.3.98	Mercia Foods	cheque	450.00	G Palmer

example of a remittance list for items received through the post

remittance lists/cash received lists

A remittance list is also used to record payments received over the counter. It is an old-fashioned method, but it serves its purpose very well. The person at the till will record each sale as it occurs; the cash and cheques are likely to be kept in a locked cash box, as there is no cash register. The total of the remittance list (or *cash received list*) should be agreed with the takings at the end of each day.

The items can either be written on a separate piece of paper or they may be entered in a book. The example below shows the sales made by a second-hand bookshop during the course of day.

FOLIO BOOKS   takings for *22 January 1998*

Milton, Paradise Lost, 1793	cash	£45.00
Hardy, Mayor of Casterbridge, 1896	cheque	£65.00
Graham Greene, Brighton Rock	cash	£1.75
Punch selections	cheque	£25.00
T S Eliot, 4 Quartets	cheque	£12.50
Haynes, Worcester within the Walls	cheque	£14.95
Culpeper, Tudor Remedies	cash	£4.95
W English, Alvechurch - a History	cheque	£9.95
TOTAL CASH		£51.70
TOTAL CHEQUES		£127.40
Total Takings		£179.10

---

example of a remittance list for items received over the counter

cash book

The cash book is the central record of money amounts received and paid out by the organisation either in the form of cash, or as items passed through the bank account. All the payments referred to in this chapter will eventually pass through the cash book. It will be dealt with in detail in Chapter 15.

CHAPTER SUMMARY

- Incoming payments can be received in a number of ways: cash, cheque, credit and debit card, inter-bank transfer.

- Receipts are often issued for cash payments; either till receipts or handwritten receipts.

- Cash in a till will be counted up at the end of each day; the amount should equal the takings for the day plus any 'float' held in the till.

- Cheques should be examined carefully when taken in payment, either over the counter or through the post. Normally they are crossed, sometimes they can be endorsed over, although this practice is becoming less common.

- Cheques received over the counter are normally only accepted with a cheque guarantee card. When this occurs, the card and the cheque should be carefully checked together.

- Payment can also be accepted by credit card – here the seller has to generate a paper sales voucher, either with an mechanical imprinter or alternatively with an electronic 'swipe' machine. A credit card enables payment to be made to the credit card company by the buyer at a later date.

- Debit cards are commonly accepted as a means of payment in place of cash or cheques. Again a sales voucher is generated, but here payment is made from the bank account of the buyer at the time of purchase by EFT (Electronic Funds Transfer)

- When payments are evidenced by documentation such as a remittance advice, the payment should be checked against the documentation. Payment in this case can be by cheque or by inter-bank transfer.

- When money is received it should be recorded, both for security purposes and also as part of the operation of the accounting system. Forms of recording include the cash till roll, remittance lists and the cash book.

KEY TERMS

cash float	the amount of cash kept in a till at the end of the day to provide change when the till is next used
cheque	a written order to the bank, signed by its customer, instructing it to pay a specified amount to a specified person
drawer of a cheque	the person who signs the front of the cheque – the customer from whose account the money is to be paid
drawee of a cheque	the bank which has to make payment – its name and address normally appear at the top of the cheque
payee of a cheque	the person to whom the cheque is payable – normally specified on the first line of the cheque amount

cheque crossing	two parallel lines on the front of a cheque, with or without writing in them – they mean that the cheque has to be paid into a bank account
endorsement	a signature on the back of the cheque (normally the payee's) meaning that the cheque can be passed to someone else to pay into their account
'account payee' crossing	two parallel lines on the face of the cheque with the words 'account payee' between them – the cheque cannot be endorsed over – it must be paid into the account of the payee
bank guarantee card	a plastic card issued by a bank to its customer which will guarantee payment of its customer's cheque up to a certain limit
debit card	a plastic card which enables customers to make payment for purchases without having to write out a cheque – payment is made electronically from the bank account straightaway
credit card	a plastic card issued by a credit card company which enables customers to make purchases and pay for them at a later date
EFT	EFT stands for Electronic Funds Transfer – the transfer of payments between banks and bank accounts by computer link
EFTPOS	EFTPOS stands for Electronic Funds Transfer at Point of Sale – the electronic transfer of payments between the bank accounts of buyer and seller which is originated at a till
BACS	BACS stands for Bankers Automated Clearing Services, a body (owned by the banks) which organises computer payments between bank accounts
remittance advice	a document sent to the recipient of a payment, advising that a payment is being made
remittance list	also known as a 'cash received list' – a record of money amounts received, either through the post, or over the counter
cash book	the central record kept by a business of cash and bank transactions

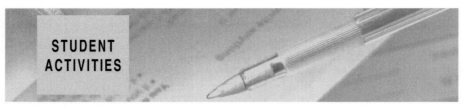

STUDENT ACTIVITIES

12.1 You operate the cash till at the firm where you work. The following are the sales for one day:

		Amount of sale £	Notes and/or coin tendered
Customer	1	8.50	£10 note
	2	3.30	£10 note
	3	2.51	£5 note
	4	1.79	£5 note
	5	0.34	£1 coin
	6	6.22	£10 note
	7	12.76	£20 note
	8	1.42	two £1 coins
	9	6.54	£10 note
	10	3.08	£5 note

Calculate
(a) the amount of change to be given to each customer
(b) the notes and/or coins that will be given in change, using the minimum number possible

12.2 If the cash till in question 1 had a float of £28.71 at the start of the day, how much cash should be held in the till after the sales from question 1 had been made? Present your answer in the following form:

	£
cash float at start	28.71
plus sales made during the day	
	———
equals amount of cash held at end of day	
	═══

12.3 You work as a shop counter assistant at New Era Lighting. You make a number of sales during the day (use today's date) which require the completion of a handwritten receipt. Complete the receipts set out on the next page. Include VAT on all purchases at the current rate. All prices quoted here are catalogue prices and exclude VAT.

(a) 2 flexilamps @ £13.99, 2
60W candlelight bulbs @
85p, to Mr George Ohm

NEW ERA LIGHTING   **977**
17 High Street Mereford MR1 2TF
VAT reg 141 7645 23

CASH RECEIPT

Customer..date............................

	VAT
	TOTAL

(b) 1 standard lamp @ £149.95,
1 3 amp plug @ 99p, to Mr
Alex Bell

NEW ERA LIGHTING   **978**
17 High Street Mereford MR1 2TF
VAT reg 141 7645 23

CASH RECEIPT

Customer..date............................

	VAT
	TOTAL

(c) 2 external Georgian lamps
@ £35.99, to Tom Edison

NEW ERA LIGHTING   **979**
17 High Street Mereford MR1 2TF
VAT reg 141 7645 23

CASH RECEIPT

Customer..date............................

	VAT
	TOTAL

Southern Bank PLC		date *9 October*	19 *97*		97-76-54

Southern Bank PLC
Mereford Branch
16 Broad Street, Mereford MR1 7TR

date *9 October* 19 *97* 97-76-54

Pay *Electron Games Limited* only

Three hundred pounds only

£ *300.00*

Account payee only

A & S SYSTEMS LTD

G Brown

Director

123456   97 76 54   68384939

12.4 Examine the cheque shown above and state who is
(a)   the drawer
(b)   the drawee
(c)   the payee
In each case, explain what the term means.

12.5 What difference does a crossing on a cheque make to the payee?

12.6 What do the following cheque crossings mean?:

(a)   _____
        _____

(b)   Barclays Bank, Hanover Square

(c)   & co

(d)   account payee

(e)   account payee only

(f)   not negotiable

12.7 Henry Enfield is the payee of a cheque which has the following crossing

        _____
        _____

(a)   What *should* happen to the cheque if it is endorsed like this:

Pay Sandra Lobb
Henry Enfield

(b)   What *could* happen to the cheque if it is endorsed like this?

> *Henry Enfield*

12.8   List three checks a cashier should make to *a cheque* when receiving it in the post for payment of an outstanding invoice.

12.9   List three checks a cashier should make when accepting a cheque over the counter when the cheque is supported by a bank guarantee card.

12.10 List three checks a cashier should make when accepting a credit card payment over the counter.

12.11 What should a cashier do if the amount of a purchase being made by a customer (£500) exceeds the cheque guarantee amount of £200 on the customer's card?
(a)   Refuse to allow the purchase to go ahead.
(b)   Ask for three cheques: £200, £200 and £100, all dated differently.
(c)   Ask the customer to use the credit card which the cashier has spotted in the customer's card wallet.
(d)   Request the customer to go and get a bank draft for £500.
Choose *one* answer.

12.12 If a credit card purchase exceeds the shop's floor limit, it should be refused. True or false?

12.13 The advantage to a shop of accepting payment by debit card is that
(a)   All cheques are automatically guaranteed.
(b)   There is no cheque.
(c)   The cheque is automatically debited to the customer' bank account.
(d)   The signature on the cheque is autgmtically verified.
Choose *one* answer.

12.14 EFT stands for:
(a)   Electronic Foreign Transfer
(b)   Electronic Financial Transaction
(c)   Electronic Funds Till
(d)   Electronic Funds Transfer
Choose *one* answer.

12.15 List three advantages to a shop of using EFTPOS.

12.16 (a)   Who is the drawer and the drawee of a bank draft?
(b)   Give examples of two transactions for which a bank draft would be suitable.

12.17 Give two examples of situations where a remittance list would be used.

13 PAYING INTO THE BANK

this chapter covers ...

This chapter explains the relationship between banks and their customers and sets out the procedures for paying money into the bank. The chapter covers the areas of

- the legal relationship between the bank and its customers

- banking services available to customers

- the bank clearing system

- paying money into the bank using paying in slips

- banking documents, including sales voucher summaries and statements

- security procedures used when handling cash

NVQ PERFORMANCE CRITERIA COVERED

unit 1: RECORDING AND ACCOUNTING FOR CASH TRANSACTIONS
element 1
record and bank monies received

❏ monies are banked in accordance with organisation's policies, regulations, procedures and timescales

❏ paying in documents are correctly prepared and reconciled to relevant records

❏ cash handling, security and confidentiality procedures are followed

❏ discrepancies, unusual features or queries are identified and either resolved or referred to the appropriate person

KNOWLEDGE AND UNDERSTANDING — THE BUSINESS ENVIRONMENT

❏ legal relationship of banker and customer

❏ general bank services and operation of bank clearing system

❏ function and form of banking documentation

BANKS AND CUSTOMERS

By way of introduction we will look briefly at the legal background to the bank and customer relationship, the main types of accounts offered by banks to their personal and business customers, and the bank clearing system.

a legal relationship

It is important to appreciate when studying and practising banking procedures that there is a distinct *legal relationship* between a bank and its customer. Normally this relationship does not give much cause for concern; it is only when something goes wrong – for example when a bank pays a cheque which its customer has stopped – that the legal relationship becomes particularly important.

bank and customer contract

In law there is said to be a *contract* between the customer and the bank. A contract may be defined as:

a legally binding agreement which is recognised in a court of law

You may wonder why a contract between a bank and a customer is important in business dealings. The answer is that the bank/customer contract means that the customer has certain rights and duties to perform, including keeping the bank account in credit (not overdrawn, unless by arrangement) and taking care when writing out cheques so that they cannot be altered by a fraudster.

If the customer fails in any of these duties and the bank loses a substantial amount of money, it has the right in law under the contract to take the customer to court to recover its money.

Similarly, the bank has certain rights and duties to perform under the contract, and if it fails to do so and the customer suffers a loss (money or reputation), the customer can take the bank to court. Examples of the bank's duties include:

* paying the customer's cheques when there is sufficient money in the account
* keeping details of the customer's account secret
* sending statements of account to the customer

Clearly a customer will not take a bank to court if a statement is not sent out! But it may do so if the bank by mistake fails to pay a business cheque issued to a supplier, and the supplier cuts off supplies to the business. This could bankrupt the customer and is a clear *breach of the contract* between the bank and the customer. For further details of the theory of contract see Chapter 18.

BANK/CUSTOMER RELATIONSHIPS

There are a number of different bank/customer relationships:

debtor and creditor

This terminology relates to whether or not the customer has any money in the bank. Remember that:

debtor = a person who owes money

creditor = a person to whom you owe money

Therefore:

customer has money in bank: *customer = creditor (is owed money)*
                                         bank = debtor (owes money)

customer is borrowing: *customer = debtor (owes money)*
                                         bank = creditor (is owed money)

This may seem complicated, but if you think it through, it is logical.

mortgagor and mortgagee

If the customer has a mortgage with the bank (a mortgage is a legal document which secures a loan), the customer is a *mortgagor* and the bank is a *mortgagee*.

bailor and bailee

If the customer deposits valuable items in the bank's safe, the customer is a *bailor* and the bank a *bailee*.

principal and agent

If the customer uses the bank to carry out a transaction, eg to arrange an insurance policy, to sell shares, then the customer is known as the *principal* and the bank the *agent*. Note that the word 'agent' is also used in 'travel agent' and 'estate agent' – businesses that arrange travel and property deals.

TYPES OF ACCOUNT

There are three main types of accounts offered by banks to its customers:

- current account
- deposit (savings) account
- loan accounts

current account

With this type of account a bank customer is issued with a cheque book and may make use of most of the services of the bank. Bank customers use a current account as a 'working account' into which receipts are paid and out of which are paid expenses by means of cheques and automated computer payments.

overdraft

Banks are often prepared to grant overdraft facilities to their current account customers on request. A business, for example, realizing that it will need overdraft facilities should contact the bank and seek agreement for an overdraft up to a certain limit for a specified time. Interest is charged on overdrawn balances and an arrangement/renewal fee is normally payable.

deposit account

A deposit account is used for savings by personal customers, or excess money held by a business, and interest is paid by the bank. Current account facilities such as cheque books, standing orders, direct debits, and overdrafts are not allowed on deposit accounts for business customers. Notice of withdrawal will normally need to be given to the bank. Other types of account may need a longer period of notice of withdrawal, perhaps one month or three months.

Many business customers have both a current and a deposit account. A business can use a deposit account as a temporary 'home' for surplus money. When the money is needed it can be transferred easily to the firm's current account.

loan accounts

Whereas an overdraft is a means of borrowing on an ordinary current account and will cover day-to-day running (revenue) expenses of the business, loan accounts are long-term loans for capital items of expenditure, eg machinery and new projects. Different banks will offer different types of loan account. Some typical examples include:

business loan

A loan for three to ten years to cover large items of expense such as new plant, premises expansion, a new project.

commercial mortgage

A loan for up to twenty five years to cover the purchase of property (the business equivalent of a 'home loan' mortgage to an individual).

CHEQUE CLEARING

Every working day each bank branch receives cheques paid in by customers. These cheques take a defined time to 'clear.' The term to 'clear' means that the cheque must have passed to the bank of the issuer of the cheque for payment before the money amount of the cheque – the amount paid in – can be used by the customer. The clearance times are normally:

- cheques paid in and issued by customers of the same branch – same day clearance

- cheques paid in by customers of other banks and branches – three working days' clearance

This means that if you are given a cheque by someone who has an account at your branch and you pay it in on Monday, you can draw against it, ie you can use the money on the account, on Monday, the same day. This assumes, of course, that the cheque is paid and does not 'bounce'. On the other hand, if you are given a cheque which is issued by someone who banks at another bank (or another branch of your bank), then if you pay it in on Monday, you will have to wait three working days, ie until Wednesday before the cheque is cleared, and you can use the money.

The reason for this delay is that the cheque will have to be sent to London for sorting. This long and expensive process, required by a law dating back to the nineteenth century, is illustrated on the next page. In this case Enigma Cafe, which banks at Midland Bank in Malvern pays a cheque for £500 to their supplier, Broadheath Bakers, who then pay it into their bank, Barclays Bank in Worcester. The diagram follows the two hundred and fifty mile journey of the cheque. The two bank branches, incidentally, are seven miles apart.

special clearance

Sometimes you may need to know quickly whether or not a cheque will be paid, for example, if you sell goods for £5,000 to an unknown buyer. The banks offer a special clearance service, known as a Special Presentation, where for a fee (around £10) a bank will send a cheque to the issuer's branch by first class post, and then telephone the following day in the morning to establish whether or not the cheque will be paid.

returned cheques

You may be in the unfortunate position of having paid in a cheque and then discovering that the cheque has been returned to your bank *unpaid*, and the amount of the cheque deducted from your account. Your bank will normally send it back to you by post. You will receive it five days after paying it in.

bank clearing system

day 1

Barclays Bank, Worcester branch

cheque for £500 paid into the account of Broadheath Bakers

↓

sent by courier to London

↓

day 2

Barclays Bank Clearing Department, London

cheques sorted into banks

delivery van ↓

Central Clearing House, London

cheques sorted into banks

delivery van ↓

Midland Bank Clearing Department, London

cheques sorted into Midland branches

↓

sent by courier to Malvern

↓

day 3

Midland Bank, Malvern Branch

cheque paid and £500 deducted from the account of Enigma Cafe

day 3

Barclays Bank, Worcester branch

cheque for £500 is now cleared and may be drawn against (ie the money may be used)

It will have one of a number of answers written along the top:

- **refer to drawer** – the person who has given you the cheque (the drawer) has no money in the bank – you will have to contact him or her for an explanation! This answer is often abbreviated to "RD"

- **refer to drawer, please represent** – (abbreviated to "RDPR") – this means that there was not enough money in the account to meet the cheque, but that the cheque has been sent through the clearing again (represented) in the hope that it will be paid when it reaches the issuers bank (note that in this case the cheque will *not* be sent back to the payee)

- **payment countermanded by order of drawer** – the cheque has been stopped – you should contact the drawer to find out the reason

- **technical problems** such as a signature required, or words and figures differ, or out of date, will mean that you will have to contact the drawer for a new cheque (if the reason is out of date) or a signature or an alteration (which will have to be signed by the drawer)

stopped cheques

We mentioned at the beginning of the chapter that it is the bank's duty in contract law to pay a customer's cheque as long as there is sufficient money in the account. A customer may order a bank not to pay a cheque; this is known as *stopping* a cheque. This often happens if a cheque is lost in the post and another cheque is issued in its place. The bank will make a charge (approximately £10) for stopping a cheque, and will return the cheque marked "payment countermanded by order of drawer" if and when it is paid in and presented for payment.

PAYING-IN SLIPS

Business customers are issued with a *paying-in* book by the bank. Details to be completed by a bank customer on a paying-in slip are:

- the name of the bank and branch where the account is held (these details are normally pre-printed)

- the name of the account to be credited, together with the account number (normally pre-printed)

- a summary of the different categories of notes or coins being paid in, the amount of each category being entered on the slip

- amounts and details of cheques being paid in, usually entered on the reverse of the slip, with the total entered on the front

- the cash and cheques being paid in are totalled to give the amount being paid in
- the counterfoil is completed
- the person paying-in will sign the slip

A completed paying-in slip (with counterfoil) is illustrated below.

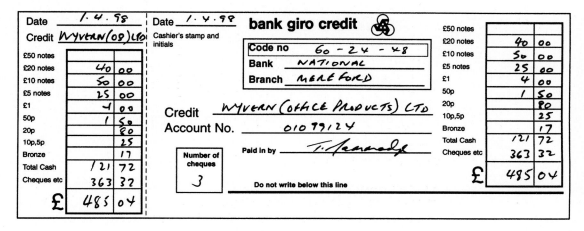

paying-in slip and counterfoil (front)

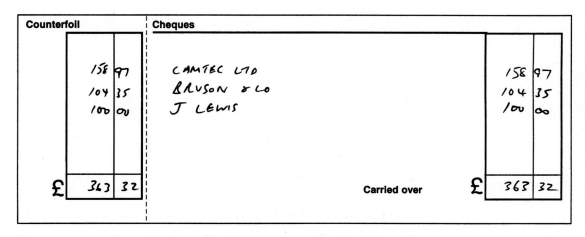

paying-in slip and counterfoil (back)

PROCEDURES FOR PAYING IN

the accounting process

Cash and cheques paid in at the bank will normally have been received by the business as cash sales and on remittance advices from debtors, and so form part of the accounting process. We will see how they are entered in the cash book in Chapter 15.

preparing the cash

The notes should be counted, checked and sorted so that they all face the same way, but should be kept separate. Defaced (damaged) notes and notes from Scotland and Northern Ireland are normally accepted by banks.

Coins should normally be sorted and placed in bags as follows:

denomination	amount in bag
£1	£20
50p	£10
20p	£10
10p	£5
5p	£5
2p	£1
1p	£1

preparing the cheques

The cheques must first be examined carefully for any irregularities, such as

- **signatures** – has the drawer signed the cheque?
- **endorsements** – if the name on the payee line is not the same as the name of the account into which it is being paid, has it been suitably endorsed?
- **crossings** – if the cheque has the "account payee" wording in the crossing and your organisation is not the payee, it will not be possible to pay it in, even if it has been endorsed
- **date** – is it out of date (over six months old)? is it post-dated? – if so, it cannot be paid in
- **words and figures** – do they agree?

The details of the cheques – the amounts and the customer names – may then be listed on the back of the paying-in slip, as in the illustration on the previous page. If the volume of cheques paid in is very large, there will not be room on the paying-in slip, so the cheque details may be listed on a separate schedule. Some banks accept instead a calculator tally-roll listing the amounts, the number of cheques, and the total money amount transferred to the front of the paying-in slip. The important point is that the organisation paying in the cheques must keep a record of the cheque details in case of future queries, and in the unfortunate event of any of the cheques 'bouncing' – ie being returned unpaid.

paying in at the bank

At the bank the completed paying-in book is handed to the bank cashier together with the notes, coins, and cheques. The cashier counts the cash, ticks off the cheques and, if everything is correct, receipt stamps and initials the paying-in slip and counterfoil. The slip is retained by the bank for the amount to be credited to the account-holder, while the paying-in book is handed back, complete with the receipted counterfoil. A business paying-in book is sometimes larger than the paying-in slip illustrated, and sometimes there is a carbon copy behind the business paying-in slip which acts as a counterfoil.

security measures for cash handling - night safes

Care must be taken when taking large amounts of cash to the bank. If possible two staff members should visit the bank. If the amount is very large, for instance the takings from a department store, a security firm may be employed to carry the cash. If the cash is received by an organisation over the weekend or, late in the day, it may be placed in a special wallet and lodged in the bank's *night safe* – a small lockable door leading to a safe in the wall of the bank. Further security measures are explained on page 218.

When a business pays in money to the bank, it will record the amount in its own records, called the cash book (see Chapter 15).

credit card voucher clearing

As we saw in the last chapter, the sales voucher is the basic document normally produced when a credit card transaction takes place (see the illustration on page 193). The sales voucher may be produced as a result of an 'over the counter' sale or from a mail order or telephone sale. The details recorded on it will enable the credit card company to charge the amount to their customer. The voucher like a cheque, is paid in at the bank and sent to the credit card company and 'cleared'.

Although there are a number of different credit card companies – Masterccard and Visa for example – the normal practice is for the organisation accepting payment to sign an agreement with a separate company which will accept all vouchers from cards issued by different companies. For example, a customer of The Royal Bank of Scotland may sign an agreement with a company called Roynet (owned by the Royal Bank of Scotland) and accept payment by Masterccard and Visa and other nominated cards. The customer will pay in all credit card vouchers on the one paying slip and schedule (see below) at The Royal Bank of Scotland. The bank will pass them to Roynet, which will then process them by sending them to the issuing card company (Masterccard or Visa, for example). Roynet is only one of a number of companies which will process credit card sales vouchers.

The customer paying in the vouchers is charged a set percentage fee – usually between 2% and 5% – of the total sales amount.

preparing credit card sales vouchers for paying-in

The vouchers are paid in after completion of a three-part Retailer Summary, illustrated below and on the next page. In this case three sales vouchers are listed on the back of the summary.

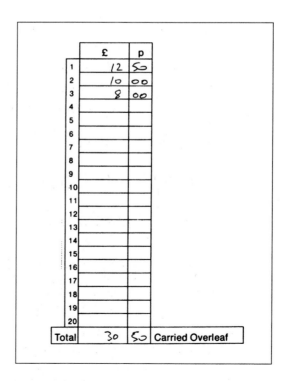

	£	p	
1	12	50	
2	10	00	
3	8	00	
4			
5			
6			
7			
8			
9			
10			
11			
12			
13			
14			
15			
16			
17			
18			
19			
20			
Total	30	50	Carried Overleaf

retailer sales voucher summary – back

**Have you imprinted the summary
with your Retailer's Card?**

VISA

Bank Processing copy of Summary
with your Vouchers in correct order:

1 Summary
2 Sales Vouchers
3 Refund Vouchers

Keep Retailer's copy and
　　　Retailer's Duplicate copy

No more than 200 Vouchers to each Summary

Do not use Staples, Pins, Paper Clips

	Items	Amount	
Sales Vouchers	3	30	50
Less Refund Vouchers			
Date 28·03·98	Total £	30 : 50	

P.Oscaro

Retailer's Signature

MasterCard   *EUROCARD*

Retailer Summary

Complete this summary for every Deposit of Sales Vouchers and enter the
Total on your normal Current Account paying-in slip

Retailer's Copy   Retailer Summary

retailer sales voucher summary – front

The procedure for listing credit card sales vouchers on the retailer's summary is as follows:

- the summary is imprinted with details of the retailer using a plastic card – the Retailer's Card – supplied with the imprinter machine

- the amounts of the sales vouchers are listed on the reverse of the summary and totalled

- the total is carried forward to the front of the summary

- any refund vouchers are listed on the front of the summary

- the summary is dated, signed and totalled

- the summary is separated into its three copies – the top two are retained by the organisation and the bottom copy (the processing copy) is placed in front of the sales vouchers

- the processing copy and sales and any refund vouchers are placed in a transparent envelope and are paid into the bank on a paying-in slip, the total from the summary listed as a single item on the paying-in slip

Organisations which accept sales by mail and telephone may use schedules rather than sales vouchers for recording and listing the credit card transactions. The procedure for paying-in for these organisations is exactly the same, except that the totals of the schedule(s) are listed on the back of the Retailer Summary rather than the individual amounts of the sales vouchers as described above.

THE IMPORTANCE OF PAYING IN PROMPTLY

Organisations realise that if money is not banked promptly and safely, problems can arise:

theft

Cash is tempting to a thief, and it must be remembered that many instances of theft are carried out by employees of an organisation rather than by criminals with stockings over their heads. An organisation will therefore have a security policy, for example:

- cash and cheques being paid in will be kept under lock and key at the place of work, normally in a cash box, under the control of the cashier
- amounts received through the post or over the counter are recorded on remittance lists or on a cash register (or equivalent)as an additional security measure – money, once it is recorded, will be missed when stolen
- larger organisations will have a system of spot checking (internal audit) to identify any theft by employees
- arranging for cash and cheques to be taken to the bank by security firm (appropriate for large businesses)
- arranging for Friday and weekend takings of cash to be lodged in the bank's night safe
- making arrangements for payroll – the organisation will have to arrange the pick up of cash from the bank, using employees or a security firm

timescale – security and cashflow

Organisations will also have a policy for the prompt paying in of money into the bank, for two main reasons – *security* and *cashflow*. Money kept on the premises is a security risk: the longer it remains there, the more likely it is that it will be stolen. Also, money not paid in is money that is not available for paying cheques and other items from the organisation's bank account: *cashflow* will be restricted. For example, it may be that the business is borrowing money on overdraft – it could save paying interest if money is banked promptly: a cheque for £50,000 lying around in the office for a week could cost the business over £100 in interest!

procedures

Because of these factors an organisation will draw up procedures for banking money. These will include the security measures mentioned above and also set timescales for paying in money, eg twice a week, one visit to coincide with the collection of the payroll cash (often a Friday). If you work in an accounts office, you will be familiar with these procedures.

confidentiality

If you work for an organisation, the importance of confidentiality will have been impressed on you. Confidentiality basically means not telling outsiders about the internal worklings of your place of work. Important aspects of this include not talking to outsiders about your customers, not disclosing secret details of your products, and most importantly to this area of your studies, not disclosing your security arrangements for handling of money. Imagine the consequences of telling a group of friends in the pub that the firm's wages are collected from the bank every Friday at 10.00 in the morning.

BANK STATEMENTS

At regular intervals the bank sends out statements of account to its customers. A business current account with many items passing through it may have weekly statements, while a less active account or a deposit account may have monthly or even quarterly statements.

A bank statement is a summary showing:

- the balance at the beginning of the statement – 'balance brought forward'
- amounts paid into (credited to) the account
- amounts paid out of (debited to) the account – eg cheques issued, cheques returned 'unpaid', bank charges and standing orders and direct debits (automatic computer payments – see the next chapter for an explanation of these).

The balance of the account is shown after each transaction. A specimen bank statement is shown on the next page.

a note on debits, credits and bank accounts

You should be aware of the fact that the terms 'credit' and 'debit' mean different things to banks and their customers.

In the double-entry system of a business customer

   debit = money received

   credit = money paid out

Banks see things from the opposite angle. To their accounting system:

   debit = money paid out from a customer's account

   credit = money paid into a customer's account

In other words a credit to a bank account is the same as a debit in the books of a customer. Think about it!

NATIONAL BANK PLC

Branch   Mereford
Account   Wyvern (Office Products) Limited
Account no.   01099124
Statement   196

DATE	PARTICULARS	PAYMENT £	RECEIPTS £	BALANCE £
1997				
1 Oct	Balance brought forward			625.50 CR
9 Oct	Cheque 352817	179.30		446.20 CR
10 Oct	Credit		485.04	931.24 CR
17 Oct	Cheque 352818	169.33		761.91 CR
23 Oct	Credit		62.30	824.21 CR
24 Oct	Credit		100.00	924.21 CR
27 Oct	Cheque 352819	821.80		102.41 CR
27 Oct	Unpaid cheque	250.00		147.59 DR
28 Oct	Credit		108.00	39.59 DR
31 Oct	Bank charges	25.00		64.59 DR

a bank statement

checking the bank statement

You will see from the specimen bank statement shown above that the balance of the account is indicated each time by the abbreviation 'CR' or 'DR'; the first of these means that the customer has a credit balance, ie has money in the bank, while 'DR' indicates a debit balance to show an overdraft, ie the customer has drawn more out of the bank than the available credit balance.

The bank charges referred to can either be calculated on an item basis (ie the number of items passing through the account) or on a turnover basis (ie the money total of all the items paid out of the account). In addition, interest will be charged on overdrawn balances.

You will see that a £250 item 'unpaid cheque' appears as an entry on 27 October. This is a cheque that has been paid in ('credited'), but has 'bounced' ie it has been returned by the issuer's bank. It has been deducted ('debited') from the bank account, pushing the account into an overdraft position.

When a bank statement is received it should be checked and reconciled with the firm's record of bank receipts and payments – the cash book – (see Chapter 15).

- The legal relationship between a bank and its customer is one of contract – a legally binding agreement.

- The legal relationship between a bank and its customer can take a number of forms: debtor and creditor, mortgagor and mortgagee, bailor and baliee, principal and agent.

- Banks offer a wide range of accounts: current accounts (including overdraft) deposit accounts and loan accounts.

- When a cheque is paid into a bank it normally takes three days to clear. When a cheque is cleared the person who has paid it in can draw on the money.

- A cheque can be returned unpaid ('bounce') for a number of reasons, eg 'refer to drawer' – which means there is no money in the drawer's bank account.

- Organisations pay money into their bank account on a paying in slip which lists the cash and cheques paid in and totals the amounts.

- Cash and cheques must be checked and listed before they are paid in.

- Credit card vouchers may also be paid into the bank account on a retailers summary form which lists all of the vouchers.

- Organisations should set up procedures to ensure that cash, cheques and credit card vouchers are kept safely on the premises and in transit to the bank.

- Money should be paid into the bank as soon as possible, both for security reasons and also to help the cashflow of the organisation.

- Bank statements are sent regularly to customers and should be checked on receipt.

- To a bank, money paid in is a 'credit' and money paid out is a 'debit.'

contract	a legally binding agreement which is recognised in a court of law
mortgagor/mortgagee	when a mortgage is signed the borrower is the mortgagor and the bank the mortgagee
bailor/bailee	when a customer deposits items of value for safe keeping with a bank the customer is the bailor and the bank the bailee
principal/agent	when a customer asks the bank to carry out something on its behalf (eg arrange insurance) the customer is the principal and the bank the agent
current account	a day-to-day transaction bank account used for paying revenue expenses

KEY TERMS (continued)	**overdraft**	a current account which is used for borrowing money for day-to-day purposes
	deposit account	an account which pays interest and is used for depositing excess funds
	loan account	a fixed loan taken for a period of years to cover capital (large item) expenses
	cheque clearing	a system used by the banks to clear cheques paid in – the process takes three working days
	paying in slip	a paper slip listing cash and cheques paid into a bank
	retailer summary	a form listing credit card sales vouchers paid into a bank account
	night safe	a wallet or bag containing cash and cheques lodged with a bank (when it is closed) through an opening in the wall of the bank – used by shops banking their takings
	bank statement	a document sent by the bank to its customer setting out transactions on the bank account

STUDENT ACTIVITIES

13.1 State two duties of a bank to its customer.

13.2 State two duties of a customer to the bank.

13.3 If a customer has an overdraft with a bank, the customer is a creditor of the bank. True or false?

13.4 If a customer has a credit balance with a bank, the customer is a debtor of the bank. True or false?

13.5 Write out and complete the following sentences:

(a) When a customer signs a mortgage to the bank, the customer is a .... and the bank is a ....

(a) When a customer deposits items of value with a bank, the bank is a .... and the customer is a ....

(c) A bank that arranges an insurance policy for a customer is known as an.................................

13.6 What type of bank account would be appropriate in the following circumstances?

(a) A business needs finance for the purchase of a new machine (capital expenditure).

(b) A business needs finance for day-to-day purchases (revenue expenditure).

(c) A business needs an account which will pay interest on a large sum of money.

13.7 A business receives a large cheque from a customer for a purchase, but wants to make sure that the cheque will be paid before releasing the goods. The business bank account is at Midland Bank, Holborn Circus and the cheque bears the name of Barclays Bank, Finsbury Circus. How long will it take to obtain clearance

(a)   through the normal bank clearing system?

(b)   by means of special clearance?

Would it make any difference if the cheque bore the name of Midland Bank, Holborn Circus?

13.8 The cheque in Question 7 is unfortunately returned unpaid. The answer on the cheque is 'Refer to Drawer, please Represent.' What are the implications of this for the business? Would the situation be any different if the answer on the cheque had been 'Refer to Drawer'?

13.9 State two advantages to the customer of using a night safe.

13.10 State two reasons why cash should not be kept on the business premises for a long period of time.

13.11 State whether the following entries are debits or credits − from the viewpoint of the bank:

(a)   an amount paid into a bank account

(b)   an amount paid out of the bank account

13.12 The firm you work for is Eveshore Traders Ltd., which has a bank account at Barclays Bank, Eveshore (sort code no. 20-23-88). The account number is 90003174. You are required to prepare the paying-in slip and counterfoil as at today's date. The cheques are to be listed on the back of the paying-in slip. The items to be banked are:

Cash	*Cheques*	
two £20 notes	£20.00	Maytree Enterprises
five £10 notes	£18.50	Bakewell Catering
eight £5 notes	£75.25	Henderson & Co
two £1 coins	£68.95	Musgrave Fine Art
six 50p coins		
four 10p coins		
two 2p coins		

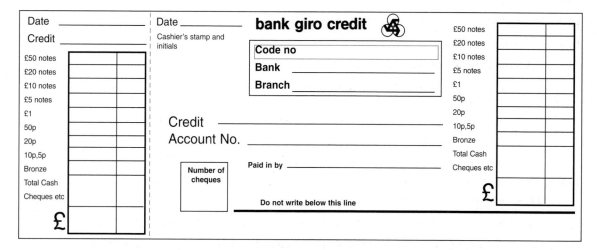

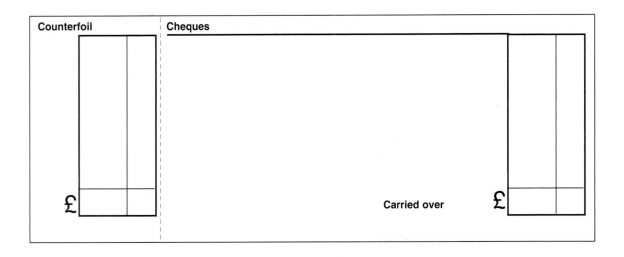

13.13 The firm you work for is Buxton Fine Wines, which has a bank account at Western Bank, Grantminster (sort code no. 47-21-95). The account number is 87163729. You are required to prepare the Retailers Summary and paying-in slip for ten credit card sales vouchers and a refund voucher. The documents are shown below and on the next page. The items to be banked are:

Sales vouchers	£45.60	£56.85
	£10.00	£56.00
	£15.50	£45.00
	£25.99	£49.50
	£67.50	£25.00
Refund voucher	£13.50	

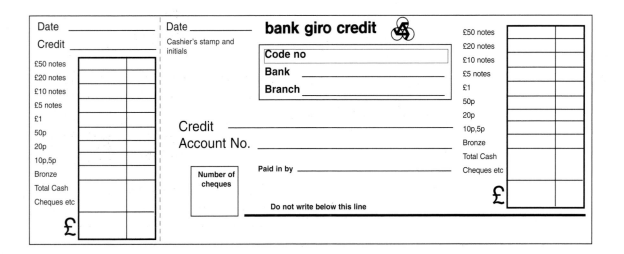

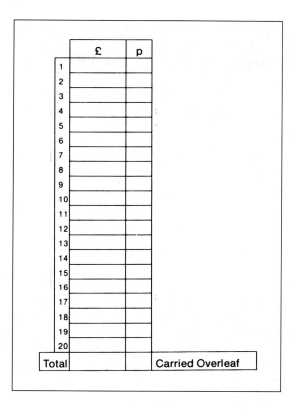

	£	p	
1			
2			
3			
4			
5			
6			
7			
8			
9			
10			
11			
12			
13			
14			
15			
16			
17			
18			
19			
20			
Total			Carried Overleaf

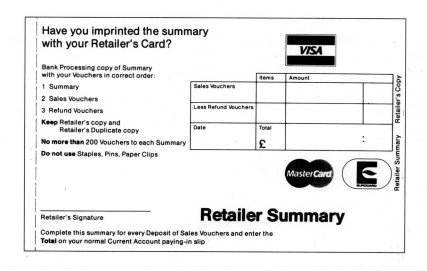

Have you imprinted the summary with your Retailer's Card?

Bank Processing copy of Summary with your Vouchers in correct order:

1 Summary

2 Sales Vouchers

3 Refund Vouchers

Keep Retailer's copy and Retailer's Duplicate copy

No more than 200 Vouchers to each Summary

Do not use Staples, Pins, Paper Clips

VISA

	Items	Amount
Sales Vouchers		
Less Refund Vouchers		
Date	Total £	

Retailer's Copy

Retailer Summary

Retailer's Signature

MasterCard   EUROCARD

Retailer Summary

Complete this summary for every Deposit of Sales Vouchers and enter the **Total** on your normal Current Account paying-in slip

14 MAKING AND RECORDING PAYMENTS

this chapter covers . . .

This chapter explains the different ways in which payments are made by an organisation and sets out the procedures followed to make sure that all payments are authorised and checked. The chapter covers the areas of:

- making payments by cheque

- making payments by inter-bank transfer: giro credits and BACS (computer) payments such as standing orders, direct debits and autopay systems

- ensuring that payments are correctly authorised and accompanied by the correct documentation, eg a remittance advice

NVQ PERFORMANCE CRITERIA COVERED

unit 1: RECORDING AND ACCOUNTING FOR CASH TRANSACTIONS

element 2

make and record payments

- ❏ payments are made and recorded in accordance with the organisation's policies, regulations, procedures and timescales
- ❏ payments are properly authorised
- ❏ cheques are prepared correctly and are signed by designated person(s) prior to despatch
- ❏ standing orders and other inter-bank transfers are correctly documented
- ❏ remittance advices are correctly prepared and despatched with payments
- ❏ totals and balances are correctly calculated and checked against documentation
- ❏ available cash discounts are identified and deducted
- ❏ documentation is correctly filed
- ❏ safety and security procedures for the handling of cash and cheques are followed
- ❏ discrepancies, unusual features or queries are identified and either resolved or referred to the appropriate person

OUTGOING PAYMENTS

If you work for an organisation, you will readily appreciate that there are different types of payments involved; some will involve the issue of cheques or cash, some will involve paying money from the organisation's bank account direct to the recipient's bank account. Here are some typical examples of these different forms of payment:

issue of cheques

- paying suppliers by cheque for goods and services against invoices and statements
- paying for 'one-off' items of expenditure, for example a computer system
- paying bills (eg telephone, gas, electricity) by cheque and bank giro credit
- paying employees for expenses incurred

paying through the bank account

- paying wages
- paying regular suppliers for goods and services
- paying bills, for example business rates

PAYING TRADE SUPPLIERS

internal procedures

Each business or organisation will have its own policies and regulations laid down to ensure that payments to suppliers of goods and services are only made when the goods and services have been received as ordered. A supplier of goods and services is therefore paid when

- the documents relating to the transaction – the purchase order, delivery note (or goods received note) and invoice have been checked against each other (they are normally filed together)
- any credit due, eg for returned goods, has been received in the form of a credit note
- all discounts, whether *cash discount* (for early payment) or *trade discount* (a set percentage reduction) have been identified and allowed for
- the payment has received the necessary authorisation – often in the form of a supervisor's initials on the invoice, or a rubber stamp

timescales – when to pay?

Each business or organisation will also have its own policies and regulations dictating *when* payment is to be made.

paying on invoice

Some businesses or organiations will pay strictly according to the *due date of the invoice*. Each invoice (and all the accompanying documentation), when it is received will be marked with the due date of payment – eg 30 days after the invoice issue date – and placed in a diary system. With this system a business may make individual payments to different suppliers on any number of days of the month. The system is best suited to small businesses which do not have too many payments to make.

payment on statement

Another widely adopted system is for suppliers to be paid monthly *on the basis of the monthly statement* issued rather than in response to individual invoices. A statement received at, say, the end of March will show all the outstanding invoices; if an organisation normally pays invoices after thirty days, it will pay all the February invoices and any dated earlier than February on receipt of the statement. It will ignore any March invoices, which will be paid at the end of April. With this system all payments are made on the same day, normally at the end of the month. This system is easy to manage, particularly if the payments are computerised (see below) as only one 'payment run' is needed each month to originate either computer-printed cheques or BACS (inter-bank) payments.

remittance advice

We have already seen that the remittance advice tells the supplier what is being paid, either

- by *cheque,* in which case the remittance advice accompanies the payment, or
- by *BACS* (inter-bank computer payment), in which case the remittance advice is sent separately by post or by Email

If your job is to make payments and prepare remittance advices, you will probably have a list of payments to make, with the payment amount already decided upon and authorised by a supervisor.

paying by cheque

If you are paying a supplier you should attach the cheque to the remittance advice. This may be a tear-off slip attached to the supplier's statement of account, or it may be a standard form used within your organisation. An example of the latter, together with the cheque issued, is illustrated below. You should note that the following details are shown:

- the date of the payment
- the amount of the cheque
- the details – ie the reference number ('your ref') and date – of the invoice(s) being paid
- the amount of any cash discount deducted for early settlement (there is none in the illustration)

In addition the remittance advice may show further details such as the cheque number, the account number of the buyer's organisation, and the buyer's order number ('our ref'). The remittance advice may also show a deduction made from the payment for a credit note issued by the supplier. The details will be recorded on the remittance advice in the normal way, as for an invoice.

REMITTANCE ADVICE
NIMROD DRAINAGE LIMITED
UNIT 6 Riverside Industrial Park Mereford MR4 5TF
Tel 01605 675187 Fax 01605 415181 Vat Reg 63 6252 27

Stourford Office Supplies
Unit 12, Avon Industrial Estate
Stourford SF5 6TD

Cheque No   000427
Date   20 April 1998
Account   9873

date	our ref.	your ref.	amount	discount	payment
18 02 98	47621	82710	47.00	00.00	47.00

| | cheque value | £ 47.00 |

---

a remittance advice accompanying a cheque payment

payment of suppliers by BACS

The use of BACS, the inter-bank computer payment system, will be dealt with in detail later in the chapter. All BACS payments must be communicated to the supplier by means of a posted remittance advice, otherwise the supplier will not know that payment has been made until the bank statement is received, and even then it may be difficult to identify the origin of the payment. If the supplier does not know payment has been received, he or she may start chasing up the debt, which could prove embarrassing!

A BACS remittance advice is illustrated on page 197.

ISSUING OF CHEQUES

Cheques may either be completed manually, or printed out on a computer printer.

When writing out (using ink, not pencil) or typing out the cheque you should take care to complete the

- correct date
- name of the payee (person receiving the money)
- amount in words
- amount in figures (which should be the same!)
- authorised signature (it may be your signature, it may be that of a more senior individual)
- counterfoil (date, amount, payee)

No room should be left on the cheque for possible fraudulent additions or alterations; any blank spaces should be ruled through. If any errors are made when you are writing out the cheque, they should be corrected and an authorised signature placed close to the alteration in order to tell the bank that it is an approved correction.

a correctly completed cheque

Computer cheque printing is increasingly used by organisations which use computer accounting programs with a purchase ledger facility. The computer will automatically indicate payments that are due and, subject to authorisation, print out the remittance advice and cheque together, ready for posting. Clearly the computer involved must be closely controlled – and possibly password protected – in order to prevent unauthorised access and fraudulent payments.

PAYING FOR 'ONE-OFF' ITEMS – CHEQUE REQUISITION FORMS

So far we have looked at the payment of trade suppliers who supply on a regular basis for the normal activities of an organisation, eg merchants who supply potatoes for crisps manufacturers. The procedure for the issue of cheques in this case is reasonably straightforward. There will be times, however, when a cheque is needed for a 'one-off' purpose, for example:

- purchase of an item of equipment, authorised by the organisation
- reimbursement of 'out-of-pocket' expenses incurred by an employee
- payment of a proforma invoice (a proforma invoice is a request for payment to be made before the supply of the goods or services – contrast this with a normal invoice when payment follows supply)

The normal procedure in these cases is the completion of a cheque requisition form by the person who needs the cheque. See below.

Mercia Pumps Limited
CHEQUE REQUISITION FORM

required by... Tom Paget ...Dept... Marketing

CHEQUE DETAILS

date... 30 March 1998

payable to... Media Promotions Ltd

amount £... 45.00

despatch to (if applicable)... Media Promotions Ltd., 145 High Street, Mereford, MR1 3TF

reason... Advert in business journal ...nominal ledger... 7556

DOCUMENTATION

invoice attached/~~to follow~~... invoice 24516

receipt attached/to follow...

other...

AUTHORISATION... *Andrew Wimbush, Marketing Director*

---

a cheque requisition form

Note the following details on the cheque requisition form:

- the cheque has been ordered by Tom Paget, but is to be sent direct to Media Promotions Ltd
- the requisition is authorised by Andrew Wimbush, the Marketing Director
- the invoice is attached
- the nominal ledger code is included – this is the category of expense for which an account is maintained in the computer accounting system of the business – 7556 is the computer account number for 'advertising account'; if the business did not have a computer accounting system the name of the nominal account – 'advertising' – would be written here

CONTROL AND AUTHORISATION OF PAYMENTS

spending limits

In order to avoid fraud or unchecked spending within an organisation, all payments must be controlled and authorised. We have seen that incoming invoices must normally be stamped, and signed or initialled by an authorised person before being passed for payment. This is part of an overall system whereby no payment can be made without the necessary authority. The system will vary from organisation to organisation, but the following elements will be usually be found:

- the larger the payment, the more senior the person who needs to authorise it; often each level of management has a money limit imposed – for example a new vehicle costing £25,000 will be authorised at senior management level, a supplier's invoice for £250 will be paid at supervisory level
- when an item of expenditure is authorised, the person giving their authority will sign or initial and date the supporting document, eg an invoice, a cheque requisition form

cheque signatures

While an organisation will have an internal system of signing for and authorising expenditure, it will also have a written agreement with the bank – a bank mandate – which will set out who can sign cheques. A limited company or partnership may, for example, allow one director or partner to sign cheques up to £5,000, but will require two to sign cheques in excess of £5,000. It is common to have a number of different signatories to allow for partners and directors going on holiday, going sick and being otherwise unavailable for signing cheques.

cash payments

Most organisations will keep a cash float – petty cash – to allow for small everyday items of expenditure such as taxi fares and coffee for customer reception. The operation of the petty cash system is strictly controlled and documented, and will be dealt with in Chapter 16. Some organisations will also use cash for the payment of wages, although this is kept to a minimum, for obvious security reasons.

BANK GIRO CREDITS

We have already seen in Chapter 13 how money can be paid into a bank account by means of a bank paying-in slip or bank giro credit. So far we have looked at an organisation which pays in at its own branch, and receives the money on the account on the same day. The banking system also allows for a *bank giro credit* – also known as a credit transfer – to be paid in at one branch and sent through a three day clearing system (like the cheque clearing system) to another bank or branch This bank giro credit can, of course, be made out to a person or organisation other than the organisation making the payment. Please note that the word giro should not be confused with the payment system of the Girobank, which has nothing to do with the bank credit clearing system. This bank credit clearing system is used widely for

- paying wages
- paying bills (electricity, gas, telephone)
- settling credit card accounts

procedure for paying by bank giro credit

You may well be familiar as a personal bank customer with paying a bill by bank giro credit; the procedure for an organisation is exactly the same. The person or organisation making payment (or payments) prepares a cheque for the total amount to be paid (payment by cash would be very unusual for an organisation) and completes a bank giro credit, or a number of credits if more than one bank account is to receive payment. If more than one credit is to be completed – for example if wages are being paid – it is usual to list and total the credits on a separate schedule for the benefit of the bank.

If you are using a blank giro credit (illustrated on the next page) the details that need to be completed are:

- the name of the bank where the beneficiary's account is held (the beneficiary is the person receiving the money)
- the branch of bank and sort code where the beneficiary's account is held. Note: the sort code is a system of numbering each bank branch. (The sort code of a bank branch appears in the top right hand corner of a cheque.)

- the name and account number of the beneficiary
- the sender's name and reference
- the amount of the payment
- the date
- the counterfoil

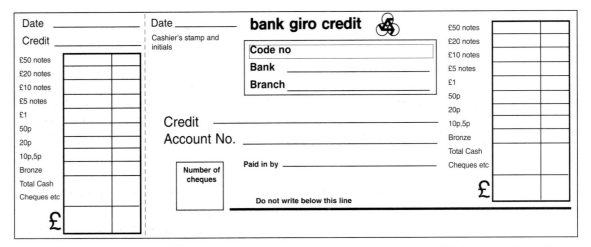

If you are using a pre-printed giro credit (to pay a bill, for example), all you need to do is complete the amount, date and name of person paying the water rates bill (see below)

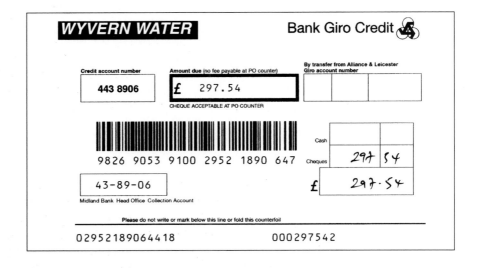

BACS: STANDING ORDERS AND DIRECT DEBITS

Bank giro credits are useful for making payments through the banking system for variable amounts, for example telephone bills, but the procedure is time-consuming because you need to visit the bank each time. To avoid this problem the banks have established an inter-bank computer money transfer system called BACS (Bankers Automated Clearing Services). Payment can take a number of forms:

standing order

The bank customer who needs to make regular payments, eg a loan repayment, completes a written authority (a mandate) instructing the bank what payments to make, to whom, and when. The bank then sets up the instructions on its computer, and the payments are made automatically by computer link on the due dates.

direct debit

Direct debits can be used for regular payments, but they differ from standing orders in two ways:

- direct debits can be used for either fixed and variable amounts and/or where the time intervals between payments vary
- it is the receiver (beneficiary) of the payment who prepares the computer instructions that request the payer's bank account for payment through the banking system; a direct debit is rather like a standing order operating backwards

The direct debit system is useful for organisations such as insurance companies and credit card companies that receive a large number of variable payments. The normal procedure is for the customer making payment to complete and sign a written authority (mandate) prepared by the beneficiary (eg insurance company); this is then returned to the beneficiary, the payment details are given to the beneficiary's bank so that the computer instructions can be set up, and the original form returned to the payer's bank.

'autopay' systems

For customers who need to make regular payments of variable amounts (eg wages, payments to established suppliers) the banks have established a system whereby they set up standing orders to the regular beneficiaries. All the customer has to do each time payment is to be made is to complete and give to the bank a schedule setting out the date, beneficiaries and amounts. The bank will then input these details direct into its computer system, and payments will be made automatically via the BACS system.

For all BACS payments – standing orders, direct debits and autopay – the bank needs written instructions (a mandate) from the customer before the amounts can be deducted from the account. The details needed by the bank – some of which may be preprinted – are:

- the name of organisation or person that is to receive the money, e.g. insurance company, hire purchase company, etc.
- the details of the recipient's bank, ie bank, branch, sort code number, and bank account number
- the reference number to be quoted
- the amount (unless it is not fixed, as in the case of direct debit and autopay)
- the frequency of payment (unless it is not fixed, as in the case of direct debit and autopay)
- the signature(s) of the customer authorising the amount to be debited to his/her bank account

If it is a business which is setting up the standing order or direct debit, it is important that the mandate form is signed by a person authorised to do so – it will often be the person(s) authorised to sign cheques. See below for examples of a standing order and a direct debit.

STANDING ORDER MANDATE

To _____ Bank

Address _____

PLEASE PAY TO

Bank _____   Branch _____   Sort code [   ]

Beneficiary _____   Account number [   ]

The sum of £ [   ]   Amount in words _____

Date of first payment _____   Frequency of payment _____

Until _____   Reference _____

Account to be debited [   ]   Account number [   ]

SIGNATURE(S) ....

.... date.............................

---

direct debit instruction

Tradesure Insurance Company
PO Box 134, Helliford, HL9 6TY

Originator's Identification Number 914208

03924540234

Reference(tobecompletedbyTradesureInsurance)...

Please complete the details <u>and return this form to Tradesure Insurance</u>

name and address of bank/building society

instructions to bank/building society

- I instruct you to pay direct debits from my account at the request of Tradesure Insurance Company
- The amounts are variable and may be debited on various dates
- I understand that Tradesure Insurance Company may change the amounts and dates only after giving me prior notice
- I will inform the bank/building society if I wish to cancel this instruction
- I understand that if any direct debit is paid which breaks the terms of this instruction, the bank/building society will make a refund.

account name

account number   sort code   signature(s)   date

COMPANY CREDIT CARDS, BANK DRAFTS AND CHAPS

If you work in an Accounts Office you may from time-to-time encounter other ways of making payment:

company credit cards

We have already examined the use of credit cards for making payments. Some organisations, particularly those which employ travelling sales representatives, may set up a company credit card scheme. This convenient and useful scheme allows nominated company representatives to have credit cards for paying for incidental expenses related to the company's business. A travelling salesperson may use one for paying for rail tickets, accommodation and food. The credit card bill is settled by the company which is then able to monitor the expenses incurred by its employees.

bank drafts

As noted in Chapter 12, an organisation may have to make a large purchase – for example new vehicles – and be asked to pay by bank draft. A bank draft is a bank cheque, a guaranteed means of payment which is as good as cash, but without the security risks. The draft is in effect 'purchased' from the bank by the organisation. If you need to order a bank draft, you will need to fill in a simple form provided by the bank, giving details of the amount and the payee. A fee is payable for this service.

CHAPS

A CHAPS (Clearing House Automated Payments System) payment is a high value payment system operated by the banks through their computer networks. It is used extensively by solicitors when they are arranging the purchase and sale of property for their clients. Businesses will use it for high value, same day, transfers. Once transmitted by a bank, a payment cannot be recalled. If you are asked to set up a CHAPS payment you will need to fill in a bank form giving details of the bank and account where the money is to be sent, the account from which the money is to be taken, and the amount. Remember to check the amount carefully, because if you make a mistake, the money cannot be recalled!

A similar system, known as SWIFT, exists for making payments abroad through the banks' computer network. The banks provide forms for setting up these payments which are sometimes known as IMT's (International Money Transfers).

CHAPTER SUMMARY

- Outgoing payments made by an organisation include payments to suppliers, payment of bills, 'one-off' items and wages.

- Before paying a supplier an organisation must see that all procedures and timescales are observed.

- When making payment by cheque or by BACS an organisation will normally send the supplier a remittance advice.

- Care must be taken when issuing cheques to ensure that the details are correct and that no room is left on the cheque for fraudulent alterations.

- If an employee needs a cheque for a 'one-off' payment, he or she will need to have a cheque requisition form completed and authorised.

- The issue of cheques should be strictly controlled; normally the larger the amount, the more senior the signatory and the greater number of signatures.

- Payments may be made through the inter-bank transfer system: paper-based paymernts include bank giro credits, computer-based payments are made through Bankers Automated Clearing Services (BACS).

- BACS payments may be made by standing order, direct debit or 'autopay' systems.

- Other methods of payment include company credit cards, bank drafts and CHAPS.

KEY TERMS

remittance advice	a document sent by the buyer to the supplier to advise the details of payment being made
cheque requisition form	an internal form which is completed and authorised when a cheque needs to be issued, normally for a 'one-off' payment
bank mandate	a form issued by a bank and completed by the organisation which sets out which employees can sign cheques and for what maximum amounts
bank giro credit	a paper slip (completed by the person making payment) which passes through the bank clearing system to the supplier's bank
BACS	the BACS system (Bankers Automated Clearing Services) passes payments through the banking system by computer transfer
standing order	a BACS payment where the person paying the money sets up a regular series of payments through his or her bank
direct debit	A BACS payment where the person paying the money authorises the supplier's bank to take money off their bank account
autopay system	a system whereby periodic payments can be made to a number of suppliers through the BACS system – the payer completes a schedule setting out the amounts and beneficiaries and passes it to the bank
company credit card	a credit card – in the name of the company – issued to an employee and used for paying expenses
bank draft	a cheque issued by a bank (and drawn on the bank) purchased by a customer as a payment which is 'as good as cash'
CHAPS	a CHAPS payment (CHAPS = Clearing House Automated Payments System) is a high-value inter-bank computer payment – often used for house purchase payments

STUDENT ACTIVITIES

14.1 A BACS remittance advice is normally attached to the cheque sent in settlement of an account. True or false?

14.2 Why should a cheque not be completed in pencil?

14.3 A cheque requisition form is used for which *one* of the following purposes?
   (a)   ordering a new cheque book
   (b)   stopping a cheque
   (c)   providing specimen signatures to the bank
   (d)   requesting a cheque within an organisation

14.4 Explain why a partnership or limited company business has to sign a bank mandate.

14.5 (a)   What is the difference between a standing order and a direct debit?

   State whether a standing order or a direct debit is the better method for the following payments, and why:
   (b)   A repayment of a fixed loan: £125 per month for five years
   (c)   A monthly insurance premium which is likely to increase over the years.

14.6 Name two commonly used methods suitable for making high value 'one-off' payments:
   (a)   a paper-based payment
   (b)   a computer-based payment

14.7 Company credit cards are popular means of making payment.
   (a)   State one advantage to the employee of the company credit card.
   (b)   State one advantage to the employer of the company credit card.

For the remainder of the activities in this chapter you are to take the role of an assistant in the Accounts Department of Nimrod Drainage Limited. Part of your day's work is the preparation of remittance advices and cheques for payments to suppliers. You are not required to sign the cheques. The date is 30 April 1997.

14.8 Your supervisor, Ivor Cash, hands you a list of authorised invoices from Jaeger Building Supplies to pay this month. Calculate the amount of the cheque you will have to make out to send with the remittance advice. You do not need to complete any documents. The date is 30 April 1997.

invoice date	payment terms	invoice total (£)
1 April	30 days	125.89
2 April	30 days	14,658.95
3 April	2.5% cash discount for settlement within 7 days	345.50
7 April	30 days	125.00

14.9 Your Supervisor hands you a statement from Mercia Wholesalers, Unit 12 Riverside Industrial Park, Mereford MR2 7GH, with a note, indicating the following invoices to be paid, and a credit note to be set off against payment:

Invoice 8765 dated 12 March 1997, your order number 5517, £765.25

Invoice 8823 dated 1 April 1997, your order number 5792, £3,567.80

Credit note C/N 3420 dated 25 April 1997 (your ref R/N 5168), £250.00

There is no cash discount. Complete the remittance advice and cheque set out below. Note that the total of the credit note should be shown in the money column in brackets, indicating that it is a deduction from the payment.

REMITTANCE ADVICE
NIMROD DRAINAGE LIMITED
UNIT 6 Riverside Industrial Park Mereford MR4 5TF
Tel 0605 675187 Fax 0605 415181 Vat Reg 63 6252 27

Cheque No
Date
Account

date	our ref.	your ref.	amount	discount	payment

cheque value £

---

date _____

National Bank PLC
Mereford Branch
10 Cathedral Street, Mereford MR1 5DE

date _____ 19 _____   35-09-75

Pay _____ only

£

NIMROD DRAINAGE LIMITED

Director   Director

£ _____

000451   000451   350975   12034875

14.10 Your supervisor, Ivor Cash, has received a memorandum from the Personnel Department stating that a new member of staff requires a refund for incidental expenses to be made direct to her bank account. The authorisation is in order, and the details are as follows:

Beneficiary   J Patel

Bank Midland Bank, Stourford Branch, sort code 40 99 87, account 87875231

Payment   cheque

Amount   £78.50

You are to complete the bank giro credit shown below. The date is 30 April 1997.

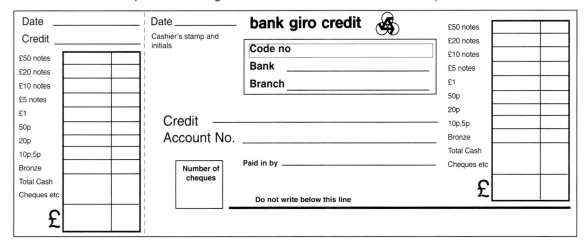

14.11 You work at a clerical grade and cannot sign cheques or other payment instructions. The date is 30 April 1997. Your supervisor, Ivor Cash, hands you two documents (shown on the next page):

- a blank standing order form provided by the bank

- a direct debit instruction received from Tradesure Insurance Company

He is in rather a rush and asks you to process the two documents, and to return them to the appropriate address with a compliments slip. He also leaves you a piece of paper with written instructions:

> *Hire Purchase Payments*
> *12 monthly instalments of £350 to Broadbent Finance from 15 May 1997, under reference BE/6637.*
> *Bank details Barclays, Eveshore, 30 98 15, Account 72627161.*
> *Debit our Account 12034875*

You are to:

(a)   complete the forms as required (look at a Nimrod Drainage cheque for your banking details)

(b)   state to which address you will send them

(c)   comment on any other procedure which you may have to carry out before sending off the forms

STANDING ORDER MANDATE

To   _____ Bank

Address   _____

PLEASE PAY TO

Bank _____ Branch _____ Sort code [   ]

Beneficiary _____ Account number [   ]

The sum of [£   ] Amount in words _____

Date of first payment _____ Frequency of payment _____

Until _____ Reference _____

Account to be debited [   ] Account number [   ]

SIGNATURE(S)   ....

  .... date..........................

— direct debit instruction —

Tradesure Insurance Company
PO Box 134, Helliford, HL9 6TY

Originator's Identification Number 914208

03924540234

Reference(tobecompletedbyTradesureInsurance)..

Please complete the details <u>and return this form to Tradesure Insurance</u>

name and address of bank/building society

instructions to bank/building society

- I instruct you to pay direct debits from my account at the request of Tradesure Insurance Company
- The amounts are variable and may be debited on various dates
- I understand that Tradesure Insurance Company may change the amounts and dates only after giving me prior notice
- I will inform the bank/building society if I wish to cancel this instruction
- I understand that if any direct debit is paid which breaks the terms of this instruction, the bank/building society will make a refund.

account name

[   ]

account number   sort code   signature(s)   date

[   ] [   ] [   ] [   ]

15 CASH BOOK

this chapter covers . . .

In this chapter we look at how the cash book brings together the separate cash and bank transactions of a business into one 'book'. The cash book is used to record the money (in the form of cash and cheques) side of book-keeping transactions and is part of the double-entry system.

Control of cash and money in the bank is important for all businesses. A shortage of money may mean that wages and other day-to-day running expenses cannot be paid as they fall due: this could lead to the rapid failure of the business.

Also in this chapter we look at the authorisation and payment of expenses claims – a task which is often carried out by a firm's cashier.

NVQ PERFORMANCE CRITERIA COVERED

unit 1: RECORDING AND ACCOUNTING FOR CASH TRANSACTIONS

element 4
account for cash and bank transactions

❏ entries in the cash book are accurately transferred to correct ledger accounts

❏ recorded transactions are supported by properly authorised primary documentation

❏ details for the relevant primary documentation are recorded in the cash book and analysed accurately

❏ totals and balances are correctly calculated

❏ security and confidentiality procedures are followed

❏ the organisation's policies, regulations, procedures and timescales are observed

❏ any discrepancies, unusual features or queries are identified and either resolved or referred to the appropriate person

THE CASH BOOK IN THE ACCOUNTING SYSTEM

For most businesses, control of cash – including both bank and cash transactions – takes place in the cash books which comprise:

* *cash book,* for receipts and payments in cash and by cheque
* *petty cash book* (see next chapter), for low-value expense payments

The cash books combine the roles of primary accounting records and double-entry book-keeping. Cash books are:

* primary accounting records for cash and bank transactions
* double-entry accounts for cash and bank

USES OF THE CASH BOOK

We have already used a separate cash account and bank account for double-entry book-keeping transactions. These two accounts are, in practice, brought together into one book under the title of cash book. This cash book is, therefore, used to record the money side of book-keeping transactions and is part of the double-entry system. The cash book is used for:

* cash transactions
    - all receipts in cash
    - most payments for cash, except for low-value expense payments (which are paid through petty cash book: see next chapter)

* bank transactions
    - all receipts by cheque (or payment of cash into the bank)
    - all payments by cheque (or withdrawal of cash from the bank)

The cash book is usually controlled by a cashier who:

* records receipts and payments by cheque and in cash
* makes cash payments, and prepares cheques for signature by those authorised to sign
* pays cash and cheques received into the bank
* has control over the firm's cash, either in a cash till or cash box
* issues cash to the petty cashier who operates the firm's petty cash book (see next chapter)
* checks the accuracy of the cash and bank balances at regular intervals

It is important to note that transactions passing through the cash book must be supported by documentary evidence. In this way an audit trail is established which provides a link that can be checked and followed through the accounting system:

- prime document
- primary accounting record
- double-entry accounts

Such an audit trail is required both as a security feature within the business (to help to ensure that fraudulent transactions cannot be made), and also for taxation purposes – both for Value Added Tax and for the Inland Revenue.

The cashier has an important role to play within the accounting function of a business – most business activities will, at some point, involve cash or cheque transactions. Thus the cash book and the cashier are at the hub of the accounting system. In particular, the cashier is responsible for:

- issuing receipts for cash (and sometimes cheques) received
- making authorised payments in cash and by cheque against documents received (such as invoices and statements) showing the amounts due
- checking expenses claims and seeking authorisation before making payment

At all times, payments can only be made by the cashier when authorised to do so by the appropriate person within the organisation, eg the accountant or the purchasing manager.

With so many transactions passing through the cash book, accounting procedures must include:

- security – of cash and cheque books, correct authorisation of payments
- confidentiality – that all cash/bank transactions, including cash and bank balances, are kept confidential

If the cashier has any queries about any transactions, he or she should refer them to the accounts supervisor.

LAYOUT OF THE CASH BOOK

Although a cash book can be set out in many formats to suit the requirements of a particular business, a common format is the columnar cash book. This is set out like other double-entry accounts, with debit and credit sides, but there may be several money columns on each side. An example of a three column cash book (three money columns on each side) is shown on the next page:

Dr							**Cash Book**					Cr
Date	Details	Folio	Discount allowed	Cash	Bank	Date	Details	Folio	Discount rec'd	Cash	Bank
			£	£	£				£	£	£

Note the following points:

- The debit side is used for receipts.

- The credit side is used for payments.

- On both the debit and credit sides there are separate money columns for cash receipts/payments and bank receipts/payments.

- A third money column on each side is used to record cash discount (that is, an allowance offered for quick settlement of the amount due, eg 2% cash discount for settlement within seven days).

- The discount column on the debit side is for discount allowed to customers.

- The discount column on the credit side is for discount received from suppliers.

- The discount columns are not part of the double-entry book-keeping system – they are used in the cash book as a listing device or memorandum column. As we will see in the Case Study which follows, the columns are totalled at the end of the week or month, and the totals are then transferred into the double-entry system.

CASE STUDY

SEVERN TRADING COMPANY – CASH BOOK

situation

The cashier at the firm for which you work, Severn Trading Company, is away on a training course this month. You are required, in her absence, to take over as the cashier. The transactions to be entered in the firm's three column cash book are:

1997

1 Apr   Balances at start of month: cash £300, bank £550

4 Apr   Received a cheque from S Wright for £98 – we have allowed her £2 cash discount

7 Apr   Paid a cheque to S Crane for £145 – he has allowed £5 cash discount

11 Apr   Paid wages in cash £275

14 Apr   Paid by cheque the account of T Lewis £120, deducting 2.5% cash discount

17 Apr   J Jones settles in cash her account of £80, deducting 5% cash discount

21 Apr   Withdrew £100 in cash from the bank for use in the business

23 Apr   Received a cheque for £45 from D Whiteman in full settlement of her account of £48

28 Apr   Paid cash of £70 to S Ford in full settlement of our account of £75

All cheques are banked on the day of receipt.

solution

The cash book records these transactions (as shown below) and, after they have been entered, is balanced on 30 April. (The other part of each double-entry book-keeping transaction is not shown here, but has to be carried out in order to record the transactions correctly.)

Dr						Cash Book						Cr
Date	Details	Folio	Discount allowed	Cash	Bank	Date	Details	Folio	Discount received	Cash	Bank
1997			£	£	£	1997			£	£	£
1 Apr	Balances b/d			300	550	7 Apr	J Crane		5		145
4 Apr	S Wright		2		98	11 Apr	Wages			275	
17 Apr	J Jones		4	76		14 Apr	T Lewis		3		117
21 Apr	Bank	C		100		21 Apr	Cash	C			100
23 Apr	D Whiteman		3		45	28 Apr	S Ford		5	70	
						30 Apr	Balances c/d			131	331
			9	476	693				13	476	693
1 May	Balances b/d			131	331						

Note: The transaction on 21 April – £100 withdrawn from the bank for use in the business – involves a transfer of money between cash and bank. As each transaction is both a receipt and a payment within the cash book, it is usual to indicate both of them in the folio column with a 'C' – this stands for contra and shows that both parts of the transaction are in the *same* book.

BALANCING THE CASH BOOK

We saw in Chapter 8 how accounts are balanced. The cash book is the ledger for cash account and bank account, and the procedure for balancing these accounts is exactly the same as for other ledger accounts.

The cash book in the Case Study above is balanced in the following way:

- add the two cash columns and subtotal in pencil (ie £476 in the debit column, and £345 in the credit column); remember to erase the subtotals afterwards

- deduct the lower total from the higher (payments from receipts) to give the balance of cash remaining (£476 – £345 = £131)

- the higher total is recorded at the bottom of both cash columns in a totals 'box' (£476)

- the balance of cash remaining (£131) is entered as a balancing item above the totals box (on the credit side), and is brought down underneath the total on the debit side as the opening balance for next month (£131)

- the two bank columns are dealt with in the same way (£693 – £362 = £331)

Notice that, in the cash book shown above, the cash and bank balances have been brought down on the debit side. It may happen that the balance at bank is brought down on the credit side: this occurs when payments exceed receipts, and indicates a bank overdraft. It is very important to appreciate that the bank columns of the cash book represent the firm's own records of bank transactions and the balance at bank – the bank statement may well show different figures (see Chapter 17).

At the end of the month, each discount column is totalled separately – no attempt should be made to balance them. At this point, amounts recorded in the columns and the totals are not part of the double-entry system. However, the two totals are transferred to the double-entry system as follows:

- the total on the debit side (£9 in the example above) is debited to discount allowed account in the general ledger

- the total on the credit side (£13 in the example) is credited to discount received account, also in the general ledger

The opposite book-keeping entries will have already been entered in the debtors' and creditors' accounts respectively (see Chapter 9). The accounts appear as follows:

Dr			Discount Allowed Account		Cr
1997		£	1997		£
30 Apr	Cash Book	9			

Dr	**Discount Received Account**		Cr
1997	£	1997	£
		30 Apr Cash Book	13

The two discount accounts represent an expense and income respectively and, at the end of the firm's financial year, the totals of the two accounts will be used in the profit statement. Where control accounts (see Chapter 10) are in use, the total of discount allowed is credited to the sales ledger control account, while the total of discount received is debited to the purchases ledger control account.

THE CASH BOOK AS A PRIMARY ACCOUNTING RECORD

The cash book performs two functions within the accounting system:

- it is a primary accounting record for cash/bank transactions
- it forms part of the double-entry book-keeping system

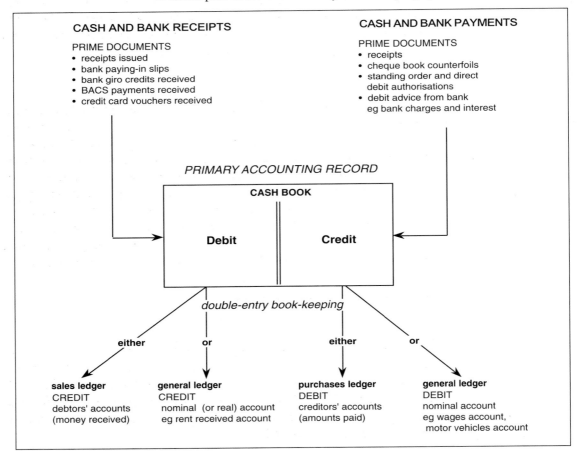

The diagram on the previous page shows the flow from:

- prime documents
- the cash book as a primary accounting record
- double-entry book-keeping, involving cash book and other ledgers

CHECKING THE CASH BOOK

As the cash book forms such an integral part of a firm's book-keeping system, it is essential that transactions are recorded accurately and that balances are calculated correctly at regular intervals, eg weekly or monthly – depending on the needs of the business. How can the cash book be checked for accuracy?

cash columns

To check the cash columns is easy. It is simply a matter of counting the cash in the cash till or box, and agreeing it with the balance shown by the cash book. In the example in the Case Study on page 248, there should be £131 in the firm's cash till at 30 April 1997. If the cash cannot be agreed in this way, the discrepancy needs to be investigated urgently.

bank columns

How are these to be checked? We could, perhaps, enquire at the bank and ask for the balance at the month-end, or we could arrange for a bank statement to be sent to us at the end of each month. However, the balance of the account at the bank may well not agree with that shown by the bank columns of the cash book. There are several reasons why there may be a difference: for example, a cheque that has been written out recently to pay a bill may not yet have been recorded on the bank statement, ie it has been entered in the cash book, but is not yet on the bank statement. To agree the bank statement and the bank columns of the cash book, it is usually necessary to prepare a bank reconciliation statement, and this topic is dealt with fully in Chapter 17.

CASH BOOK INCORPORATING VAT

A cash book can be adapted to suit the needs of a business – already we have seen how a three-column cash book uses a memorandum column for discounts allowed and received. Another common layout uses a fourth money column, for VAT, as shown in the Case Study which follows. The VAT columns act as memorandum columns and, at the end of the week or month, are transferred to VAT account.

CASE STUDY

CASH BOOK INCORPORATING VAT

situation

On Monday, 2 June 1997, the cash book of Eveshore Growers showed balances of £86 in cash and £248 in the bank. Transactions for the week were:

2 June	Paid insurance premium of £130 by cheque
3 June	Cash sales of £282, including Value Added Tax
3 June	Paid travel expenses in cash £47 (no Value Added Tax)
3 June	Paid an invoice for £100 from A–Z Supplies by cheque after deducting £5 cash discount
4 June	Received a cheque for £117 from a debtor, P Leech, who was settling his account balance of £120 after deducting £3 cash discount
5 June	Cash sales of £423, including Value Added Tax
6 June	Cash purchase of £188, including Value Added Tax
6 June	Paid wages of £205, partly by cheque for £105 and partly in cash £100
6 June	Transferred £250 of cash into the bank

The rate of Value Added Tax is 17.5%.
All cheques are banked on the day of receipt.

As cashier to Eveshore Growers, you are to:

* write up the cash book for the week commencing 2 June 1997, using separate columns for discount, VAT, cash and bank

* balance the cash book at 6 June 1997

* explain how the totals for the discount and VAT columns will be entered in the ledger of Eveshore Growers

solution

Dr													Cr
						Cash Book							
Date	Details	Folio	Disc allwd	VAT	Cash	Bank	Date	Details	Folio	Disc recd	VAT	Cash	Bank
1997			£	£	£	£	1997			£	£	£	£
2 Jun	Balances b/d				86	248	2 Jun	Insurance	GL				130
3 Jun	Sales	GL		42	282		3 Jun	Travel exp	GL			47	
4 Jun	P Leech	SL	3			117	3 Jun	A–Z Supplies	PL	5			95
5 Jun	Sales	GL		63	423		6 Jun	Purchases	GL		28	188	
6 Jun	Cash	C				250	6 Jun	Wages	GL			100	105
							6 Jun	Bank	C			250	
							6 Jun	Balances c/d				206	285
			3	105	791	615				5	28	791	615
7 Jun	Balances b/d				206	285							

notes to the Case Study

- The folio columns have been completed as follows:

  GL = general ledger (or NL for nominal ledger)

  SL = sales ledger

  PL = purchases ledger

  C = contra (both parts of the transaction in the same book)

- With transactions involving sales ledger (ie P Leech) and purchases ledger (ie A–Z Supplies), no amount for VAT is shown in the VAT columns. This is because VAT has been charged on invoices issued and received and was recorded in the VAT account (via the day books) when the sale or purchase was made.

- VAT on cash sales and purchases, and other transactions, is recorded in the two VAT analysis columns.

The discount and VAT columns:

- *discount allowed column* – the total of £3 will be debited to discount allowed account in the general ledger

- *discount received column* – the total of £5 will be credited to discount received account in the general ledger

- *VAT columns* – the total of £105 will be credited to VAT account in the general (or nominal) ledger, while the total of £28 will be debited to VAT account

ANALYSED CASH BOOK

Many businesses use an analysed cash book to provide more information. An analysed cash book divides receipts and payments between a number of categories.

Receipts could be divided between:

- the main sections of a business, such as (1) furniture, and (2) carpets, for a home furnishing shop

- (1) discount allowed, (2) Value Added Tax (where a business is registered for VAT), (3) sales paid for immediately in cash or by cheque, (4) sales ledger, ie receipts from debtors, (5) sundry items

Payments could be divided between:

- the main sections of a business, such as (1) compact discs, (2) audio tapes, and (3) video tapes, for an audio/video shop

- (1) discount received, (2) Value Added Tax, (3) purchases paid for immediately in cash or by cheque, (4) purchases ledger, ie payments to creditors, (5) sundry items

A business will use whatever analysis columns suit it best: the cash book should be adapted to meet the needs of the business in the best possible way.

CASE STUDY

ANALYSED CASH BOOK

situation

Wyvern Auto Spares Limited buys car parts from manufacturers, and sells to local garages and to members of the public. The company is registered for VAT.

The business uses a cash book which analyses receipts and payments as follows:

RECEIPTS	PAYMENTS
• discount allowed	• discount received
• VAT	• VAT
• sales	• purchases
• sales ledger	• purchases ledger
• sundry receipts	• sundry payments

The following transactions are to be entered for the first week of December 1997:

1 Dec	Balances from previous week: cash £255, bank £875
1 Dec	Sales for cash £240 + VAT
1 Dec	A debtor, Main Street Garage, settles an invoice for £195, paying by cheque
2 Dec	Paid rent on premises £325 (no VAT) by cheque
2 Dec	Sales for cash £200 + VAT
2 Dec	Paid an invoice for £250 from Boxhall Supplies Limited (a creditor) by cheque for £240, £10 being received for prompt settlement
3 Dec	Transferred £500 of cash into the bank
3 Dec	Paid for office stationery in cash, £40 + VAT
3 Dec	A debtor, A45 Service Station, settles an invoice for £143, paying £140 by cheque and receiving £3 discount for prompt settlement
4 Dec	Sales £320 + VAT, received half in cash, and half by cheque
4 Dec	Paid for urgently needed spares in cash, £80 + VAT
5 Dec	Paid an invoice for £155 from Vord Supplies (a creditor) by cheque for £150, £5 being received for prompt settlement
5 Dec	Sales for cash £200 + VAT
5 Dec	Paid wages £385 in cash
5 Dec	Balanced the cash book at the end of the week

The rate of Value Added Tax is 17.5%

All cheques are banked on the day of receipt.

solution

Dr (Receipts)

Date	Details	Folio	Cash	Bank	Discount allowed	VAT	Sales	Sales ledger	Sundry
1997			£	£	£	£	£	£	£
1 Dec	Balances b/d		255	875					
1 Dec	Sales	GL	282			42	240		
1 Dec	Main Street Garage	SL		195				195	
2 Dec	Sales	GL	235			35	200		
3 Dec	Cash	C		500					
3 Dec	A45 Service Station	SL		140	3			140	
4 Dec	Sales	GL	188	188		56	320		
5 Dec	Sales	GL	235			35	200		
			1,195	1,898	3	168	960	335	
6 Dec	Balances b/d		169	1,183					

Cr (Payments)

Date	Details	Folio	Cash	Bank	Discount received	VAT	Purchases	Purchases ledger	Sundry
1997			£	£	£	£	£	£	£
2 Dec	Rent	GL		325					325
2 Dec	Boxhall Supplies Limited	PL		240	10			240	
3 Dec	Bank	C	500						
3 Dec	Office stationery	GL	47			7			40
4 Dec	Purchases	GL	94			14	80		
5 Dec	Vord Supplies	PL		150	5			150	
5 Dec	Wages	GL	385						385
5 Dec	Balances c/d		169	1,183					
			1,195	1,898	15	21	80	390	750

NOTES:

- The analysed cash book analyses each receipt and payment between a number of headings. A business will adapt the cash book and use whatever analysis columns suit it best.

- For transactions involving sales ledger and purchases ledger, no amount for VAT is shown in the VAT columns. This is because VAT has been charged on invoices issued and received and was recorded in the VAT account (via the day books) when the sale or purchase was made.

- The cash and bank columns are balanced in the way described on page 249.

- The analysis columns are totalled at the end of the week and transferred to other accounts as follows:

- – *discount allowed* column total of £3 is debited to discount allowed account in the general ledger
- – *discount received* column total of £15 is credited to discount received account in the general ledger
- – *Value Added Tax* columns, the total of £168 is credited to VAT account in the general ledger, while the total of £21 is debited to the VAT account
- – *sales* column total of £960 is credited to sales account in the general ledger
- – *purchases* column total of £80 is debited to purchases account in the general ledger
- For a business which uses control accounts (see Chapter 10), the totals from the columns are also transferred directly to the control accounts as follows:
  - – *discount allowed*, to the credit side of sales ledger control account
  - – *discount received*, to the debit side of purchases ledger control account
  - – *sales ledger*, to the credit side of sales ledger control account
  - – *purchases ledger*, to the debit side of purchases ledger control account

EXPENSES CLAIMS

A further duty of the cashier (or the petty cashier – see Chapter 16) is the checking of *expenses claims*.

Often an employee is required to pay for expenses incurred on behalf of the business or organisation, and then to claim back the amount already paid from the business. Typically, expenses which can be reclaimed include:

- Travel, eg rail, bus, air and taxi fares, mileage allowance where a private car or motorbike has been used. (Note that the costs of travel to and from work are not paid, except under special circumstances, eg the burglar alarms go off in the middle of the night and the police request the presence of the keyholder).
- Hotel bills, including meals.
- Subsistence allowance – to cover the costs of working away from the normal place of employment, often paid at a daily rate.
- Other expenses, eg part of the employee's domestic telephone bill.

A business will establish the terms under which it will reimburse an employee. For example, travel claims might have to be at the cheapest form of travel, such as a bus, even if the employee uses his/her private car; first-class travel is likely to be available only to senior employees. Before refunding expenses, the business will usually require proof of the expense, eg a receipt, or the travel ticket.

WYVERN TRADERS LIMITED
EXPENSES CLAIM FOR THE MONTH ENDING ....

Name:

Department:

Date	Item	Travelling £	Subsistence £	Entertaining £	Miscellaneous £	Total £	OFFICE USE ONLY	
							VAT £	Net £
Total								

Signed:

Date:

Authorised by:

Date:

expenses claim form

claims procedure

At regular intervals – perhaps monthly – an employee will be required to submit an expenses claim (see previous page). The procedure is likely to be:

- Employee completes and signs expenses claim form.

- Receipts for the expenses are attached to the expenses claim form.

- The form is passed to the employee's manager or section head for authorisation.

- The form is then sent to the accounts department where the amounts will be checked against the company's policies. The calculations on the form will also be checked. The various expenses will then be coded for the appropriate general ledger account, eg travel expenses, telephone expenses, etc. The book-keeping will be:

    – *debit* appropriate expense account (in the general ledger)

    – *credit* cash book (cash or bank column, as appropriate)

- The amount will either be paid direct to the employee in cash, by cheque or bank giro credit (small amounts can be paid out of petty cash – see Chapter 16), or the employee's pay will be credited and the amount paid at the next payroll run.

- The firm's general ledger expenses accounts will be debited with the cost. Where an expense includes VAT, a VAT-registered business will debit the appropriate expense account with the net amount of the expense, and debit the VAT amount to VAT account; in this way, the business claims back the VAT paid on the expense.

income tax and expenses

Most expenses are wholly incurred on behalf of the business or organisation. As such, their reimbursement does not form a part of the employee's salary, and is not subject to income tax. However, some expenses incurred are only partly used on behalf of the business, the other part is a benefit to the employee. Examples include the provision of a company car, or payment of the employee's telephone bill. The Inland Revenue lays down guidelines which, depending on the circumstances, state the employee's liability for income tax, together with the employee's and employer's liability for National Insurance Contributions.

**CHAPTER
SUMMARY**

- The cash book records receipts (debits) and payments (credits) both in cash (except for low-value expense payments) and by cheque.

- A basic layout for a cash book has money columns for cash transactions and bank transactions on both the debit and credit sides, together with a further column on each side for discounts.

- In the discount columns are recorded cash discounts: discounts allowed (to customers) on the debit side, and discounts received (from suppliers) on the payments side.

- Another common cash book layout incorporates columns for VAT.

- An analysed cash book is used to provide more information: it divides receipts and payments between a number of categories.

- The cashier may be responsible for checking expenses claims.

**KEY
TERMS**

cash book	records both cash and bank transactions; combines the roles of primary accounting records and double-entry book-keeping
columnar cash book	commonly-used layout for cash books which incorporates several money columns on the debit and credit sides, eg columns for cash discount, VAT, cash, bank
analysed cash book	cash book which divides receipts and payments between a number of categories, eg the main sections of the business
expenses claims	forms used by employees to claim back expenses paid by the employee but incurred on behalf of the business or organisation

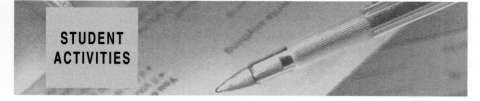

**STUDENT
ACTIVITIES**

15.1 The cash book records:

(a) receipts and payments in cash only

(b) receipts and payments by cheque only

(c) all receipts and payments both in cash and by cheque

(d) receipts and payments both in cash (except for low-value expense payments) and by cheque

Answer (a) or (b) or (c) or (d)

15.2 The cash book is:

(a)   a prime document

(b)   a primary accounting record only

(c)   part of double-entry book-keeping only

(d)   combines primary accounting records and double-entry book-keeping

Answer (a) or (b) or (c) or (d)

15.3 You work as the cashier for Wyvern Publishing, a company which publishes a wide range of travel and historical books. As cashier, your main responsibility is for the firm's cash book.

Explain to a friend what your job involves and the qualities required of a cashier.

15.4 On 1 August 1997, the balances in the cash book of Metro Trading Company were:

Cash   £276 debit

Bank   £4,928 debit

Transactions for the month were:

1 Aug	Received a cheque from Wild & Sons Limited, £398
5 Aug	Paid T Hall Limited a cheque for £541 in full settlement of a debt of £565
8 Aug	Paid wages in cash £254
11 Aug	Withdrew £500 in cash from the bank for use in the business
12 Aug	Received a cheque for £1,755 from A Lewis Limited in full settlement of their account of £1,755
18 Aug	Paid F Jarvis £457 by cheque
21 Aug	Received a cheque for £261 from Harvey & Sons Limited
22 Aug	Paid wages in cash £436
25 Aug	Paid J Jones a cheque for £628 in full settlement of a debt of £661
27 Aug	Paid salaries by cheque £2,043
28 Aug	Paid telephone account by cheque £276
29 Aug	Received a cheque for £595 from Wild & Sons Limited in full settlement of their account of £610
29 Aug	Withdrew £275 in cash from the bank for use in the business

All cheques are banked on the day of receipt.

You are to:

*   Enter the above transactions in the three column cash book of Metro Trading Company.

*   Balance the cash and bank columns at 31 August, and carry the balances down to 1 September.

*   Total the two discount columns.

15.5 On 1 April 1997, the balances in the cash book of Johnson Brothers were:

Cash £85 debit

Bank £718 credit (the business has a bank overdraft limit of £2,000)

Transactions for the month were:

3 Apr	Paid travelling expenses of £65 in cash
4 Apr	Paid the telephone bill of £235 (including £35 of Value Added Tax) by cheque
7 Apr	Jim Bowen, a debtor, settles an invoice for £90, paying £85 in cash and receiving £5 discount for prompt settlement
10 Apr	Cash sales £470 (including Value Added Tax) received by cheque and paid into the bank
14 Apr	Paid an invoice for £190 from M Hughes (a creditor) by cheque for £180, £10 being received for prompt settlement
17 Apr	Cash purchases of £94 (including Value Added Tax) paid by cheque
18 Apr	Received a cheque for £575 from J Burrows, a debtor, in full settlement of an invoice for £600
21 Apr	Cash sales of £188 (including Value Added Tax) received in cash
22 Apr	Withdrew £200 in cash from the bank for use in the business
24 Apr	Paid a cheque for £245 to Wilson Limited, a creditor, in full settlement of an invoice for £255
25 Apr	Paid wages in cash £350

You are to:

- Enter the above transactions in the cash book of Johnson Brothers, using columns for dates, details, discount, VAT, cash and bank.
- Balance the cash book at 30 April 1997.
- Show how the totals for the discount and VAT columns will be entered in the accounts in the general ledger.

Notes:

Calculate Value Added Tax at the current rate (17.5% at the time of writing).

All cheques are banked on the day of receipt.

15.6 David Lewis runs a shop selling carpets. He buys carpets from the manufacturers and sells to the public on cash terms and also to a few trade customers – such as carpet fitters – on credit terms. His business is registered for VAT.

He uses a cash book which analyses *receipts* between:

- discount allowed
- VAT
- sales
- sales ledger
- sundry

Payments are analysed between:

- discount received
- VAT
- purchases
- purchases ledger
- sundry

The following transactions take place during the week commencing 12 May 1997 (all cheques are banked on the day of receipt):

12 May	Balances from previous week: cash £205.75, bank £825.30
12 May	Sales £534.62 (including VAT), cheque received
12 May	Paid shop rent by cheque £255.50 (no VAT)
13 May	Sales £164.50 (including VAT), cash received
13 May	A debtor, T Jarvis, settles an invoice for £157.50, paying £155.00 by cheque, £2.50 discount being allowed for prompt settlement
13 May	Paid an invoice for £368.20 from Terry Carpets Limited (a creditor) by cheque for £363.55 and receiving £4.65 discount for prompt settlement
14 May	Sales £752.00 (including VAT), cheque received
14 May	Paid for stationery in cash, £28.20 (including VAT)
15 May	Transferred £250 of cash into the bank
15 May	Sales £264.37 (including VAT), cash received

15 May   Paid an invoice for £295.80 from Longlife Carpets Limited (a creditor), paying £291.50 by cheque, £4.30 discount being received for prompt settlement

16 May   Paid wages £314.20 in cash

16 May   A debtor, Wyvern District Council, settles an invoice for £565.45, paying £560.45 by cheque and receiving £5.00 discount for prompt settlement

You are to:

*   Enter the above transactions in the analysed cash book of David Lewis (VAT amounts should be rounded down to the nearest penny).

*   Balance the cash book at 16 May 1997.

*   Explain how the totals for the columns will be entered in the accounts in the general ledger (David Lewis does not use control accounts).

Notes:

Calculate Value Added Tax at the current rate (17.5% at the time of writing).

All cheques are banked on the day of receipt.

16 PETTY CASH BOOK

this chapter covers . . .

A petty cash book is used to record low-value cash payments for various small purchases and expenses incurred by a business or other organisation.

An amount of cash is handed by the main cashier to a member of staff, the petty cashier, who will be responsible for security of the money, and will make payments as appropriate against authorised petty cash vouchers.

In the context of the accounting system, the petty cash book is both

- the primary accounting record
- part of the double-entry system

NVQ PERFORMANCE CRITERIA COVERED

unit 1: RECORDING AND ACCOUNTING FOR CASH TRANSACTIONS
element 3
maintain petty cash records

- ❏ *transactions are accurately recorded and analysed to the correct expenditure heads*
- ❏ *cash withdrawals from the main cash account are accurately recorded*
- ❏ *claims are properly authorised, are within prescribed limits and are supported by adequate evidence*
- ❏ *totals and balances are correctly calculated*
- ❏ *the balance of cash in hand is reconciled with the petty cash records at appropriate intervals*
- ❏ *documentation is correctly filed*
- ❏ *analysed totals of petty cash expenditure are transferred to the correct ledger accounts*
- ❏ *cash handling, security and confidentiality procedures are followed*
- ❏ *any discrepancies, unusual features or queries are identified and either resolved or referred to the appropriate person*

THE PETTY CASH PROCEDURE

The petty cash book is used to record low-value cash payments for purchases and expenses such as small items of stationery, postages, etc, items which it would not be appropriate to enter in the main cash book. Instead, an amount of cash is handed by the main cashier to a member of staff, the petty cashier, who is responsible for control of the petty cash, making cash payments when appropriate, keeping records of payments made and balancing the petty cash book at regular intervals.

In order to operate the petty cash system, the petty cashier needs the following:

- a *petty cash book* in which to record transactions
- a lockable *cash box* in which to keep the money
- a stock of blank *petty cash vouchers* (see page 268) for claims on petty cash to be made
- a *lockable desk drawer* in which to keep these items

making a claim

As an employee you are most likely to encounter the petty cash system when making claims for money for small purchases you have made. Before studying the form-filling procedures in detail, read the summary of a typical petty cash transaction set out below:

your supervisor asks you to go and buy a box of computer disks from an office supplies shop

you go to the shop and buy the computer disks; having paid for them, you retain the receipt (for £5.50) which you hand to the petty cashier on your return to the office

the supervisor authorises a petty cash voucher which contains details of the purchase

the petty cashier gives you £5.50 in cash

the petty cashier attaches the receipt to the petty cash voucher and enters the details in the petty cash book

WHAT ITEMS CAN BE PASSED THROUGH PETTY CASH BOOK?

Petty cash is used to make small cash payments for purchases and expenses incurred by the business. Examples of the type of payments made from petty cash include:

- stationery items
- small items of office supplies
- casual wages
- window cleaning
- bus, rail and taxi fares (incurred on behalf of the business)
- meals and drinks (incurred on behalf of the business)
- postages
- tips and donations

Note that petty cash should not be used to pay for private expenses of employees, eg tea, coffee, and milk, unless the business has agreed these in advance. Usually the petty cashier will have a list of approved expenses which can be reimbursed.

A business will also decide on the maximum value of each transaction that can be paid out of petty cash; for example, £25 is a common figure.

CASE STUDY

PETTY CASH EXPENSES

situation

You are working as an accounts clerk for Wyvern Engineering Limited. One of your duties is that of petty cashier. Which of the following expenses would you allow to be paid out of petty cash?

- envelopes for use in the office, £2.50
- postage on an urgent parcel of engineering parts, £3.75
- bus fare to work claimed by secretary £1.20
- car mileage to work of office manager called in late at night when the burglar alarm went off (false alarm!), £5.50
- tea and coffee for use in the office, £3.70
- office window cleaning, £2.80
- pot plant bought for reception area, £5.50
- computer disks, £35.00
- donation to local charity by the business, £5.00
- meal allowance paid to a member of staff required to work during the lunch hour, £3.50

solution

For most expenses it is clear whether or not they can be drawn from petty cash. However, there are points to consider for some of the expenses.

Envelopes	pay from petty cash
Postage	pay from petty cash
Bus fare to work	this is a personal expense and cannot be drawn from petty cash
Car mileage	travel to work is a personal expense, as seen with the previous item; however, as this expense was a special journey in the middle of the night in order to resolve a business problem, it can be paid from petty cash
Tea and coffee	this is a personal expense of employees and cannot normally be paid out of petty cash; however, if the ingredients were used to make drinks for official visitors and customers, it can be paid from petty cash
Window cleaning	pay from petty cash
Pot plant	pay from petty cash (but plants for the general office cannot be bought with the company's money)
Computer disks	this is a business expense but, in view of the amount (too large for petty cash), it should be paid by cheque from the cash book
Donation	pay from petty cash
Meal allowance	pay from petty cash, provided that it is company policy to make an allowance in these circumstances

notes on the case study

- If the petty cashier is unable to resolve whether or not an expense can be paid from petty cash, the item should be referred to the accounts supervisor for a decision.
- Before payments can be made for petty cash expenses, they must be:
  - within the prescribed limit for petty cash expenses (for example, £25 maximum for any one expense item)
  - supported by documentary evidence, such as a receipt or a rail/bus ticket
  - authorised by the appropriate supervisor or manager

THE IMPREST SYSTEM

Most petty cash books operate on the imprest system. With this method the petty cashier starts each week (or month) with a certain amount of money – the imprest amount. As payments are made during the week (or month) the amount of money will reduce and, at the end of the period, the cash will be made up by the main cashier to the imprest amount. For example:

Started week with imprest amount	£100.00
Total of petty cash amounts paid out during week	£80.50
Cash held at end of week	£19.50
Amount drawn from cashier to restore imprest amount	£80.50
Cash at start of next week, ie imprest amount	£100.00

If, at any time, the imprest amount proves to be insufficient, further amounts of cash can be drawn from the cashier. Also, from time-to-time, it may be necessary to increase the imprest amount so that regular shortfalls are avoided.

PETTY CASH VOUCHER

Payments out of petty cash are made only against correct documentation – usually a petty cash voucher (see below). Petty cash vouchers are completed as follows:

- details and amount of expenditure
- signature of the person making the claim and receiving the money
- signature of the person authorising the payment to be made
- additionally, most petty cash vouchers are numbered, so that they can be controlled, the number being entered in the petty cash book
- relevant documentation, eg receipt, should be attached to the petty cash voucher

petty cash voucher		No. 807	
	date	12 May 1997	
description		amount (£)	
C5 Envelopes		1	50
10 Floppy disks		6	50
		8	00
	VAT	1	40
		9	40
signature	T Harris		
authorised	R Singh		

Petty cash vouchers are the *prime documents* for the petty cash book.

LAYOUT OF A PETTY CASH BOOK

The petty cash book is both the *primary accounting record* and part of the *double-entry system* for petty cash transactions. Petty cash book can be set out as follows:

Receipts	Date	Details	Voucher No	Total Payment	Analysis columns				
					VAT	Postages	Stationery	Travel	Ledger
£				£	£	£	£	£	£

The layout shows that:

- receipts from the main cashier are entered in the column on the extreme left
- there are columns for the date and details of all receipts and payments
- there is a column for the petty cash voucher number
- the total payment (ie the amount paid out on each petty cash voucher) is in the next column
- then follow the analysis columns which analyse each transaction entered in the 'total payment' column (note that VAT may need to be calculated – see below)

A business or organisation will use whatever analysis columns are most suitable for it and, indeed, there may be more columns than shown in the example. It is important that expenses are analysed to the correct columns so that the contents show a true picture of petty cash expenditure.

PETTY CASH AND VAT

Value Added Tax is charged by VAT-registered businesses on their taxable supplies. Therefore, there will often be VAT included as part of the expense paid out of petty cash. However, not all expenses will have been subject to VAT. There are four possible circumstances:

- VAT has been charged at the standard rate
- VAT has not been charged because the supplier is not VAT-registered
- the zero rate of VAT applies, eg food and drink (but not meals which are standard-rated), books, newspapers, transport (but not taxis and hire cars)
- the supplies are exempt (eg financial services, postal services)

Often the indication of the supplier's VAT registration number on a receipt or invoice will tell you that VAT has been charged at the standard rate.

Where VAT has been charged, the amount of tax might be indicated separately on the receipt or invoice. However, for small money amounts it is quite usual for a total to be shown without indicating the amount of VAT. An example of a receipt which does not show the VAT content is illustrated below. The receipt is for a box of envelopes purchased from Wyvern Stationers. It shows:

- the name and address of the retailer

- the date and time of the transaction

- the VAT registration number of the retailer

- the price of the item – £4.70

- the amount of money given – a £10 note

- the amount of change given – £5.30

| Wyvern Stationers |
| 25 High St Mereford |
| 08 10 97 16.07 |
| VAT Reg 454 7106 34 |
| |
| Salesperson Rashid |
| |
| Stationery   4.70 |
| |
| TOTAL   4.70 |
| CASH   10.00 |
| CHANGE   5.30 |

What it does not show, however, is the VAT content of the purchase price – it only shows the price after the VAT has been added on.

How do you calculate purchase price before the VAT is added on?

The formula, with VAT at 17.5%, is:

price including VAT ÷ 1.175 = price before VAT is added on

in this case ...

£4.70 ÷ 1.175 = £4.00 = price before VAT is added on

The VAT content is therefore

£4.70 less £4.00 = 70p

Here £0.70 will be entered in the VAT column in the petty cash book, £4.00 in the appropriate expense column, and the full £4.70 in the total payment column.

Remember when calculating VAT amounts that fractions of a penny are ignored, ie the tax is rounded *down* to a whole penny.

CASE STUDY

PETTY CASH BOOK

situation

You work in the accounts office of Wyvern Traders. One of your tasks is to keep the petty cash book, which is operated on the imprest system. There are a number of authorised transactions (all of which, unless otherwise indicated, include VAT at 17.5%) to be entered for the week in the petty cash book:

1997	
7 Apr	Started the week with an imprest amount of £50.00
7 Apr	Paid stationery £3.76 on voucher no. 47
7 Apr	Paid taxi fare £2.82 on voucher no. 48
8 Apr	Paid postages £0.75 (no VAT) on voucher no. 49
9 Apr	Paid taxi fare £4.70 on voucher no. 50
9 Apr	Paid J Jones, a creditor, £6.00 (no VAT shown in petty cash book – amount will be on VAT account already) on voucher no. 51
10 Apr	Paid stationery £3.76 on voucher no. 52
10 Apr	Paid postages £2.85 (no VAT) on voucher no. 53
11 Apr	Paid taxi fare £6.11 on voucher no. 54
11 Apr	Cash received to restore imprest amount, and petty cash book balanced at the end of the week

solution

The petty cash book is written up as follows:

Receipts	Date	Details	Voucher No	Total Payment	Analysis columns				
					VAT	Postages	Stationery	Travel	Ledger
£	1997			£	£	£	£	£	£
50.00	7 Apr	Balance b/d							
	7 Apr	Stationery	47	3.76	0.56		3.20		
	7 Apr	Taxi fare	48	2.82	0.42			2.40	
	8 Apr	Postages	49	0.75		0.75			
	9 Apr	Taxi fare	50	4.70	0.70			4.00	
	9 Apr	J Jones	51	6.00					6.00
	10 Apr	Stationery	52	3.76	0.56		3.20		
	10 Apr	Postages	53	2.85		2.85			
	11 Apr	Taxi fare	54	6.11	0.91			5.20	
				30.75	3.15	3.60	6.40	11.60	6.00
30.75	11 Apr	Cash received							
	11 Apr	Balance c/d		50.00					
80.75				80.75					
50.00	11 Apr	Balance b/d							

notes on the case study

- The totals of the analysis columns add up to the total payment
- the amount of cash received from the main cashier to restore the imprest amount is the same as the total paid out during the week
- The petty cashier will give the firm's book-keeper a posting sheet giving details of the total of each analysis column – see below – so that the amounts can be recorded in the double-entry book-keeping system

PETTY CASH AND DOUBLE-ENTRY BOOK-KEEPING

When the petty cash book has been balanced, the petty cashier will prepare a posting sheet (see page 108) which shows:

- *debits* to expenses accounts (and VAT account) in the general ledger in respect of each expenses column
- *debits* to creditors' accounts in the purchases ledger in respect of the ledger column (eg J Jones in the Case Study)
- *credit* to cash book, being the amount drawn from the main cashier to restore the imprest amount of the petty cash book

For example, the postages in the above Case Study will be debited as follows:

Dr			Postages Account		Cr
1997		£	1997		£
11 Apr	Petty cash book	3.60			

From the petty cash book, debits are passed to the general ledger accounts as follows:

- VAT account, £3.15
- stationery account, £6.40
- postages account, £3.60
- travel expenses account, £11.60

The amount in the ledger column, £6.00, is debited to the account of J Jones in the purchases ledger.

Total debits in the Case Study are £30.75 and this is the amount that has been drawn from the main cashier on 11 April. The petty cashier will complete a cheque requisition form either for the cash itself, or for a cheque made payable to cash. The petty cashier will take the cheque to the bank and obtain the cash. An example of a cheque requisition is shown on the next page.

The cheque is credited in the firm's cash book, so completing double-entry :

– *debit* petty cash book £30.75   – *credit* cash book £30.75

```
WYVERN TRADERS        CHEQUE REQUISITION

Amount              £30.75

Payee               Cash

Date                11 April 1997

Details             Reimbursement of petty cash

Signature           Jane Watkins, petty cashier

Authorised by       Natalie Wilson, supervisor

Cheque no           017234
```

cheque requisition form

If a trial balance is extracted on 11 April (after the analysis columns have been debited to the respective accounts, and a credit entered in the cash book to restore the imprest amount) the balance of petty cash, £50.00, must be included as a debit balance in the trial balance – this is because petty cash book is part of the double-entry system.

CASE STUDY

CONTROL OF PETTY CASH

situation

You are an accounts clerk in the office of Osborne Engineering Limited. As part of your duties you are required to be responsible for the petty cash.

The office manager is reviewing the way in which work is carried out in the office. She asks you to set out the procedures for the operation and control of petty cash. She explains that this will be of help to the person who takes over from you when you go on holiday. She also says that she doesn't require details of how to balance the petty cash book.

solution

The main procedures for the operation and control of petty cash are:

• On taking over, check that the petty cash book has been balanced and that the amount of cash held agrees with the balance shown in the book. If there is any discrepancy, this should be referred to the office manager immediately.

• Ensure that you start each week with the imprest amount of cash which has been agreed with the office manager.

- Keep the petty cash secure in a locked cash box, and keep control of the keys.

- Provide petty cash vouchers (in number order) on request.

- Pay out of petty cash against correctly completed petty cash vouchers ensuring that:

    - the voucher is signed by the person receiving the money

    - the voucher is signed by the person authorising payment (a list of authorised signatories will be provided)

    - a receipt (whenever possible) is attached to the petty cash voucher, and that receipt and petty cash voucher are for the same amount

- Write up the petty cash book (to include calculation of VAT amounts when appropriate); it is important that the petty cash book is *accurate*.

- Store the completed petty cash vouchers safely – file them in numerical order. The vouchers will need to be kept for at least six years in the company's archives. They may be needed by the firm's auditors or in the event of other queries. Completed petty cash books will also need to be retained.

- Expect a surprise check of petty cash from the office manager – at any one time the cash held plus amounts of petty cash vouchers should equal the imprest amount.

- At the end of each week (or month) balance the petty cash book and draw an amount of cash from the cashier equal to the amount of payments made, in order to restore the imprest amount.

- Prepare a posting sheet for the totals of each analysis column, so that the book-keeper can enter the amount of each expense into the double-entry system.

- Present the petty cash book and cash in hand for checking by the office manager.

- Deal with any discrepancies promptly; these can include:

    - a receipt and petty cash voucher total differing – raise the matter with the person who made the purchase

    - a difference between the totals of the analysis columns and the total payments column in the petty cash book – check the addition of the columns, check the figures against the vouchers, check your VAT calculations (does the VAT plus the analysis column amount equal the total payment amount?)

    - a difference between the cash in the petty cash box and the balance shown in the petty cash book – if this is not an arithmetic difference it may be a case of theft, and should be reported promptly to the office manager

    - where discrepancies and queries cannot be resolved, they should be referred to the office manager

- Remember that all aspects of petty cash are confidential and should not be discussed with others.

CHAPTER SUMMARY

- The petty cash book records payments for a variety of low-value business expenses.

- The person responsible for maintaining the petty cash book is the petty cashier.

- Payment can only be made from the petty cash book against correct documentation – usually a petty cash voucher, which must be signed by the person authorising payment.

- Where a business is registered for Value Added Tax, it must record VAT amounts paid on petty cash purchases in a separate column in the petty cash book.

- At regular intervals – weekly or monthly – the petty cash book will be balanced; the main cashier will restore the imprest amount of cash and the total of each analysis column will be debited to the relevant account in the book-keeping system.

KEY TERMS

petty cash book	the primary accounting record and part of the double-entry system for recording low-value business expenses
petty cashier	the person responsible for the petty cash system
imprest system	where the money held in the petty cash float is restored to the same amount for the beginning of each week or month
petty cash voucher	the prime document used to claim amounts from petty cash

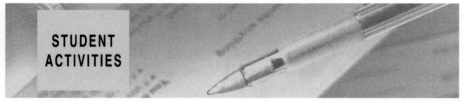

STUDENT ACTIVITIES

16.1 Most petty cash books operate on the imprest system. This means that:

(a) the petty cashier draws money from the main cashier as and when required

(b) the main cashier has to authorise each petty cash payment

(c) a copy has to be kept of each petty cash voucher

(d) the petty cashier starts each week or month with a fixed amount of money

Answer (a) or (b) or (c) or (d)

16.2   A petty cash book is balanced at the end of each week and the petty cash float restored by the main cashier. At the start of this week the cash float is £50. Petty cash vouchers for the week total £34.56. How much will be received from the main cashier at the end of the week?

   (a)   £50.00

   (b)   £15.44

   (c)   £34.56

   (d)   £84.56

   Answer (a) or (b) or (c) or (d)

16.3   You work as an accounts clerk in the office of Temeside Printers Limited. One of your duties is that of petty cashier. Which of the following expenses will you allow to be paid out of petty cash?

   (a)   postage on a parcel of printing sent to a customer, £3.85

   (b)   a rubber date stamp bought for use in the office, £4.60

   (c)   rail fare to work claimed by the office manager's secretary, £2.50

   (d)   donation to charity, £5.00

   (e)   tea and coffee for use by office staff, £5.50

   (f)   mileage allowance claimed by works foreman who had to visit a customer, £4.80

   (g)   meal allowance paid to assistant who had to work her lunch hour, £4.00

   (h)   window cleaning, £3.50

   (i)   purchase of shelving for the office, £55.00

   (j)   taxi fare claimed for delivering an urgent parcel of printing to a customer, £6.25

   Explain any expenses that you will refer to the accounts supervisor.

16.4   You are going on holiday and handing your job as petty cashier to a colleague who is not familiar with the security and confidentiality aspects of the job, although she can manage the paperwork. Prepare a checklist of the security and safety aspects of the job so that she can learn them more easily. Write them out as bullet points rather than as solid text – they will be more easily remembered in this format.

16.5   As petty cashier, prepare the petty cash vouchers shown on the next page under today's date for signature by the person making the claim. You are authorised to approve payments up to £10.00.

   Voucher no. 851: £4.45 claimed by Jayne Smith for postage (no VAT) on an urgent parcel of spare parts sent to a customer, Evelode Supplies Limited.

   Voucher no. 852: £2.35 (including VAT) claimed by Tanya Howard for air mail envelopes bought for use in the office. Show on the petty cash voucher the amount of VAT.

   What documentation will you require to be attached to each voucher?

petty cash voucher

No. 851

date

description	amount (£)	
VAT		

signature ....

authorised ....

petty cash voucher

No. 852

date

description	amount (£)	
VAT		

signature ....

authorised ....

16.6 The business for which you work is registered for VAT. The following petty cash amounts include VAT at 17.5% and you are required to calculate the amount that will be shown in the VAT column and the appropriate expense column (remember that VAT amounts should be rounded down to the nearest penny):

(a) £9.40

(b) £4.70

(c) £2.35

(d) £2.45

(e) £5.60

(f) £3.47

(g) £8.75

(h) 94p

(i) 99p

(j) £9.41

16.7 On returning from holiday, you are told to take over the petty cash book. This is kept on the imprest system, the float being £75.00 at the beginning of each month. Analysis columns are used for VAT, travel, postages, stationery, meals, and miscellaneous.

Enter the following transactions for the month. The voucher amounts include VAT at 17.5% unless indicated. You can assume that all payments have been authorised by the office manager:

1997

1 Aug	Balance of cash £75.00
4 Aug	Voucher no. 39: taxi fare £3.80
6 Aug	Voucher no. 40: parcel postage £2.35 (no VAT)
7 Aug	Voucher no. 41: pencils £1.26
11 Aug	Voucher no. 42: travel expenses £5.46 (no VAT)
12 Aug	Voucher no. 43: window cleaner £8.50 (no VAT)
14 Aug	Voucher no. 44: large envelopes £2.45
18 Aug	Voucher no. 45: donation to charity £5 (no VAT)
19 Aug	Voucher no. 46: rail fare £5.60 (no VAT); meal allowance £5.00 (no VAT)
20 Aug	Voucher no. 47: recorded delivery postage £0.75 (no VAT)
22 Aug	Voucher no. 48: roll of packing tape £1.50
25 Aug	Voucher no. 49: excess postage paid £0.55 (no VAT)
27 Aug	Voucher no. 50: taxi fare £5.40
29 Aug	Petty cash book balanced and cash received from cashier to restore imprest amount to £75.00

You are to show how the following will be recorded in the double-entry book-keeping system:

- the totals of the analysis columns
- the transfer of cash from the main cashier on 29 August

16.8 Prepare a petty cash book with analysis columns for VAT, postages, travel, meals, and sundry office expenses. Enter the following authorised transactions for the week. The voucher amounts include VAT at 17.5% unless indicated.

1997

2 June	Balance of cash £100.00
2 June	Postages £6.35 (no VAT), voucher no. 123
3 June	Travel expenses £3.25 (no VAT), voucher no. 124
3 June	Postages £1.28 (no VAT), voucher no. 125
4 June	Envelopes £4.54, voucher no. 126
4 June	Window cleaning £5.50, voucher no. 127
5 June	Taxi fare £4.56, meals £10.85, voucher no. 128
5 June	Postages £8.56 (no VAT), packing materials £3.25, voucher no. 129
5 June	Taxi fare £4.50, meals £7.45, voucher no. 130
6 June	Marker pens £2.55, envelopes £3.80, voucher no. 131
6 June	Petty cash book balanced and cash received from cashier to restore imprest amount to £100.00

You are to show how the following will be recorded in the double-entry book-keeping system:

- the totals of the analysis columns
- the transfer of cash from the main cashier on 6 June

BANK RECONCILIATION STATEMENTS

this chapter covers . . .

Bank reconciliation statements form the link between the balance at bank shown in the cash book of a firm's book-keeping system and the balance shown on the bank statement received from the bank.

The reasons why the cash book and bank statement may differ are because:

- there are timing differences caused by

  – unpresented cheques, ie the time delay between writing out (drawing) a cheque and recording it in the cash book, and the cheque being entered on the bank statement

  – outstanding lodgements, ie amounts paid into the bank, but not yet recorded on the bank statement

- the cash book has not been updated with items which appear on the bank statement and which should also appear in the cash book, eg bank charges

Assuming that there are no errors, both cash book and bank statement are correct, but need to be reconciled with each other, ie the closing balances need to be agreed.

NVQ PERFORMANCE CRITERIA COVERED

unit 1: RECORDING AND ACCOUNTING FOR CASH TRANSACTIONS

element 4

account for cash and bank transactions

❑ bank reconciliation statements are accurately prepared and are presented within specified timescales

❑ any discrepancies, unusual features or queries are identified and either resolved or referred to the appropriate person

TIMING DIFFERENCES

The two main timing differences between the bank columns of the cash book and the bank statement are:

- *unpresented cheques*, ie cheques drawn, not yet recorded on the bank statement

- *outstanding lodgements*, ie amounts paid into the bank, not yet recorded on the bank statement

The first of these – unpresented cheques – is caused because, when a cheque is written out, it is immediately entered on the payments side of the cash book, even though it may be some days before the cheque passes through the bank clearing system and is recorded on the bank statement. Therefore, for a few days at least, the cash book shows a lower balance than the bank statement in respect of this cheque. When the cheque is recorded on the bank statement, the difference will disappear. We have looked at only one cheque here, but a business will often be issuing many cheques each day, and the difference between the cash book balance and the bank statement balance may be considerable.

With the second timing difference – outstanding lodgements – the firm's cashier will record a receipt in the cash book as he or she prepares the bank paying-in slip. However, the receipt may not be recorded by the bank on the bank statement for a day or so, particularly if it is paid in late in the day (when the bank will put it into the next day's work), or if it is paid in at a bank branch other than the one at which the account is maintained. Until the receipt is recorded by the bank the cash book will show a higher bank account balance than the bank statement. Once the receipt is entered on the bank statement, the difference will disappear.

These two timing differences are involved in the calculation known as the bank reconciliation statement. The business cash book must not be altered for these because, as we have seen, they will correct themselves on the bank statement as time goes by.

UPDATING THE CASH BOOK

Besides the timing differences described above, there may be other differences between the bank columns of the cash book and the bank statement, and these do need to be entered in the cash book to bring it up-to-date. For example, the bank might make an automatic standing order payment on behalf of a business – such an item is correctly debited by the bank, and it might be that the bank statement acts as a reminder to the business cashier of the payment: it should then be entered in the cash book.

Examples of items that show in the bank statement and need to be entered in the cash book include:

receipts

- standing order and BACS (Bankers' Automated Clearing Services) receipts credited by the bank, eg payments from debtors (customers)
- bank giro credit (credit transfer) amounts received by the bank, eg payments from debtors (customers)
- dividend amounts received by the bank
- interest credited by the bank

payments

- standing order and direct debit payments
- bank charges and interest
- unpaid cheques debited by the bank (ie cheques from creditors paid in by the business which have 'bounced' and are returned by the bank marked 'refer to drawer')

For each of these items, the cashier needs to check to see if they have been entered in the cash book; if not, they need to be recorded (provided that the bank has not made an error). If the bank has made an error, it must be notified as soon as possible and the incorrect transactions reversed by the bank in its own accounting records.

THE BANK RECONCILIATION STATEMENT

This forms the link between the balances shown in the bank statement and the cash book.

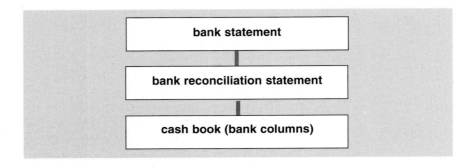

Upon receipt of a bank statement, reconciliation of the two balances is carried out in the following way:

- tick off the items that appear in both cash book and bank statement
- the unticked items on the bank statement are entered into the bank columns of the cash book to bring it up-to-date (provided none are errors made by the bank)
- the bank columns of the cash book are now balanced to find the revised figure
- the remaining unticked items from the cash book will be the timing differences
- the timing differences are used to prepare the bank reconciliation statement, which takes the following format (with example figures):

XYZ TRADING LIMITED
Bank Reconciliation Statement as at 31 October 1997

		£	£
Balance at bank as per bank statement			245
Less: unpresented cheques			
J Lewis	cheque no. 0012378	60	
ABC Limited	cheque no. 0012392	100	
Eastern Oil Company	cheque no. 0012407	80	
			240
			5
Add: outstanding lodgements		220	
		300	
			520
Balance at bank as per cash book			525

Notes:

- The layout shown above starts from the bank statement balance, and works towards the cash book balance. A common variation of this layout is to start with the cash book balance and to work towards the bank statement balance (see page 287).
- If a bank overdraft is involved, brackets should be used around the numbers to indicate this for the bank statement or cash book balance. The timing differences are still added or deducted, as appropriate.
- Once the bank reconciliation statement agrees, it should be filed because it proves that the bank statement and cash book were reconciled at a particular date. If, next time it is prepared, it fails to agree, the previous statement is proof that reconciliation was reached at that time.

CASE STUDY

BANK RECONCILIATION STATEMENT

situation

The cashier of Severn Trading Company has written up the firm's cash book for the month of February 1997, as follows (the cheque number is shown against payments):

Cash Book

Dr   Cr

Date	Details	Cash	Bank	Date	Details	Cash	Bank
1997		£	£	1997		£	£
1 Feb	Balances b/d	250.75	1,340.50	3 Feb	Appleton Ltd 123456		675.25
7 Feb	A Abbott		208.50	5 Feb	Wages	58.60	
10 Feb	Sales	145.25		12 Feb	Rent 123457		125.00
13 Feb	Sales	278.30		14 Feb	Transfer to bank C	500.00	
14 Feb	Transfer from cash C		500.00	17 Feb	D Smith & Co 123458		421.80
20 Feb	Sales	204.35		24 Feb	Stationery	75.50	
21 Feb	D Richards Ltd		162.30	25 Feb	G Christie 123459		797.55
26 Feb	Sales	353.95		27 Feb	Transfer to bank C	500.00	
27 Feb	Transfer from cash C		500.00	28 Feb	Balances c/d	98.50	954.00
28 Feb	P Paul Ltd		262.30				
		1,232.60	2,973.60			1,232.60	2,973.60
1 Mar	Balances b/d	98.50	954.00				

The cash balance of £98.50 shown by the cash columns on 1 March has been agreed with the cash held in the firm's cash box. The bank statement for February 1997 has just been received:

National Bank plc

Branch ..Bartown..............

TITLE OF ACCOUNT ....Severn Trading Company......

ACCOUNT NUMBER ....67812318.............   STATEMENT NUMBER 45

DATE	PARTICULARS	PAYMENTS	RECEIPTS	BALANCE
1997		£	£	£
1 Feb	Balance brought forward			1340.50 CR
8 Feb	Credit		208.50	1549.00 CR
10 Feb	Cheque no. 123456	675.25		873.75 CR
17 Feb	Credit		500.00	1373.75 CR
17 Feb	Cheque no. 123457	125.00		1248.75 CR
24 Reb	Credit		162.30	1411.05 CR
24 Feb	BACS credit: J Jarvis Ltd		100.00	1511.05 CR
26 Feb	Cheque no. 123458	421.80		1089.25 CR
26 Feb	Direct debit: A-Z Finance	150.00		939.25 CR
28 Feb	Credit		500.00	1439.25 CR
28 Feb	Bank charges	10.00		1429.25 CR

solution

As the month-end balance at bank shown by the cash book, £954.00, is not the same as that shown by the bank statement, £1,429.25, it is necessary to prepare a bank reconciliation statement. The steps are:

1. Tick off the items that appear in both cash book and bank statement.
2. The unticked items on the bank statement are entered into the bank columns of the cash book to bring it up-to-date. These are:
    *   receipt   24 Feb   BACS credit, J Jarvis Limited £100.00
    *   payments   26 Feb   Direct debit, A-Z Finance £150.00
                         28 Feb   Bank Charges, £10.00

    In double-entry book-keeping, the other part of the transaction will need to be recorded in the accounts, eg in J Jarvis Ltd's account in the sales ledger, etc.

3. The cash book is now balanced to find the revised balance:

Dr			**Cash Book (bank columns)**		Cr
1997		£	1997		
	Balance b/d	954.00	26 Feb	A-Z Finance	150.00
24 Feb	J Jarvis Ltd	100.00	28 Feb	Bank Charges	10.00
			28 Feb	Balance c/d	894.00
		1,054.00			1,054.00
1 Mar	Balance b/d	894.00			

4. The remaining unticked items from the cash book are used in the bank reconciliation statement:
    *   receipt 28 Feb – P Paul Limited £262.30
    *   payment 24 Feb – G Christie (cheque no 123459) £797.55

    These items are timing differences, which should appear on next month's bank statement.

5. The bank reconciliation statement is now prepared, starting with the bank statement balance of £1,429.25 .

SEVERN TRADING COMPANY
Bank Reconciliation Statement as at 28 February 1997

	£
Balance at bank as per bank statement	1,429.25
Less: unpresented cheque, no. 123459	797.55
	631.70
Add: outstanding lodgement, P Paul Limited	262.30
Balance at bank as per cash book	894.00

This statement has been produced which starts with the bank statement balance, and finishes with the amended balance from the cash book, ie the two figures are reconciled.

notes on the case study

• The *unpresented cheque* is deducted from the bank statement balance because, until it is recorded by the bank, the bank statement shows a higher balance than the cash book.

• The *outstanding lodgement* is added to the bank statement balance because, until it is recorded by the bank, the bank statement shows a lower balance than the cash book.

PREPARING A BANK RECONCILIATION STATEMENT

In order to help you with the Student Activities at the end of the chapter, here is a step-by-step summary of the procedure. Reconciliation of the bank statement balance with that shown in the cash book should be carried out in the following way:

1. From the bank columns of the cash book tick off, in both cash book and bank statement, the receipts that appear in both.

2. From the bank columns of the cash book tick off, in both cash book and bank statement, the payments that appear in both.

3. Identify the items that are unticked on the bank statement and enter them in the cash book on the debit or credit side, as appropriate. (If, however, the bank has made a mistake and debited or credited an amount in error, this should not be entered in the cash book, but should be notified to the bank for them to make the correction. The amount will need to be entered on the bank reconciliation statement – see section below, dealing with unusual items on bank statements: bank errors.)

4. The bank columns of the cash book are now balanced to find the up-to-date balance.

5. Start the bank reconciliation statement with the final balance figure shown on the bank statement.

6. In the bank reconciliation statement *deduct* the unticked payments shown in the cash book – these will be unpresented cheques.

7. In the bank reconciliation statement, *add* the unticked receipts shown in the cash book – these are outstanding lodgements.

8. The resultant money amount on the bank reconciliation statement is the balance at bank as per the cash book.

The layout which is often used for the bank reconciliation statement is that shown on page 283. The layout starts with the bank statement balance and finishes with the cash book balance. However, there is no reason why it should not commence with the cash book balance and finish with the bank statement balance: with this layout it is necessary to:

- *add* unpresented cheques
- *deduct* outstanding lodgements

The bank reconciliation statement of Severn Trading Company (see page 285) would then appear as:

	£
SEVERN TRADING COMPANY	
Bank Reconciliation Statement as at 28 February 1997	
Balance at bank as per cash book	894.00
Add: unpresented cheque, no 123459	797.55
	1,691.55
Less: outstanding lodgement, P Paul Limited	262.30
Balance at bank as per bank statement	1,429.25

DEALING WITH UNUSUAL ITEMS ON BANK STATEMENTS

The following are some of the unusual features that may occur on bank statements. As with other accounting discrepancies and queries, where they cannot be resolved they should be referred to a supervisor for guidance.

out-of-date cheques

As noted above, these are cheques that are more than six months' old. Where a business has a number of out-of-date – or 'stale' – cheques which have not been debited on the bank statement, they will continue to appear on the bank reconciliation statement. As the bank will not pay these cheques, they can be written back in the cash book, ie debit cash book (and credit the other double-entry account involved).

returned cheques

A cheque received by a business is entered as a receipt in the cash book and then paid into the bank, but it *may be returned* by the drawer's (issuer's) bank to the payee's bank because:

- the drawer (the issuer) has stopped it
- the drawer has no money (the cheque may be returned 'refer to drawer') – ie the cheque has 'bounced'

A cheque returned in this way should be entered in the book-keeping system:

- as a payment in the cash book on the *credit* side
- as a *debit* to the account of the drawer of the cheque in the sales ledger (if it is a credit sale), or sales account if it is a cash sale

On the other hand, if the business itself stops a cheque, the cheque drawn by the business will have been entered as a payment in the cash book (a *credit*). It should now be entered as

- a receipt on the *debit* side
- a *credit to* the account of the payee, most probably in the purchases ledger (if it is a credit purchase)

bank errors

Errors made by the bank can include:

- A cheque debited to the bank account which has not been drawn by the business – look for a cheque number on the bank statement that is different from the current cheque series: care, though, as it could be a cheque from an old cheque book.
- A BACS payment (or other credit) shown on the bank statement for which the business is not the correct recipient. If in doubt, the bank will be able to give further details of the sender of the credit.
- Standing orders and direct debits paid at the wrong time or for the wrong amounts. A copy of all standing order and direct debit mandates sent to the bank should be kept by the business for reference purposes.

When an error is found, it should be queried immediately with the bank. The item and amount should not be entered in the firm's cash book until the issue has been resolved. If, in the meantime, a bank reconciliation statement is to be prepared, the bank error should be shown separately:

- if working from the bank statement balance to the cash book balance, add payments and deduct receipts that the bank has applied to the account incorrectly
- if working from the cash book balance to the bank statement balance, deduct payments and add receipts that the bank has applied to the account incorrectly

bank charges and interest

From time-to-time the bank will debit business customers' accounts with an amount for:

- – service charges, ie the cost of operating the bank account
- – interest, ie the borrowing cost when the business is overdrawn

Banks usually notify customers in writing before debiting the account.

reconciliation of opening cash book and bank statement balances

If you look back to the Case Study on page 284, you will see that both the cash book (bank columns) and the bank statement balance both started the month with the same balance: 1 February 1997 £1,340.50. In reality, it is unlikely that the opening cash book and bank statement balances will be the same. It will be necessary, in these circumstances, to prepare an opening bank reconciliation statement in order to prove that there are no errors between cash book and bank statement at the start of the month. This is set out in the same format as the end-of-month bank reconciliation statement, and is best prepared immediately after ticking off the items that appear in both cash book and bank statement. The earliest unpresented cheques drawn and outstanding lodgements will comprise the opening bank reconciliation statement. Of course, where last month's bank reconciliation statement is available, such as in business, there is no need to prepare an opening reconciliation.

IMPORTANCE OF BANK RECONCILIATION STATEMENTS

1. A bank reconciliation statement is important because, in its preparation, the transactions in the bank columns of the cash book are compared with those recorded on the bank statement. In this way, any errors in the cash book or bank statement will be found and can be corrected (or advised to the bank, if the bank statement is wrong).

2. The bank statement is an independent accounting record, therefore it will assist in deterring fraud by providing a means of verifying the cash book balance.

3. By writing the cash book up-to-date, the organisation has an amended figure for the bank balance to be shown in the trial balance.

4. Unpresented cheques over six months old – out-of-date cheques – can be identified and written back in the cash book (any cheque dated more than six months' ago will not be paid by the bank).

5. It is good business practice to prepare a bank reconciliation statement each time a bank statement is received. The reconciliation statement should be prepared as quickly as possible so that any queries – either with the bank statement or in the firm's cash book – can be resolved. Many firms will specify to their accounting staff the timescales for preparing bank reconciliation statements – as a guideline, if the bank statement is received weekly, then the reconciliation statement should be prepared within five working days.

- A bank reconciliation statement is used to agree the balance shown by the bank statement with that shown by the bank columns of the cash book.

- Certain differences between the two are timing differences. The main timing differences are:
  - unpresented cheques
  - oustanding lodgements

  These differences will be corrected by time and, most probably, will be recorded on the next bank statement.

- Certain differences appearing on the bank statement need to be entered in the cash book to bring it up-to-date. These include:

  Receipts – standing order and BACS receipts credited by the bank
  – bank giro credit amounts received by the bank
  – dividend amounts received by the bank
  – interest credited by the bank

  Payments – standing order and direct debit payments
  – bank charges and interest
  – unpaid cheques debited by the bank

- The bank reconciliation statement makes use of the timing differences.

- Once prepared, a bank reconciliation statement is proof that the bank statement and the cash book (bank columns) were agreed at a particular date.

bank reconciliation statement	forms the link between the balances shown in the bank statement and the cash book
timing differences	discrepancies between the bank statement and the cash book that will be corrected over time, such as unpresented cheques and outstanding lodgements
unpresented cheques	cheques drawn, but not yet recorded on the bank statement
outstanding lodgements	amounts paid into the bank, but not yet recorded on the bank statement

STUDENT
ACTIVITIES

17.1 When preparing a bank reconciliation statement, which one of the following is a timing difference?

(a) unpresented cheques

(b) direct debit payments

(c) bank charges and interest

(d) BACS receipts

Answer (a) or (b) or (c) or (d)

17.2 A firm's bank statement shows a balance of £400. Unpresented cheques total £350; outstanding lodgements total £200. What is the balance at bank shown by the cash book?

(a) £100

(b) £200

(c) £250

(d) £400

Answer (a) or (b) or (c) or (d)

17.3 The bank columns of Tom Reid's cash book for December 1997 are as follows:

1997	Receipts	£	1997	Payments		£
1 Dec	Balance b/d	280	9 Dec	W Smith	345123	40
12 Dec	P Jones	30	12 Dec	Rent	345124	50
18 Dec	H Homer	72	18 Dec	Wages	345125	85
29 Dec	J Hill	13	19 Dec	B Kay	345126	20
			31 Dec	Balance c/d		200
		395				395

He then received his bank statement which showed the following transactions for December 1997:

BANK STATEMENT		Payments	Receipts	Balance
1997		£	£	£
1 Dec	Balance brought forward			280 CR
12 Dec	Credit		30	310 CR
15 Dec	Cheque no. 345123	40		270 CR
17 Dec	Cheque no. 345124	50		220 CR
22 Dec	Credit		72	292 CR
23 Dec	Cheque no. 345125	85		207 CR

You are to prepare a bank reconciliation statement which agrees the bank statement balance with the cash book total.

17.4 The bank columns of P Gerrard's cash book for January 1997 are as follows:

1997	Receipts	£	1997	Payments		£
1 Jan	Balance b/d	800.50	2 Jan	A Arthur Ltd	001351	100.00
6 Jan	J Baker	495.60	10 Jan	C Curtis	001352	398.50
31 Jan	G Shotton Ltd	335.75	13 Jan	Donald & Co	001353	229.70
			14 Jan	Bryant & Sons	001354	312.00
			23 Jan	P Reid	001355	176.50
			31 Jan	Balance c/d		415.15
		1,631.85				1,631.85

He received his bank statement which showed the following transactions for January 1997:

BANK STATEMENT		Payments	Receipts	Balance
1997		£	£	£
1 Jan	Balance brought forward			800.50 CR
6 Jan	Cheque no. 001351	100.00		700.50 CR
6 Jan	Credit		495.60	1,196.10 CR
13 Jan	BACS credit: T K Supplies		716.50	1,912.60 CR
20 Jan	Cheque no. 001352	398.50		1,514.10 CR
23 Jan	Direct debit: Omni Finance	207.95		1,306.15 CR
24 Jan	Cheque no. 001353	229.70		1,076.45 CR

You are to:

(a) write the cash book up-to-date at 31 January 1997

(b) prepare a bank reconciliation statement at 31 January 1997

17.5   The bank columns of Jane Doyle's cash book for May 1997 are as follows:

1997	Receipts	£	1997	Payments		£
1 May	Balance b/d	300	2 May	P Stone	867714	28
7 May	Cash	162	14 May	Alpha Ltd	867715	50
16 May	C Brewster	89	29 May	E Deakin	867716	110
23 May	Cash	60			Bal c/d	463
30 May	Cash	40				

She received her bank statement which showed the following transactions for May 1997:

BANK STATEMENT		Payments	Receipts	Balance
1997		£	£	£
1 May	Balance brought forward			326 CR
1 May	Credit		54	380 CR
5 May	Cheque no. 867714	28		352 CR
6 May	Cheque no. 867713	80		272 CR
7 May	Credit		162	434 CR
16 May	Standing order: A-Z Insurance	25		409 CR
19 May	Credit		89	498 CR
20 May	Cheque no. 867715	50		448 CR
26 May	Credit		60	508 CR
31 May	Bank Charges	10		498 CR

You are to:

(a)   write the cash book up-to-date at 31 May 1997

(b)   prepare an opening bank reconciliation statement at 1 May 1997

(c)   prepare a bank reconciliation statement at 31 May 1997

17.6   You work as an accounts clerk in the office of H James (Precision Engineering) Limited. One of your tasks at the end of each month is to reconcile the bank statement with the bank columns of the company's cash book. As you will be away on holiday over the next month-end, the office manager has asked you to write clear instructions in the form of a memorandum for the person who is to undertake this task when you are away.

COMMUNICATING FOR ACCOUNTING

this chapter covers . . .

This chapter explains the importance of accurate and prompt communication both within an organisation and also in its dealings with outsiders. It covers:

- the sources of information – particularly in relation to accounting information

- the extraction of correct and appropriate information

- the need to communicate to the right person and to keep to deadlines

- dealing with delays in communication

- the different forms of written communication – notes, letters and memoranda

NVQ REQUIREMENTS

unit 24 COMMUNICATING FOR ACCOUNTING

element 1

supply information for a specific purpose

- ❑ relevant sources of information are correctly identified and accessed
- ❑ appropriate data is abstracted, listed and classified correctly
- ❑ information is supplied to appropriate person within required deadlines
- ❑ difficulties in achieving targets are promptly reported and politely explained

element 2

draft routine business communications

- ❑ legible letters and memos containing all essential information drafted within specified deadlines
- ❑ draft communications are presented in an approved format

TYPES OF INFORMATION NEEDED

If you are working in an accounting office or are a sole trader dealing with the accounting side of the business you will need to organise your records so that information can be easily retrieved. You will need to have access to this information for a number of reasons:

- queries raised by customers
- information needed by the auditors (if you use them)
- you will need to monitor what is going on the business – eg credit control, bank reconciliation, paying your suppliers

Examples of the data you are likely to need on a regular basis are:

banking data

These include chequebook stubs, paying in slip details, standing order and direct debit instructions, BACS payment schedules and bank statements.

sales ledger management

You will need to keep track of dealings with your customers, eg entries on individual ledger accounts, customer discounts, customer contact details and last but not least credit control – the aged debtor summary.

purchase ledger management

You will also need to keep track of dealings with your suppliers, eg entries on ledger accounts, discounts available to you, contact details and a diary system to make sure that you pay your suppliers on time.

stock data

You will need to keep an up-to-date record of the stock that you keep, or, if you offer a service, the details of those services. The type of information that will be enquired about is the nature of the stock, its stock code, current price, whether you have it in stock, and if not, when you can get it.

SOURCES OF THE INFORMATION

paper and computer systems

Data can be stored in a variety of ways. The traditional method is the paper-based system, but increasingly low priced computers enable businesses to store data electronically. An accounting office may use a computer (single or networked) for a variety of functions:

- accounting programs, such as Sage, to process payments, sales, purchases and stock records
- a database for customer records
- a spreadsheet for specific numerical tasks

It is critical, however, that you keep a paper back-up of the computer system as well as computer data back-ups. This means an organised filing system for documents, eg bank statements, sales invoices, purchase invoices, customer correspondence. This will ensure that when the inevitable happens and the computer breaks down or you have a power cut, you can access your accounting records to enable the work to continue and customer enquiries to be answered. The paper records may also be needed for audit purposes.

filing systems

Filing can be carried in a number of different ways to suit different purposes; these include:

- alphabetic filing – eg sales ledger customers by surname or organisation name
- numeric filing – eg invoices filed by invoice number
- date order – eg bank statements filed in chronological order

Some larger organisations use electronic filing systems; here each document is electronically scanned as a digital image for storage on computer file. With this system a copy of each document can be called up on computer screen.

other sources of information

You are likely to encounter other ways of accessing information. Many of these will already be familiar to you. These include:

- *reference books* – trade directories, timetables, dictionaries
- *Web sites* – information accessed through the computer 'internet' – your computer will need to be linked to other computers by means of a modem to obtain on-line information
- *Viewdata* – information accessed through the telephone and viewed onscreen, eg Prestel, Ceefax and Teletext
- *microfiche* – sheets of film which can be viewed on a special viewer – each sheet has a large number of pages very much reduced in size – library catalogues and commercial stock records are often kept on microfiche
- *microfilm* – a continuous strip of film on which data is printed in greatly reduced size; like microfiche, microfilm is viewed on a special reader

EXTRACTING ACCURATE INFORMATION

This may seem an obvious subject area, but it is one that is too often taken for granted. If you deal with an inefficient organisation you will see that problems arise in the areas of providing

- correct and accurate information
- within given timescales
- to the correct person

Examples of problems of this type are shown in the table below. You will no doubt be able to add examples of your own.

the problem

You are ordering goods and are quoted an incorrect stock code.

the result

You are supplied with the wrong goods, or encounter a delay when the mistake is realised.

the problem

You are asked for a quote for your product but send it in after the deadline.

the result

You do not get the order!

the problem

You are asked for a quote for your product but forget to apply the customer discount.

the result

You do not get the order!

You will no doubt understand the importance of providing accurate information on time.

You may encounter the situation of being faced with a problem you cannot deal with yourself, eg being asked for a higher customer discount than is shown on the list. The answer here is always to refer the matter to a more senior person. If you are a sole trader, however, the answer is always readily to hand – you make your own decisions!

THE MEMORANDUM

format

The memorandum (plural memoranda) is a formal written note used for internal communication within an organisation. It may be typed or handwritten, and will often be produced in a number of copies which can be circulated as necessary. A memorandum may be sent by e-mail within an organisation.

A memorandum can be used for situations such as:

• giving instructions

• requesting information

• making suggestions

• recording of opinions

• confirming telephone conversations

A memorandum is normally pre-printed by the organisation with all the headings in place, and can be half page or full page in size.

elements of the memorandum

'to' and 'from'	the name and job title of the sender and the recipient are entered in full, and the formal phrases you find on letters, eg 'Dear......' and 'Yours ....' are not necessary
copies to	memoranda are frequently sent (as in the example on the next page) to a large number of people; the recipients will be indicated in this section of the document
subject	the subject matter of the memorandum must be stated concisely
text	the message of the memorandum should be clear and concise
signature	a memorandum can be signed, initialled, or even – as is often the case – left blank
enclosures	if material is circulated with the memorandum, the abbreviation 'enc' or 'encl' should be used

MEMORANDUM

To

From   **Ref**

Copies to   **Date**

Subject

---

a blank memorandum

MEMORANDUM

To   Edgar Pound, Accounts Supervisor

From   K Perch, Finance Director   **Ref**   34345

Copies to   Managers and Supervisors   **Date**   7 July 1997

Subject   COMPUTERISATION OF ACCOUNTING RECORDS

Please attend a meeting on 14 July in the Conference Room. Attendance is
vital as the new system comes on line on 1 September. Summary details of
the new system are attached.

enc

a completed memorandum

INTERNAL COMMUNICATIONS – THE NOTE

One of the most common forms of communication within an organisation is the *note.* This can be:

- an informal written note, passing on a message or an instruction
- an e-mail message
- a telephone message (some organisations use preprinted telephone message pads)

The importanty elements of a written note are

- the name of the person who is sending the note
- the name of the person who is to receive the note
- the time and date that the note is written
- a clearly stated message
- a clear indication of any action to be taken as a result of the message

Examine the examples set out below and see how they contain all these elements.

```
To Tim Blackstock,
Order Processing

Please remember to allow PDT
Ltd an extra 10% trade discount
on invoices this month.

John Tregennick, Sales
01.04.97    10.30
```

```
           TELEPHONE MESSAGE

TO      Karin Schmidt, Accounts
FROM    H Khan, Sales
DATE    2 April 1997
TIME    12.30

Please ring Jim Stoat at RF
Electronics - he is complaining
that they have not received a
credit note for returned damaged
stock (order ref 823423).

Please treat urgently - he is
not very happy!

HK
```

THE LETTER

When you deal with business letters you will see that the appearance and format of each letter is in a uniform 'house' style, a style which identifies that business, and is common to all letters that it sends. The letter will normally be on standard printed stationery showing the name, address and details of the business, and will be set out with headings, paragraphs, signatures – the 'elements' of the letter – in a uniform way.

There are a number of different ways of setting out the text of a letter. The most of common of these – the 'fully blocked' style is illustrated and explained on the next two pages.

characteristics of a fully blocked letter

- the most commonly used style of letter

- all the lines start at the left margin

- the use of open punctuation, ie there is no punctuation, except in the main body of the letter, which uses normal punctuation

- paragraphs are divided by a space, and are not indented

- a fully blocked letter is easy to type as all the lines are set uniformly to the left margin

elements of the letter

The explanations which follow refer to the illustration of the letter on page 303.

printed letterhead　　The name and address of the business is normally pre-printed, and must be up-to-date.

reference　　The reference on the letter illustrated –DH/SB/69 – is a standard format

- DH (Derek Hunt), the writer

- SB (Sally Burgess), the secretary

- 69, the number of the file where Mr Smart's correspondence is kept

If you need to quote the reference of a letter to which you are replying, the references will be quoted as follows: Your ref TR/FG/45 Our ref DH/SB/69.

date	The date is typed in date (number), month (word), year (number) order.
recipient	The name and address of the person to whom the letter is sent. This section of the letter may be displayed in the window of a window envelope, so it is essential that it is accurate.
salutation	'Dear Sir. . . Dear Madam' if you know the person's name and title (ie Mr, Mrs, Miss, Ms) use it, but check that it is correct – a misspelt name or an incorrect title will ruin an otherwise competent letter.
heading	The heading sets out the subject matter of the letter – it will concentrate the reader's mind.
body	The body of the letter is an area where the message of the letter is set out. The text must be • laid out in short precise paragraphs and short clear sentences • start with a point of reference (eg referring to an invoice) • set out the message in a logical sequence • be written in plain English – but avoid 'slang' expressions and, equally, avoid 'posh' words. • finish with a clear indication of the next step to be taken (eg please telephone, please arrange appointment, please buy our products, please pay our invoice).
complimentary close	The complimentary close (signing off phrase) must be consistent with the salutation: 'Dear Sir/Dear Madam' followed by 'Yours faithfully' 'Dear Mr Sutton/Dear Ms Jones' followed by 'Yours sincerely'.
name and job title	It is essential for the reader to know the name of the person who sent the letter, and that person's job title, because a reply will need to be addressed to a specific person.
enclosures	If there are enclosures with the letter, the abbreviation 'enc' or 'encl' is used at the bottom of the letter.

Wyvern Electrical Services Limited
107 High Street
Mereford MR1 9SZ

Tel 01605 675365 Fax 01605 675576 Email dh@wyvern.u-net.com

reference   Ref DH/SB/69

date   15 December 1997

name and
address of   J D Smart Esq
recipient   23 Pedmore Close
of letter   Sinton Green
Mereford MR4 7ER

salutation   Dear Mr Smart

heading   Invoice 8288 £1,589.50

We note from our records that we have not yet received
payment of our invoice 8288 dated 30 September 1997. Our
up-to-date statement of account is enclosed.

body of
the letter   Our payment terms were strictly 30 days from date of the
invoice. We shall be grateful if you will settle the
overdue £1,589.50 without further delay.

We look forward to receiving your cheque.

close   Yours sincerely

signature   *D Hunt*

name and
job title   Derek Hunt
of sender   Accounts Manager

enclosure
indicator   enc

a business letter – chasing up an unpaid invoice

TYPES OF BUSINESS LETTER

Different types of business letter require different treatment. We will look at four situations and in each case give an examples of how the text of the letter might read:

- providing information
- chasing a debt
- making a complaint
- dealing with a complaint

a letter providing information

The body of a letter providing information in answer to enquiry will be structured in a number of stages:

1   Refer to the original enquiry, eg 'Further to your telephone enquiry/visit/letter' and give the enquiry a date ... 'of 1 April.'

2   Provide the information, either in the text, or by enclosing promotional literature, eg a catalogue.

3   Finish the text of the letter on a positive note or 'selling' note, eg 'Please let us know if we can be of further help' ... 'We look forward to your order' ... 'If you wish to order the goods, please contact Mr Eden in our Sales Department, telephone 01908 384983.'

Here is an extract from a letter following a telephone enquiry to a bathroom centre. Note that the text is not particularly lengthy, but is polite and to the point. It follows the three stages set out above.

Dear Mr Knott

Shower Enclosures

Thank you for your telephone enquiry today.

I am now pleased to enclose a brochure and price list for the Niagara range of shower enclosures.

If you require further information, please do not hesitate to give me a call.

Yours sincerely

J Waterman

J Waterman
Sales Executive

---

a letter chasing a debt

This type of letter is used by an accounts department or by a sole trader chasing up overdue invoices. Often the letter will be a 'set' letter, already formatted on a word processor. There may be a number of set letters on file: a gentle reminder, a firm reminder, a threat of legal action and a formal demand.

Each letter is set out in a number of stages:

1   Details of the amount owing is clearly stated: the amount itself and the date of the original invoice(s). Sometimes a copy invoice(s) will be included in the letter to avoid the common problem of the customer claiming that the original invoice has been lost!

Mention will often be made of the fact that statements of account have also been sent.

2   The terms of the invoice will be stated and the fact that the terms have not been complied with will be stressed.

3   Payment will be firmly requested – often a time limit will be stated.

4   Sometimes it may be necessary to threaten what will happen if the money is not received, eg 'If we do not receive settlement by this date we regret we will have no alternative but to place the matter in the hands of our solicitors.'

Here is an example of a chaser for a long overdue invoice.

---

31 March 1998

Dear Mr Khan

Invoice 23846 £1,250

We note from our records that invoice 23846 (copy enclosed) for £1,250, dated 1 December 1997, has not yet been settled.

The terms of this invoice were strictly 30 days and therefore it is well overdue.

We shall be grateful if you will kindly settle this amount by return of post.

Yours sincerely

N Wakefield

N Wakefield
Accounts Manager

a letter making a complaint

This type of letter sometimes has to be written: goods supplied may be faulty or the bank may have made a mistake. The important point about this type of letter is that it must be polite and factually accurate. You may feel extremely angry or upset about the situation, but this must not show in the letter.

The letter will follow set stages:

1   The details of the problem must be set out in full. If goods are involved, the order number must be quoted, if an invoice is wrong, the invoice number must be referred to, and so on. The actual problem must be set out in strictly factual form … not 'the carrier you used was so hopeless that the parcel was mangled on arrival' but 'the goods (delivery note 3477) were received damaged.'

2   Explain how the problem has inconvenienced you – again in factual terms.

3   State what action you are looking for to remedy the situation.

Here is an example of a letter to a bank. The writer has found a number of errors on the business account bank statement.

Dear Sir

<u>Account 12039834 Bank Statement 120</u>

We have just received our bank statement dated 31 March 1997 and note the following errors:

Cheque 894439 for £350 was paid on 11 March. We stopped payment of this cheque on 10 March.

A standing order for £120 to the Martley Chamber of Commerce was paid on 3 March as well as on 3 February. This was an annual standing order due to be paid at the beginning of February each year.

I shall be grateful if you will look into these matters and refund the amounts to the bank account as soon as possible.

Yours faithfully

N Wakefield

N Wakefield
Accounts Manager

a letter making an apology

If you receive a letter of complaint you are likely to have to write a letter of apology. There are a number of points to bear in mind:

- get the facts right first – the person making the complaint may be in the wrong and may be distorting the truth!

- decide what is to be done to put the situation right – refer to a superior authority if necessary

- when writing the apology be polite, but do not overdo it – if you are over-apologetic the reader will lose all respect for you!

The letter will follow set stages:

1 Acknowledge receipt of the complaint.

2 Acknowledge the problem and apologise (but not too much). Do not go into long explanations of how the problem arose – the reader will not be interested.

3 Explain what you are going to do to put the matter right.

4 Conclude with a further brief apology.

Here is a letter a clothes supplier might write when a shop has not been sent the correct colour T shirts.

Dear Mrs Lockwood

<u>Purchase Order 1283892</u>

Thank you for your fax of 11 March pointing out that we had supplied the wrong colour T shirts on your Purchase Order 1283892.

As we stated on the telephone, we expect delivery of the red T shirts into our warehouse on 17 March. We have therefore arranged for our carrier to deliver the red T shirts on 18 March and to collect the incorrect ones at the same time.

We apologise for the inconvenience this has caused you.

Yours sincerely

A Gaffe

Ann Gaffe
Sales Manager

**CHAPTER
SUMMARY**

- Communicating for accounting involves being able to access a wide variety of data which is both paper-based and maintained in electronic (computer) records.

- Data is normally maintained for the following accounting areas: banking, sales ledger management, purchases and stock.

- Filing systems can be organised in alphabetic, numeric and date order systems.

- Other sources of data include reference books, Web sites, Viewdata, microfiche and microfilm.

- When information is extracted it needs to be accurate, appropriate and it needs to be communicated to the right person.

- Keeping to deadlines is important when communicating information.

- There are a number of different forms of written communication which are used both within an organisation and also when dealing with outsiders.

- The memorandum is a formal written note used within an organisation; it may be typed, wordprocessed or handwritten. Memoranda may also sent by internal e-mail. Examples of its use include giving information, asking for information, giving instructions and recording.

- Informal written notes (and e-mail messages) are also widely used for communicating information. It is important that they record the date and time of writing. They range from informal scribbled messages to the pre-printed telephone message.

- The written letter, sent by post or by fax, is still a widely used form of business communication. Letters can be used for a variety of purposes in the context of accounting, including giving information, making a complaint, writing an apology and chasing debts.

**KEY
TERMS**

Web site	an external source of data maintained on a computer and accessed through a computer
Viewdata	a source of data accessed through the telephone and viewed on-screen
microfiche	a sheet of film containing pages of data which can be read on a special reader
microfilm	a continuous strip of film containing pages of data which can be read on a special reader
salutation	the 'Dear Sir' type of greeting at the beginning of a letter
complimentary close	the 'Yours sincerely' type of ending to a letter

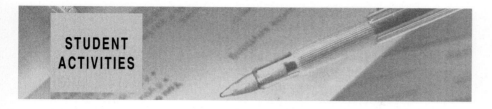

STUDENT ACTIVITIES

18.1 State three types of accounting data that may be used in communicating within a business.

18.2 What forms of back-up are needed for computer-based filing systems and why are they necessary?

18.3 Give two examples of each of the following filing systems: alphabetic, numeric, date order. In each case state why these systems have been chosen.

18.4 What is the difference between

(a) a Web site and Viewdata?

(b) microfilm and microfiche?

18.5 It is 14.30 and you feel very ill after a curry you had at lunchtime. You need to tell your supervisor Ms Helga Thurmann (who is out at a meeting) that you are going home. You still have the monthly statements to print out from the computer for despatch today and also need to list the cheques received ready for banking. Write her a suitable note – use your own name and today's date.

18.6 You are an Accounts Supervisor and you need to circulate to all the Sales Managers in the business a list of the customers who are more than 2 months behind in settling their accounts. These customers should be referred to the Accounts Manager before any further credit sales are made. You are to write a suitable memorandum, using your own name and today's date.

Note: you do not need to produce the list (which has been produced on your computer).

18.7 Draft a letter chasing up an overdue invoice. The letter is a 'gentle' reminder and follows previous statements of account. Complete the letter with details of a specimen invoice. The letter is for signature by you as Accounts Manager.

18.8 You have just received a bank statement from The National Bank, 10 High Street, Mereford, MR1 5FD, dated 31 December. You notice the following problems:

(a) A direct debit for £50 to Allied Insurance was paid on 15 December. On 1 December you had written to the bank cancelling the direct debit.

(b) On 31 December you were charged £125.65 in overdraft interest. According to your calculations the sum should have been approximately £75.

Draft a suitable letter to the Manager of the bank. The letter is for signature by you as Accounts Manager.

18.9 You are an Accounts Supervisor in the Accounts Department of Janus Fabrics. You receive the following e-mail message from your Customer Services Department on 1 April:

'Mrs Joan Pearce of Lizard Designs telephoned. She is furious. She placed an urgent customer order for 25 square metres of Roma velvet curtain fabric, colour burgundy, and has only received 15 square metres. I have sent a further 10 square metres today . Please write to her - she is a valued customer and needs keeping happy.'

You check your records and find that on her purchase order (no. 6234) the figure '25' could be read as '15' because the first digit is indistinct. Write her a suitable letter, using your own name and today's date. Her address is Lizard Designs, 13 Regency Passage, Mereford, MR2 6DA.

19 BUSINESS CONTRACTS

this chapter covers . . .

This chapter explains what a contract is, and how it affects everyday business dealings. It covers:

- the definition of a contract

- the agreement in a contract – the offer and the acceptance

- the bargain in a contract – the need for both parties to provide something (known as 'consideration')

- the need for both sides to a contract to intend it to be legally binding

- breach of contract – what to do when things go wrong

- types of contract, eg sale contracts

- protection given in law when someone purchases goods or services

NVQ REQUIREMENTS

unit 2 RECORDING AND ACCOUNTING FOR CREDIT TRANSACTIONS

knowledge and understanding – the business environment

❑ Basic law of contract

A CONTRACT DEFINED

Part of your course involves the understanding of the legal framework which enables buying and selling to take place and which states what can happen if there is a dispute. The agreement between the parties is known as a *contract.*

what is a contract?

a contract is a legally binding agreement enforceable in a court of law

Contracts, which may be in writing, or by word of mouth (oral), are agreements between two parties. Examples include:

- a written contract which you sign if you buy a house
- a written contract for a loan agreement if you borrow money
- a written contract of employment
- an oral contract if you buy goods in a shop
- an oral contract if you order goods over the telephone
- an oral contract if you hire a decorator to paint your house

In each case somebody does something for which some kind of payment is made. A contract is *an agreement with legal consequences* because if the work done is not satisfactory, or if the payment is not made, the wronged party can take the other person to court for *breach of contract.*

You may rightly wonder how all this affects you in the workplace. The answer is that the principles of contract affect any person carrying out normal business activities. For example if you quote an incorrect price to a customer, they may be able to hold your business to that price, under the terms of the contract of sale. If you fail to finish a job for a customer, they may be able to go to court to obtain a court order for your business to complete the work under the contract.

the three elements of contract

There are three elements which are common and essential to all contracts:

agreement – an offer and an acceptance

bargain – some value (consideration) passes

intention to create legal relations – the agreement is commercial

THE AGREEMENT - OFFER AND ACCEPTANCE

the offer

A firm and clear offer must be made either to a single party, a group, or to the world at large. In a famous legal case in 1893, a manufacturer of medicines (the Carbolic Smoke Ball Company) advertised a patented smoke ball and promised to pay a £100 reward to any person who contracted a specified illness having used the ball three times a day for two weeks. A Mrs Carlill used the ball for eight weeks and still contracted 'flu. She claimed her £100, the company refused, and she had to take the matter to the court which ruled that she should be granted her £100, as the offer of £100 had been to the "whole world" and needed no communicated acceptance from Mrs Carlill. It formed part of a valid contract which the company had to honour. Note that this is *not* the same situation as an *advertised price* which is not an offer but information which will enable a purchase – the contract – to be made (see below).

invitation to treat

An offer is quite different from an *invitation to treat* which is an invitation for a person to make an offer. Goods on supermarket shelves are an invitation for a customer to take them to the checkout where that customer can offer to purchase them at the price indicated at the checkout, which is where the contract takes place. That is the reason why shop tills indicate the price for each item, normally on an illuminated display; it is also the reason why a shop is not obliged to sell the goods at the price shown on the shelves.

---

practical example - invitation to treat

problem
Basil sees a holiday advertised in the local paper for £50. He telephones the travel company which tells him that the figure is a printing error – it should have been £500. Basil is angry and insists on booking his week in Menorca for £50. The problem is, does a contract exist on the basis of the £50 quoted?

answer
Basil has no rights here. There is no contract because the £50 quoted is only *an invitation to treat*, an invitation for Basil to make an agreement for booking the holiday. The company will clearly not agree to £50 for a week in Menorca!

termination of an offer

An offer may only be accepted while it is still open for acceptance. An offer may be terminated in the following circumstances:

- the time limit (if there is one) expires; if there is no time limit the offer lapses after a reasonable period of time

- the offeror – the person making the offer – may revoke (cancel) the offer

- an offer may be rejected by the making of a counter-offer; for instance, if you offer your car for sale for £1,500 and someone offers you £1,350, that is a counter-offer

- by acceptance or rejection of the offer

acceptance of an offer

Acceptance of an offer must be firm and unambiguous; it may be in spoken words, written form or even implied by action. Acceptance cannot be assumed from silence on the part of the person to whom the offer is made. For instance, if you say "I offer you my car for £1,500; if I have not heard from you within a week I will assume the deal is done," there is no acceptance. The offeree may go on holiday, or forget it even happened. Acceptance must also be *unconditional*. Any new term introduced - "I will agree to buy your car as long as the wing is resprayed" - amounts to a counter-offer (see above) and revokes the original offer.

practical example - conditional acceptance

problem
Basil works for Martley Garden Centre and has recently sent a quotation for a fountain to Mrs Waters: the cost will be £250.00 plus VAT and the fountain will have to be ordered from an outside supplier. Mrs Waters writes back saying she wants to accept the price, but the fountain must be delivered before the end of the month. Is there a valid contract between Mrs Waters and the garden centre?

answer
No. There is no contract because the acceptance has been conditional. *Acceptance must be unconditional.* Any new term introduced amounts to a counter-offer: "I will pay £250 plus VAT if the fountain is delivered by the end of the month."

The term "subject to contract", often seen on estate agents' boards, means that the terms of the offer to the offeree are agreeable, but have not been finally accepted. The two parties involved have agreed to draw up a formal contract for signature at a later date. There is no binding contract at this point.

communication of acceptance

The rules relating to communication of acceptance are largely dictated by what is required by the offer:

- the acceptance must normally be communicated to the person making the offer
- if the offer requires acceptance by a specific means (letter/fax/verbal message) then that means must be used

the postal rule

An acceptance by post is effective as long as the letter of acceptance is correctly addressed, correctly stamped and actually posted

The time of acceptance is when the letter is posted (not when it is received). Given that letters may be delayed or lost in the post, this rule may seem unjust to the offeror! The postal rule only applies to an acceptance, it does not apply to a posted offer which must reach the offeree.

practical example - acceptance by post

problem
On 1 April Cotheridge Conifers telephones Basil at Martley Garden Centre to offer a job lot of 150 Leylandii trees at a knock-down price of £1.50 each. Basil needs time to think about this and says he will drop a line in the post. On 3 April he posts a reply to Cotheridge Conifers accepting the offer and placing an order for the trees. On 5 April the order is received. The question is, what is the date on which the contract was formed?

answer
3 April. The postal rule states that the date of posting of an acceptance of an offer is the effective date of the contract.

THE BARGAIN: CONSIDERATION

definition of consideration

A valid contract involves a bargain, a passing of value, known in law as consideration. If a business buys goods there is a two way process involved:

- the supplier promises to deliver the goods
- the buyer agrees to pay for them

The parties involved are:

- the promisor, the supplier that promises to supply the goods
- the promisee, the buyer who has to make payment

The consideration here is the payment, the price paid for the service provided. The principle is simple in itself, but there are a number of rules which relate to consideration.

consideration must be sufficient

Consideration must by law be sufficient. This means that:

- it must have value, although the value need not be adequate in some eyes; for example, you could sell this book for 5p; many would consider the amount to be inadequate, but the 5p still has value and is therefore consideration
- it must be sufficient, ie it must be in return for the promise; money due for some other reason or obligation is not sufficient consideration

consideration must move from the promisee

This legal phrase means, in effect, that the person who is promised goods or a service must themselves provide payment if the promise is to be enforceable as a contract. If you buy goods, you must make the payment. If someone else pays for you (an unlikely event!) you cannot take the supplier to court if the goods do not arrive.

consideration cannot be past

This legal phrase means that the consideration should not precede the promise. If you mend someone's car without any mention of payment, and the car owner the following week promises to give you £5, and subsequently refuses to pay you, there is no contract. The promise of payment followed the good turn done, consideration (the repair) was past as it had taken place the previous week.

practical example - consideration

problem

Basil promises to cut down some trees for a friend free of charge one weekend. Unfortunately Basil cuts down the wrong trees. His friend is very upset and says he will sue Basil. Can he? Is there a contract?

answer

No. There is no contract because there is no consideration - no money has been paid. Basil has made a mistake but he cannot be sued.

THE INTENTION TO CREATE LEGAL RELATIONS

A contract is an agreement involving consideration which the parties intend to be legally binding. In other words the parties entering a contract can reasonably expect the agreement to be enforced in a court of law if the necessity arises. The law assumes:

- commercial agreements are intended to be legally binding
- social and domestic arrangements are not intended to be legally binding

In short, if a man enters a contract to buy your car and then, without reason, refuses to pay for it, you can take him to court. If you ask a friend out for the evening, promising to take him or her out for a meal, and your friend doesn't turn up, you can hardly take court action. The sale of a car involves the intention to create legal relations, the invitation out does not.

BREACH OF CONTRACT

A contract normally contains certain terms which must be fulfilled as part of the agreement. If a person breaks one of those terms, that person is in *breach of contract.* For example, if a supplier undertakes to supply goods, it must send the goods on the due date, and in turn expects the goods to be paid for by a certain time. If the customer does not pay, he or she is in breach of contract and may be taken to court for damages (money compensation).

Contract terms may be classified as follows:

express terms	explicitly stated terms which are binding on both parties to the contract
conditions	fundamental terms of the contract which, if broken, will enable the injured party to reject the contract and to go to court to sue for damages
warranties	minor terms which if broken can be cause for an action for damages for loss suffered; the contract, however, remains in force
implied terms	terms which are not stated, but which are implied by trade custom or by law; for instance, goods sold should be of "merchantable quality," in accordance with the Sale of Goods Act 1979.

In short:

- express terms are written into the contract; implied terms are not
- conditions are important terms, warranties are less important

---

practical example - breach of contract

problem

Martley Garden Centre orders 1500 flower arrangements from a London wholesale supplier for delivery two days before Mothers Day. Unfortunately, because of a transport strike they arrive during the week following Mothers Day. Martley Garden Centre threatens to sue the supplier. Is the garden centre within its rights to do so?

answer

There is a clear breach of contract – the delivery date is a term of the contract and has not been met. Martley Garden Centre could sue.

CONTRACTS OF SALE

When a business orders goods, the order is normally placed on a purchase order , and the goods are sent with a delivery note followed by an invoice. It is rare for a formal written contract of sale to be drawn up, except in the case of large items of equipment or a long-term contract of supply. What normally happens is that the supplier will send a copy of its "Terms and Conditions" to the buyer at the time of intended purchase, either as a separate document, or printed on the back of the quotation. If the buyer does not object to these terms and conditions, or offer an alternative set of terms and conditions, these are then assumed to be the terms and conditions of the contract.

The following terms and conditions are typical – as you will see they are very much weighted in favour of the supplier:

specifications	the supplier can change the specifications of its products without notice
prices	prices can change without notice, they exclude VAT and carriage
orders	orders (and cancellations) must be notified in writing
damaged goods	notification of goods received damaged must reach the supplier within three days of delivery, or the supplier will accept no responsibility for damage
return of goods	goods may not be returned without the written permission of the supplier
settlement terms	strictly cash with order, credit accounts settled within 30 days of invoice date, or as otherwise agreed

risk	the risk of damage or loss to the goods while in transit will be borne by the buyer
retention of title	the goods will remain the property of the supplier until they are paid for; if the buyer goes into liquidation (goes 'bust') the supplier can enter the premises of the buyer and seize back the goods if they are not paid for

You will see from these terms and conditions that the supplier has the advantage in dictating terms. If there were a dispute, the terms and conditions would be upheld in a court of law. It would be possible for the buyer to object when the order was being placed, but it would depend on how anxious the supplier was to sell whether or not the objections were accepted!

SELLING AND STATUTE LAW

Statute law is law set down in an Act of Parliament.

There are a number of statutes which govern the way in which goods and services are sold, and they obviously affect the way in which businesses operate. The principal statutes are the Trades Descriptions Act, the Sale of Goods Act and the Unfair Contract Terms Act.

Trades Descriptions Act

The Trade Descriptions Act makes it a criminal offence:

• to make false statements about goods offered for sale

• to make misleading statements about services

Examples of offences therefore include:

• stating that a car for sale has clocked up 15,000 miles, when in fact the figure is 25,000 miles

• making a misleading statement about the price of goods, eg saying 'Now only £49.95, was £99.95' when it has only ever sold for £69.95

• making a misleading statement about a service, eg 'our dry cleaning is guaranteed to remove every stain' when it does not, or 'our apartments are within easy reach of the sea' when they are fifteen miles away

Sale of Goods Act

This Act states that you are entitled to expect any goods that you buy from a shop to be:

of 'satisfactory quality'

This means they must meet the standard that a 'reasonable' person would expect given the description and the price.

'fit for the purpose'

The goods must do what they are supposed to do, or what the shop claims they can do: an umbrella should keep the rain out, a watch should keep accurate time.

'as described'

The goods must be what they are claimed to be: a 'leather coat' must be made of leather, a 'stereo TV' must provide stereo sound.

If any of these three conditions is not met, the purchaser is entitled to a full or a part refund, depending on how soon the fault appears, how serious it is and how quickly the matter is taken up. Note also the following practical points:

- the buyer can accept a replacement, but can also insist on a refund if a replacement is not wanted

- the buyer does not have to accept a credit note for spending on other purchases

- a shop is not entitled to put up a notice saying "No Refunds!"

---

practical example - Sale of Goods Act

problem

Jason buys a watering can from Martley Garden Centre but finds that it leaks. He returns it to the Garden Centre, asking for a refund. The sales assistant refuses, pointing to a sign on the counter which states "No refunds given!" What is Jason's position?

answer

Jason *is* entitled to a refund. The Sale of Goods Act clearly states that goods must be of 'satisfactory quality.' The shop has no right to try and avoid statute law.

Unfair Contract Terms Act

Any organisation that tries to insist on *unfair* terms (eg in small print on the back of a sales contract) may be in breach of the Unfair Contract Terms Act. This would protect, for example, holidaymakers who are not put up in the hotel they booked because the small print stated that the holiday company had the right to move them to another resort. This would be seen as an 'unfair term' and would enable the holidaymaker to seek compensation. In short, a business cannot 'contract out' through the small print.

- A contract is an agreement between two people ('parties') with legal consequences – if something goes wrong with the agreement, the matter can go to court if necessary.

- A contract therefore has to contain three elements: an agreement made between two parties, a bargain struck involving each party giving up something of value, and an intention that the agreement is a legal one.

- A contract involves an offer being made and accepted. An offer may be made to an individual, a group of people or to everyone. For a contract to exist, an offer must be accepted clearly and without any conditions attached.

- The bargain in a contract – the passing of something of value – must involve both parties and must follow the contract.

- The intention behind a contract should be to form a legal agreement; arrangements such as 'doing someone a favour' do not form a contract.

- If one of the parties breaks the terms of a contract – eg does not pay, does not do the work required – the matter can be taken to court as a breach of contract, either for damages (money compensation) or to ensure the work is done.

- Sellers sometimes draw up a contract of sale, the terms of which will apply to the transaction. Often these terms are very much in favour of the seller. These contracts usually apply to high value items or services. Normally buyers and sellers do not have a covering written contract of sale.

- Statute law (laws passed in Parliament) protects buyers of goods and services. Examples include the Trades Descriptions Act and the Sale of Goods Act.

contract	a legally binding agreement enforceable in a court of law
parties	the people directly involved in a contract
consideration	value which is passed between the parties to a contract, eg money, doing a job
invitation to treat	an invitation for someone to make an offer, eg priced goods on a shop shelf
subject to contract	the stage reached when the terms of an offer are said to be acceptable but the final agreement has not been finalised
postal rule	if an acceptance of an offer is made by post, the contract comes into being when the acceptance is correctly posted

breach of contract	the situation where one of the parties to a contract breaks one or more of the terms of the contract
damages	money compensation awarded in a court of law

STUDENT
ACTIVITIES

19.1 Write down a sentence defining a contract – use your own words.

19.2 State the three elements of a contract, writing down a sentence describing each of the three elements.

19.3 State in each of the following situations whether a contract exists. In each case give reasons for your answer.

(a) You order goods over the phone and agree a price but do not issue a purchase order.

(b) You order goods by sending a signed purchase order by fax to the supplier who then despatches them.

(c) You do a job for someone free of charge and as a favour. She later gives you £10 but then complains that the job has not been done properly.

(d) You do a job for a friend and agree a price, but after you have done the job he refuses to pay you.

19.4 You go to a local DIY store and see a power drill on the shelves with a price sticker of £39.95. You think it is a good buy and take it to the till. The cashier says that the price is now £49.95; the lower price was for a special offer that has now expired. Is the cashier right to insist on charging the higher price or can you insist that the contract is based on the lower price being the offer price? Give *legal reasons* for your answer.

19.5 You fill in an order form for some stationery. The order form is contained in the catalogue sent to you by the supplier. At the bottom of the form you write in red "We are only placing this order on the basis that we will receive the goods by 4 April." The order form says "Allow 28 days for delivery." The date is 15 March. Is this a valid acceptance of the offer for sale made by the stationery company in its catalogue?

19.6 You telephone for a mail order catalogue on 15 March, complete the order form on 16 March and post the order form on 17 March. On what date is the contract formed?

19.7 You buy a word processor from Zenith Office Supplies. Unfortunately the machine will not work – it appears to be damaged. You take it back to Zenith. The salesman says "Sorry - nothing we can do – you will have to get in touch with the manufacturer!" Is he right? What is the legal position?

19.8 You buy an office chair from Summit Office Furniture. It is advertised as having an adjustable back. When you get it back to your office, you find it does not. You telephone the supplier to complain and are told "Sorry we can't change it – you saw what it was like when you picked it up." Is the supplier right?

ANSWERS TO STUDENT ACTIVITIES

CHAPTER 1: INTRODUCTION TO ACCOUNTING

1.1 (c)

1.2 revenue: (a) (c) (d); capital: (b) (e)

1.3 cash: (a) (b) (d) credit: (c) (e)

1.4 See key terms page 14.

1.5 Assets minus liabilities equals capital. See pages 9 - 10. The capital would increase.

1.6 See page 11.

1.7 (a) Jo's pay packet, income tax and national insurance will be incorrect; if Jo does not check the payslip, the error may go undetected.

  (b) The invoice will be incorrect, the customer may exceed the credit limit, the business may lose the customer!

  (c) The bank account may go overdrawn, the business may be charged extra interest and fees, cheques may be 'bounced' resulting in the withdrawal of credit by suppliers.

CHAPTER 2: DOCUMENTS – SELLING ON CREDIT

2.1 (a) delivery note   (b) returns note   (c) invoice
   (d) statement   (e) credit note   (f) purchase order

2.2

	total	discount	net total	VAT	invoice total
	£	£	£	£	£
(a)	160.00	32.00	128.00	22.40	150.40
(b)	400.00	80.00	320.00	56.00	376.00
(c)	40.00	none	40.00	7.00	47.00
(d)	8000.00	1600.00	6400.00	1120.00	7520.00

2.3

	net total	discount deducted	total after cash discount	VAT	invoice total*
(a)	128.00	3.20	124.80	21.84	149.84
(b)	320.00	8.00	312.00	54.60	374.60
(c)	40.00	1.00	39.00	6.82	46.82
(d)	6400.00	160.00	6240.00	1092.00	7492.00

*Remember that the VAT is normally added to the total before deduction of cash discount.

2.4 Net monthly = payment of net amount one month after the invoice date.

E & OE = Errors and Omissions Excepted (a supplier has the right to correct an invoice after issue).

Carriage paid = Delivery costs paid to the delivery address (contrast with Ex-Works).

2.5 Examples: Purchase order number, delivery note number, invoice number, stock code, account number, credit note number.
The main importance of coding is for accurate cross referencing.

2.6 The problems are the urgency and the need for accuracy. If the wrong goods are sent the problems will be compounded.

Solutions: telephone or e-mail, and fax a copy of the order pointing out the error.

Best and quickest solution - telephone.

Important point – ask for a replacement corrected order to be sent (marked 'confirmation' to avoid duplication), preferably by fax so that a further check can be made. This is to make sure your position is strong, just in case the customer gets it wrong again! This type of problem can be sorted out at assistant level, but should be reported to the supervisor when he/she returns.

2.7 (a) Incorrect discount rate applied (10%), wrong addition for total. Goods total should be £76.00, VAT £13.30 and final total £89.30.

(b) Total before discount should be £250.00. VAT has also been rounded up (should have been rounded down to £35.43). Corrected figures: goods total £225.00 (after deduction of 10% discount), VAT £39.37, final total £264.37.

2.8

	Net amount £	VAT £	Total £
(a)	40.00	7.00	47.00
(b)	34,613.60	6,057.38	40,670.98
(c)	34.03	5.95	39.98
(d)	80.00	14.00	94.00
(e)	0.40	0.07	0.47
(f)	1.03	0.17	1.20

CHAPTER 3: DOCUMENTS – BUYING ON CREDIT

3.1   (a)   purchase order

(b)   delivery note

(c)   goods received note

(d)   remittance advice

(e)   invoice

(f)   returns note

3.2   An unauthorised purchase order cannot be used as the basis for raising an order. The purchase order will have to be returned to the purchaser for signature, or alternatively, if the order is urgent, the purchaser could be contacted and a new order faxed through.

3.3   (d)

3.4   A returns note accompanies any goods returned by the purchaser to the seller; a credit note is issued by the seller when credit has to be given to the purchaser, eg for returned goods. Hence a credit note is usually issued when a returns note is received.

3.5   The buyer would effectively be overcharged. The buyer would request a credit note. Under no circumstances should the invoice be altered.

3.6   The errors are:

(a)   the goods were delivered to the wrong address

(b)   an incorrect customer discount has been applied (10% instead of 15%)

(c)   the wrong goods were sent (product code 4574 instead of 4573)

The total should have been £95 less 15% discount = £80.75 plus VAT of £14.13 = £94.88

The letter should point out these errors and state that the disks are being returned for credit.

CHAPTER 4: ACCOUNTING RECORDS

4.1   (a)

4.2   (c)

4.3 • Start with a *prime document*. For credit transactions, the prime documents are:
  – sales invoices
  – purchases invoices
  – credit notes issued
  – credit notes received
- Enter the prime document in the appropriate *primary accounting record*, which is the first accounting book – or book of original entry – in which the prime document is recorded and summarised. For credit transactions, the primary accounting records are:
  – sales day book
  – purchases day book
  – sales returns day book
  – purchases returns day book
- Transfer the information from the prime document and the primary accounting record into the *double-entry accounts.* For credit transactions the ledgers and accounts used are:
  – sales ledger, which contains separate accounts for each debtor (customer)
  – purchases ledger, which contains separate accounts for each creditor (supplier)
  – general (or nominal) ledger, which contains – amongst other accounts – sales account, purchases account, and Value Added Tax account

  When payment is made to creditors or received from debtors, the transaction will also be recorded in cash account or bank account (collectively these two accounts form the ledger called *cash book*).

4.4 • Book-keeping is organised on the basis of a number of *accounts* which record the money amounts of financial transactions.
- Accounts are kept in the names of debtors (customers) and creditors (suppliers), and also for other transactions.
- Each account has a debit side (on the left), and a credit side (on the right). An alternative style of account has three money columns: debit, credit and balance – this is known as a *running balance account.*
- The principle of double-entry book-keeping is that, for every financial transaction, two entries are made, usually in different accounts:
  – one account is debited } with the money amount
  – one account is credited   of the financial transaction
- The debit entry is made on the left-hand side of the account which gains value, or records an asset, or an expense.
- The credit entry is made on the right-hand side of the account which gives value, or records a liability, or an income item.
- Thus, with double-entry book-keeping the money amount of the debit entries is equal to the money amount of the credit entries.

4.5
(a)	J Williams, a creditor	purchases ledger
(b)	purchases account	general (or nominal) ledger
(c)	H Wilson, a debtor	sales ledger
(d)	sales account	general (or nominal) ledger
(e)	cash account	cash book
(f)	VAT account	general (or nominal) ledger

4.6

prime document
Source document for the accounting records; for credit transactions, prime documents are sales invoices, purchases invoices, credit notes issued, credit notes received.

primary accounting record
The first accounting books in which transactions are recorded; for credit transactions, the primary accounting records are sales day book, purchases day book, sales returns day book, purchases returns day book.

double-entry book-keeping
System of book-keeping, organised on the basis of a number of accounts which record the money amounts of financial transactions. Two entries are made for every financial transaction, usually in different accounts:

– one account is debited
– one account is credited
} with the money amount of the financial transaction

With double-entry book-keeping, the money amount of the debit entries is equal to the money amount of the credit entries.

account
Accounts are an integral part of the book-keeping system where the money amounts of financial transactions are recorded. Accounts are kept in the names of debtors (customers) and creditors (suppliers), and also for other transactions such as the receipt and payment of money for various purposes.

An account is debited when it gains value, or records an asset, or an expense. An account is credited when it gives value, or records a liability, or an income item.

ledger
A ledger is a collection of accounts. In a larger book-keeping system the accounts are separated into four main sections:

• sales ledger
• purchases ledger
• cash book
• general (or nominal) ledger

CHAPTER 5: ACCOUNTING FOR CREDIT SALES AND SALES RETURNS

5.1 (a)

5.2 (a)
• The prime documents for credit sales transactions are the sales invoices or copy invoices, that have been checked and authorised.
• The details and amounts of the invoices are entered into the sales day book. In the money columns of the sales day book is recorded:

-    gross column, the final total of each invoice
-    VAT column, the VAT amount shown on each invoice
-    net column, the net ('goods or services total') amount of each invoice

- After the sales day book has been written up for the week or month, it is totalled and the information from it is transferred into the double-entry system.
- The book-keeping entries are:
  -    the amounts from the gross column for each separate transaction are debited to the accounts of the debtors (customers) in the sales ledger
  -    the total of the VAT column is credited to VAT account in the general ledger
  -    the total of the net column is credited to sales account in the general ledger

(b)
- The prime documents for sales returns transactions are credit notes (or copies of credit notes) issued, that have been checked and authorised.
- The details and amounts of the credit notes are entered into the sales returns day book. In the money columns of the sales returns day book is recorded:
  -    gross column, the final total of each credit note
  -    VAT column, the VAT amount shown on each credit note
  -    net column, the net ('goods or services total') amount of each credit note
- After the sales returns day book has been written up for the week or month, it is totalled and the information from it is transferred into the double-entry system.
- The book-keeping entries are:
  -    the amounts from the gross column for each separate transaction are credited to the accounts of the debtors (customers) in the sales ledger
  -    the total of the VAT column is debited to VAT account in the general ledger
  -    the total of the net column is debited to sales returns account in the general ledger

5.3   (a)

Sales Day Book						
Date	Customer	Invoice No	Folio	Gross	VAT	Net
1997				£ p	£ p	£ p
2 Apr	Malvern Stores	4578		64.62	9.62	55.00
4 Apr	Pershore Retailers	4579		76.37	11.37	65.00
7 Apr	E Grainger	4580		32.90	4.90	28.00
10 Apr	P Wilson	4581		68.15	10.15	58.00
11 Apr	M Kershaw	4582		89.30	13.30	76.00
14 Apr	D Lloyd	4583		77.55	11.55	66.00
18 Apr	A Cox	4584		38.77	5.77	33.00
22 Apr	Dines Stores	4585		119.85	17.85	102.00
24 Apr	Malvern Stores	4586		55.22	8.22	47.00
25 Apr	P Wilson	4587		41.12	6.12	35.00
29 Apr	A Cox	4588		96.35	14.35	82.00
30 Apr	Totals for month			760.20	113.20	647.00

(b)

SALES LEDGER

Dr	Malvern Stores		Cr
1997	£ p	1997	£ p
2 Apr Sales	64.62		
24 Apr Sales	55.22		

Dr	Pershore Retailers		Cr
1997	£ p	1997	£ p
4 Apr Sales	76.37		

Dr	E Grainger		Cr
1997	£ p	1997	£ p
7 Apr Sales	32.90		

Dr	P Wilson		Cr
1997	£ p	1997	£ p
10 Apr Sales	68.15		
25 Apr Sales	41.12		

Dr	M Kershaw		Cr
1997	£ p	1997	£ p
11 Apr Sales	89.30		

Dr	D Lloyd		Cr
1997	£ p	1997	£ p
14 Apr Sales	77.55		

Dr	A Cox		Cr
1997	£ p	1997	£ p
18 Apr Sales	38.77		
29 Apr Sales	96.35		

Dr	Dines Stores		Cr
1997	£ p	1997	£ p
22 Apr Sales	119.85		

GENERAL LEDGER

Dr	Sales Account		Cr
1997	£ p	1997	£ p
		30 Apr Sales Day Book	647.00

Dr	Value Added Tax Account		Cr
1997	£ p	1997	£ p
		30 Apr Sales Day Book	113.20

5.4 (a)

Sales Returns Day Book						
Date	Customer	Credit Note No	Folio	Gross	VAT	Net
1997				£ p	£ p	£ p
8 Apr	Pershore Retailers	CN 572		23.50	3.50	20.00
10 Apr	E Grainger	CN 573		32.90	4.90	28.00
16 Apr	D Lloyd	CN 574		38.77	5.77	33.00
28 Apr	Malvern Stores	CN 575		23.50	3.50	20.00
30 Apr	A Cox	CN 576		47.00	7.00	40.00
30 Apr	Totals for month			165.67	24.67	141.00

(b)

SALES LEDGER

Dr	Pershore Retailers		Cr
1997	£ p	1997	£ p
4 Apr Sales	76.37	8 Apr Sales Returns	23.50

Dr	E Grainger		Cr
1997	£ p	1997	£ p
7 Apr Sales	32.90	10 Apr Sales Returns	32.90

Dr	D Lloyd		Cr
1997	£ p	1997	£ p
14 Apr Sales	77.55	16 Apr Sales Returns	38.77

Dr	Malvern Stores		Cr
1997	£ p	1997	£ p
2 Apr Sales	64.62	28 Apr Sales Returns	23.50
24 Apr Sales	55.22		

Dr	A Cox		Cr
1997	£ p	1997	£ p
18 Apr Sales	38.77	30 Apr Sales Returns	47.00
29 Apr Sales	96.35		

GENERAL LEDGER

Dr	Sales Returns Account				Cr
1997		£ p	1997		£ p
30 Apr	Sales Returns Day Book	141.00			

Dr	Value Added Tax Account				Cr
1997		£ p	1997		£ p
30 Apr	Sales Returns Day Book	24.67	30 Apr	Sales Day Book	113.20

CHAPTER 6: ACCOUNTING FOR CREDIT PURCHASES AND PURCHASES RETURNS

6.1 (d)

6.2 (a)

6.3 (a)
- The prime documents for credit purchases transactions are the purchases invoices received from suppliers, that have been checked and authorised.
- The details and amounts of the invoices are entered into the purchases day book. In the money columns of the purchases day book is recorded:
  - gross column, the final total of each invoice
  - VAT column, the VAT amount shown on each invoice
  - net column, the net ('goods or services total') amount of each invoice
- After the purchases day book has been written up for the week or month, it is totalled and the information from it is transferred into the double-entry system.
- The book-keeping entries are:
  - the amounts from the gross column for each separate transaction are credited to the accounts of the creditors (suppliers) in the purchases ledger
  - the total of the VAT column is debited to VAT account in the general ledger
  - the total of the net column is debited to purchases account in the general ledger

(b)
- The prime documents for purchases returns transactions are credit notes received from suppliers, that have been checked and authorised.
- The details and amounts of the credit notes are entered into the purchases returns day book. In the money columns of the purchases returns day book is recorded:
  - gross column, the final total of each credit note
  - VAT column, the VAT amount shown on each credit note
  - net column, the net ('goods or services total') amount of each credit note
- After the purchases returns day book has been written up for the week or month, it is totalled and the information from it is transferred into the double-entry system.
- The book-keeping entries are:
  - the amounts from the gross column for each separate transaction are debited to the

accounts of the creditors (suppliers) in the purchases ledger
- the total of the VAT column is credited to VAT account in the general ledger
- the total of the net column is credited to purchases returns account in the general ledger

6.4   (a)

Purchases Day Book						
Date	Supplier	Invoice No	Folio	Gross	VAT	Net
1997				£ p	£ p	£ p
2 Apr	Severn Supplies	6789		293.75	43.75	250.00
4 Apr	I Johnstone	A241		246.75	36.75	210.00
10 Apr	L Murphy	2456		217.37	32.37	185.00
15 Apr	Mercia Manufacturing	X457		211.50	31.50	180.00
18 Apr	AMC Enterprises	AMC 456		405.37	60.37	345.00
24 Apr	S Green	2846		464.12	69.12	395.00
30 Apr	Totals for month			1,838.86	273.86	1,565.00

(b)

PURCHASES LEDGER

Dr		**Severn Supplies**		Cr
1997	£ p	1997		£ p
		2 Apr	Purchases	293.75

Dr		**I Johnstone**		Cr
1997	£ p	1997		£ p
		4 Apr	Purchases	246.75

Dr		**L Murphy**		Cr
1997	£ p	1997		£ p
		10 Apr	Purchases	217.37

Dr		**Mercia Manufacturing**		Cr
1997	£ p	1997		£ p
		15 Apr	Purchases	211.50

Dr		**AMC Enterprises**		Cr
1997	£ p	1997		£ p
		18 Apr	Purchases	405.37

Dr		S Green			Cr
1997		£ p	1997		£ p
			24 Apr	Purchases	464.12

GENERAL LEDGER

Dr		Purchases Account		Cr
1997		£ p	1997	£ p
30 Apr	Purchases Day Book	1,565.00		

Dr		Value Added Tax Account		Cr
1997		£ p	1997	£ p
30 Apr	Purchases Day Book	273.86		

6.5 (a)

	Purchases Returns Day Book					
Date	Supplier	Credit Note No	Folio	Gross	VAT	Net
1997				£ p	£ p	£ p
7 Apr	Severn Supplies	CN225		58.75	8.75	50.00
14 Apr	L Murphy	X456		94.00	14.00	80.00
21 Apr	AMC Enterprises	C3921		146.87	21.87	125.00
29 Apr	S Green	CN/SG247		79.90	11.90	68.00
30 Apr	Totals for month			379.52	56.52	323.00

(b)

PURCHASES LEDGER

Dr		Severn Supplies				Cr
1997		£ p	1997			£ p
7 Apr	Purchases Returns	58.75	2 Apr	Purchases		293.75

Dr		L Murphy				Cr
1997		£ p	1997			£ p
14 Apr	Purchases Returns	94.00	10 Apr	Purchases		217.37

Dr	AMC Enterprises		Cr
1997		1997	
	£ p		£ p
21 Apr Purchases Returns	146.87	18 Apr Purchases	405.37

Dr	S Green		Cr
1997		1997	
	£ p		£ p
29 Apr Purchases Returns	79.90	24 Apr Purchases	464.12

GENERAL LEDGER

Dr	Purchases Returns Account		Cr
1997		1997	
	£ p		£ p
		30 Apr Purchases Returns Day Book	323.00

Dr	Value Added Tax Account		Cr
1997		1997	
	£ p		£ p
30 Apr Purchases Day Book	273.86	30 Apr Purchases Returns Day Book	56.52

6.6

						Purchases Day Book		
Date	Supplier	Invoice No	Folio	Gross	VAT	Furniture	Carpets	
1997				£ p	£ p	£ p	£ p	
2 Apr	T Table Ltd			1,465.81	218.31	1,247.50		
7 Apr	Eastern Imports			936.24	139.44		796.80	
10 Apr	Minster Carpets Ltd			2,203.40	328.16		1,875.24	
14 Apr	Pegasus Ltd			585.30	87.17	498.13		
16 Apr	United Carpets Ltd			559.55	83.33		476.22	
21 Apr	Gerrard Furniture			977.00	145.51	831.49		
23 Apr	T Table Ltd			762.45	113.55	648.90		
28 Apr	Eastern Imports			1,524.33	227.02		1,297.31	
30 Apr	Totals for month			9,014.08	1,342.49	3,226.02	4,445.57	

CHAPTER 7: FURTHER ASPECTS OF DOUBLE-ENTRY ACCOUNTS

7.1 (c)

7.2 (b)

7.3 *Computer*

- The double-entry book-keeping transaction for the purchase of a computer is:
  - *debit* computer account
  - *credit* cash account or bank account

  (This assumes that the computer has been bought as a fixed asset, ie for use in the business, and that it has been paid for either in cash or by cheque.)

- Thus, the computer account records an asset, while cash/bank account has given value.

- The computer, being an asset, is recorded in the accounts by a debit transaction; the method of paying for it is recorded in cash/bank account by a credit transaction.

Capital

- The double-entry book-keeping transaction for the introduction of capital into a business is:
  - *debit* cash account or bank account
  - *credit* capital account

  (This assumes that the capital was in the form of money rather than other assets.)

- Thus, the cash/bank account has gained value, while capital account records a liability to the owner. It is a liability that is unlikely to be repaid immediately as the business would then be unable to operate.

7.4

	transaction	how the bank sees it	how the business sees it
(a)	a cheque is paid into the bank	credit	debit
(b)	bank charges	debit	credit
(c)	a loan taken out from the bank	debit	credit
(d)	cash is paid into the bank	credit	debit
(e)	the business buys an asset, paying by cheque	debit	credit

7.5

JAMES ANDERSON

Dr			**Capital Account**			Cr
1997			£	1997		£
				3 Feb	Bank	7,500

Dr			**Computer Account**			Cr
1997			£	1997		£
6 Feb	Bank		2,000			

Dr			**Rent Paid Account**			Cr
1997			£	1997		£
7 Feb	Bank		750			

Dr		Wages Account			Cr
1997		£	1997		£
12 Feb	Bank	425			
25 Feb	Bank	380			

Dr		Bank Loan Account			Cr
1997		£	1997		£
			14 Feb	Bank	2,500

Dr		Commission Received Account			Cr
1997		£	1997		£
			20 Feb	Bank	145

Dr		Drawings Account			Cr
1997		£	1997		£
24 Feb	Bank	200			

Dr		Van Account			Cr
1997		£	1997		£
28 Feb	Bank	6,000			

7.6

TONY LONG

Dr		Bank Account			Cr
1997		£	1997		£
1 May	Capital	6,000	5 May	Machinery	3,500
12 May	L Warner: loan	1,000	6 May	Office equipment	2,000
19 May	Commission received	150	9 May	Rent paid	350
			15 May	Wages	250
			20 May	Drawings	85
			26 May	Wages	135

Dr		Capital Account			Cr
1997		£	1997		£
			1 May	Bank	6,000

Dr Machinery Account Cr

1997		£	1997		£
5 May	Bank	3,500			

Dr Office Equipment Account Cr

1997		£	1997		£
6 May	Bank	2,000			

Dr Rent Paid Account Cr

1997		£	1997		£
9 May	Bank	350			

Dr Lucy Warner: Loan Account Cr

1997		£	1997		£
			12 May	Bank	1,000

Dr Wages Account Cr

1997		£	1997		£
15 May	Bank	250			
26 May	bank	135			

Dr Commission Received Account Cr

1997		£	1997		£
			19 May	Bank	150

Dr Drawings Account Cr

1997		£	1997		£
20 May	Bank	85			

7.7   **JEAN LACEY**

Dr Bank Account Cr

1997		£	1997		£
1 Aug	Capital	5,000	4 Aug	Computer	2,115
15 Aug	S Orton: loan	1,000	7 Aug	Rent paid	100
20 Aug	Office fittings	282	12 Aug	Office fittings	2,350
25 Aug	Commission received	188	27 Aug	S Orton: loan	150

Dr	Capital Account		Cr
1997	£	1997	£
		1 Aug Bank	5,000

Dr	Computer Account		Cr
1997	£	1997	£
4 Aug Bank	1,800		

Dr	Value Added Tax Account		Cr
1997	£	1997	£
3 Aug Bank (computer)	315	10 Aug Cash (commission received)	35
12 Aug Bank (office fittings)	350	20 Aug Bank (office fittings)	42
		25 Aug Bank (commission received)	28

Dr	Rent Paid Account		Cr
1997	£	1997	£
7 Aug Bank	100		

Dr	Commission Received Account		Cr
1997	£	1997	£
		10 Aug Cash	200
		25 Aug Bank	160

Dr	Cash Account		Cr
1997	£	1997	£
10 Aug Commission received	235	17 Aug Drawings	100

Dr	Office Fittings Account		Cr
1997	£	1997	£
12 Aug Bank	2,000	20 Aug Bank	240

Dr	Sally Orton: Loan Account		Cr
1997	£	1997	£
27 Aug Bank	150	15 Aug Bank	1,000

Dr	Drawings Account		Cr
1997	£	1997	£
7 Aug Cash	100		

CHAPTER 8: BALANCING ACCOUNTS AND THE TRIAL BALANCE

8.1 (b)

8.2 (c)

8.3 (d)

8.4

Dr		Sales Account				Cr
1997			£	1997		£
30 Apr	Balance c/d		17,170	1 Apr	Balance b/d	12,550
				30 Apr	Sales Day Book	4,620
			17,170			17,170
				1 May	Balance b/d	17,170

Dr		Wages Account				Cr
1997			£	1997		£
1 Apr	Balance b/d		3,710	30 Apr	Balance c/d	5,180
11 Apr	Bank		780			
25 Apr	Bank		690			
			5,180			5,180
1 May	Balance b/d		5,180			

Dr		Wyvern Traders				Cr
1997			£	1997		£
1 Apr	Balance b/d		375	24 Apr	Bank	375

Dr		T Johnson				Cr
1997			£	1997		£
15 Apr	Bank		240	1 Apr	Balance b/d	240
18 Apr	Purchases Returns		45	10 Apr	Purchases	180
30 Apr	Balance c/d		350	29 Apr	Purchases	215
			635			635
				1 May	Balance b/d	350

8.5 (a)

Dr			Bank Account			Cr
1997			£	1997		£
1 Apr	Capital		1,000	2 Apr	Purchases	255
7 Apr	Sales		195	4 Apr	Advertising	60
10 Apr	Sales		248	8 Apr	Rent paid	125
16 Apr	J Couchman: loan		1,000	11 Apr	Drawings	100
18 Apr	Sales		220	14 Apr	Purchases	240
25 Apr	Sales		312	21 Apr	Shop fittings	1,250
				23 Apr	Purchases	180
				24 Apr	Advertising	90
				28 Apr	Rent	125
				30 Apr	Drawings	125
				30 Apr	Balance c/d	425
			2,975			2,975
1 May	Balance b/d		425			

(b) and (c)

GENERAL LEDGER

Dr		Capital Account			Cr
1997		£	1997		£
			1 Apr	Bank	1,000

Dr		Purchases Account			Cr
1997		£	1997		£
2 Apr	Bank	255	30 Apr	Balance c/d	675
14 Apr	Bank	240			
23 Apr	Bank	180			
		675			675
1 May	Balance b/d	675			

Dr		Advertising Account			Cr
1997		£	1997		£
4 Apr	Bank	60	30 Apr	Balance c/d	150
24 Apr	Bank	90			
		150			150
1 May	Balance b/d	150			

Dr		Sales Account			Cr
1997		£	1997		£
30 Apr	Balance c/d	975	7 Apr	Bank	195
			10 Apr	Bank	248
			18 Apr	Bank	220
			25 Apr	Bank	312
		975			975
			1 May	Balance b/d	975

Dr		Rent Paid Account			Cr
1997		£	1997		£
8 Apr	Bank	125	30 Apr	Balance b/d	250
28 Apr	Bank	125			
		250			250
1 May	Balance b/d	250			

Dr		Drawings Account			Cr
1997		£	1997		£
11 Apr	Bank	100	30 Apr	Balance c/d	225
30 Apr	Bank	125			
		225			225
1 May	Balance b/d	225			

Dr		J Couchman: Loan Account			Cr
1997		£	1997		£
			16 Apr	Bank	1,000

Dr		Shop Fittings Account			Cr
1997		£	1997		£
21 Apr	Bank	1,250			

(d)

Trial balance of Andrew Jarvis as at 30 April 1997

Name of account	Dr £	Cr £
Bank	425	
Capital		1,000
Purchases	675	
Advertising	150	
Sales		975
Rent paid	250	
Drawings	225	
J Couchman: Loan		1,000
Shop fittings	1,250	
	2,975	2,975

8.6

Trial balance of Jane Greenwell as at 28 February 1997

Name of account	Dr £	Cr £
Bank		1,250
Purchases	850	
Cash	48	
Sales		730
Purchases returns		144
Creditors		1,442
Equipment	2,704	
Van	3,200	
Sales returns	90	
Debtors	1,174	
Wages	1,500	
Capital (missing figure)		6,000
	9,566	9,566

CHAPTER 9: DEBTORS AND CREDITORS

9.1 (a)

9.2 *Before the goods are supplied*

- As the potential buyer is not known, the seller should ask for two referees. One of these should be the buyer's bank, and the other a trader with whom the buyer has previously done business.
- The seller should take up both references and obtain satisfactory replies before goods are supplied on credit.
- Once satisfactory replies have been received, a credit limit for the customer should be established, eg £1,000.

- Larger businesses often require their customers to sign a credit agreement, which sets out the terms of payment.

Subsequent dealings with the customer

- The credit limit should not normally be exceeded – in larger firms the accounts supervisor or accountant should be asked to approve any transactions above the limit.
- Invoices should be sent out promptly and should state clearly the terms of trade.
- Month-end statements of account should be sent out promptly with an analysis of how long the balance has been outstanding, eg current, 30 days, 60 days, older.
- If the customer does not pay within a reasonable time, established procedures should be followed to chase the debt. These include:
  - telephone calls
  - letters
  - threat of legal action
- If the amount is unpaid, consideration should be given to taking legal action – although whether this is carried out will depend on the size of the debt.
- Where the debt is still unpaid it will have to be written off as a bad debt (ie a cost to the seller) and, clearly, no further goods should be supplied to the customer.

9.3

Date	Details	Folio	Dr £	Cr £
1997				
21 Oct	Bad debts written off	GL	18	
	J Roberts	SL		18
	Bad debt written off as per memo from accounts supervisor dated 21 October 1997			

SALES LEDGER

Dr			James Roberts		Cr
1997		£	1997		£
1 Jan	Balance b/d	70	17 Feb	Bank	40
			20 Mar	Cash	10
			20 Oct	Bank	2
			21 Oct	Bad debts written off	18
		70			70

GENERAL LEDGER

Dr			Bad Debts Written Off Account		Cr
1997		£	1997		£
21 Oct	J Roberts	18			

9.4 *Tutorial note:* VAT relief is not available here as the debt is less than six months overdue.

Date	Details	Folio	Dr	Cr
1997			£	£
22 Dec	Bad debts written off	GL	25	
	N Watson	SL		25
	Bad debt written off as per memo from accounts supervisor dated 22 December 1997			

SALES LEDGER

Dr   **Natalie Wilson**   Cr

1997		£	1997		£
1 Nov	Balance b/d	320	3 Nov	Bank	312
10 Nov	Sales	200	3 Nov	Discount allowed	8
			15 Nov	Sales returns	50
			20 Nov	Bank	100
			3 Dec	Cash	25
			22 Dec	Bad debts written off	25
		520			520

GENERAL LEDGER

Dr   **Bad Debts Written Off Account**   Cr

1997		£	1997	£
22 Dec	N Watson	25		

9.5 (a)

ELECTRALARM LIMITED
67 Newtown Road, West Roxton, WR6 6YP
Tel .... Fax ....

Date ....

T Gunsmith Esq
8 Tresham Close
West Roxton
WR3 5FG

Dear Mr Gunsmith

Overdue account

We note from our records that we have not yet received payment of our invoice no .... for £785.00 dated .... A statement of account is enclosed.

Our payment terms were strictly 30 days from date of the invoice. We shall be grateful if you will settle the overdue amount of £785.00 without further delay.

We look forward to receiving your remittance.

Yours sincerely

....
Accounts Department
enc

(b) If no payment is received, the following procedure could be adopted:
- telephone the customer to ask for payment
- if no payment is forthcoming, write again threatening legal action
- if still no payment is made, and you think that there is a chance of getting some money back, commence legal action:
  - either take Mr Gunsmith to the Small Claims Court
  - or place the debt in the hands of a solicitor or debt collecting agency
- if you suspect that the customer is in financial difficulties or bankrupt, legal action may not be worth the time and costs involved in which case the amount may have to be written off as a bad debt

9.6

Dr		£		**Apple Supplies Limited**		Cr £
1997		£	1997			£
6 May	Bank	780	1 May	Balance b/d		800
6 May	Discount	20	5 May	Purchases		255
12 May	Purchases returns	55	26 May	Purchases		150
30 May	Bank	195				
30 May	Discount	5				
31 May	Balance c/d	150				
		1,205				1,205
			1 Jun	Balance b/d		150

Reconciliation of Apple Supplies Limited's statement of account as at 31 May 1997		
	£	£
Balance of account at 31 May 1997		150
Add: payment sent on 30 May 1997	195	
discount received	5	200
Balance of statement at 31 May 1997		350

9.7

GENERAL LEDGER

Dr		£	**Purchases Account**		Cr £
1997		£	1997		£
2 Feb	G Lewis	200			
17 Feb	G Lewis	160			

Dr		£	**Sales Account**		Cr £
1997		£	1997		£
			4 Feb	L Jarvis	150
			7 Feb	G Patel	240

Dr   **Discount Received Account**   Cr

1997	£	1997		£
		10 Feb	G Lewis	10
		24 Feb	G Lewis	8

Dr   **Discount Allowed Account**   Cr

1997		£	1997	£
12 Feb	L Jarvis	3		
20 Feb	G Patel	6		

PURCHASES LEDGER

Dr   **G Lewis**   Cr

1997		£	1997		£
10 Feb	Bank	190	2 Feb	Purchases	200
10 Feb	Discount received	10	17 Feb	Purchases	160
24 Feb	Bank	152			
24 Feb	Discount received	8			
		360			360

SALES LEDGER

Dr   **L Jarvis**   Cr

1997		£	1997		£
4 Feb	Sales	150	12 Feb	Bank	147
			12 Feb	Discount allowed	3
		150			150

Dr   **G Patel**   Cr

1997		£	1997		£
7 Feb	Sales	240	20 Feb	Bank	234
			20 Feb	Discount allowed	6
		240			240

CASH BOOK

Dr   **Bank Account**   Cr

1997		£	1997		£
12 Feb	L Jarvis	147	10 Feb	G Lewis	190
20 Feb	G Patel	234	24 Feb	G Lewis	152

CHAPTER 10: CONTROL ACCOUNTS

10.1   (d)

10.2   (b)

10.3   *Principles of control accounts*
- Control accounts are 'master' accounts which control a number of subsidiary ledger accounts.
- Control accounts use total figures:
  - total of opening balances
  - total of amounts increasing the balances
  - total of amounts decreasing the balances

  In this way, the total of the closing balances for the subsidiary accounts can be calculated and then checked against a separate listing of the balances of the subsidiary accounts to ensure that the two figures agree.
- Two commonly used control accounts are:
  - sales ledger control account, the total of the debtors
  - purchases ledger control account, the total of the creditors

Control accounts as an aid to management
- The figures for debtors and creditors are available immediately from the sales ledger and purchases ledger control accounts – there is no need to add up the balances of all the individual debtors' or creditors' accounts.
- Control accounts can help in locating errors. The balance of the control account can be checked against the separate listing of balances of the subsidiary accounts to ensure that the two figures agree. However, this only proves the arithmetical accuracy of the control account and subsidiary accounts – there could still be errors, such as misposts and compensating errors, within the ledger section.
- Fraud is made more difficult when control accounts are used – this especially applies to a manual accounting system. The reason for this is that any fraudulent transaction to be recorded on the personal account of a debtor or creditor must also be entered in the control account. As the control account will be either maintained by a supervisor, or checked regularly by the manager, the control accounts add another level of security within the accounting system.

Control accounts and book-keeping
- Control accounts can be:
  - either, incorporated into the book-keeping system
  - or, used as memorandum accounts
- The first approach uses the control account as the double-entry system, ie the balances of the sales ledger control account and the purchases ledger control account are recorded in the trial balance as the figures for debtors and creditors respectively. The personal accounts of debtors and creditors are not part of double-entry but are kept as memorandum accounts which record how much each debtor owes, and how much is owed to each creditor. From time-to-time, the balances of the memorandum accounts are agreed with the balance of the appropriate control account.
- The second method uses the opposite approach. Personal accounts of debtors and creditors

are included in the double-entry system, while the control accounts are memorandum accounts used as checking devices.

- Both methods follow the principles of double-entry book-keeping. Both are acceptable and it is for a business to decide how to incorporate control accounts into its book-keeping system.

10.4

Dr			**Sales Ledger Control Account**			Cr
1997		£	1997			£
1 Jun	Balances b/d	17,491	30 Jun	Sales returns		1,045
30 Jun	Credit sales	42,591	30 Jun	Payments received from debtors		39,024
			30 Jun	Cash discount allowed		593
			30 Jun	Bad debts written off		296
			30 Jun	Balances c/d		19,124
		60,082				60,082
1 Jul	Balances b/d	19,124				

10.5

Dr			**Purchases Ledger Control Account**		Cr
1997		£	1997		£
30 Apr	Purchases returns	653	1 Apr	Balances b/d	14,275
30 Apr	Payments made to creditors	31,074	30 Apr	Credit purchases	36,592
30 Apr	Cash discount received	1,048			
30 Apr	Set-off	597			
30 Apr	Balances c/d	17,495			
		50,867			50,867
			1 May	Balances b/d	17,495

10.6 (a)

SALES LEDGER

Dr			**Arrow Valley Retailers**		Cr
1997		£ p	1997		£ p
1 Feb	Balance b/d	826.40	20 Feb	Bank	805.74
3 Feb	Sales	338.59	20 Feb	Discount allowed	20.66
			28 Feb	Balance c/d	338.59
		1,164.99			1,164.99
1 Mar	Balance b/d	338.59			

Dr		B Brick (Builders) Limited		Cr
1997		£ p	1997	£ p
1 Feb	Balance b/d	59.28	28 Feb Bad debts written off	59.28

Dr		Mereford Manufacturing Company		Cr
1997		£ p	1997	£ p
1 Feb	Balance b/d	293.49	24 Feb Sales returns	56.29
3 Feb	Sales	127.48	28 Feb Set-off	364.68
		420.97		420.97

Dr		Redgrove Restorations		Cr
1997		£ p	1997	£ p
1 Feb	Balance b/d	724.86	7 Feb Sales returns	165.38
17 Feb	Sales	394.78	28 Feb Balance c/d	954.26
		1,119.64		1,119.64
1 Mar	Balance b/d	954.26		

Dr		Wyvern Warehouse Limited		Cr
1997		£ p	1997	£ p
1 Feb	Balance b/d	108.40	15 Feb Bank	105.69
17 Feb	Sales	427.91	15 Feb Discount allowed	2.71
			28 Feb Balance c/d	427.91
		536.31		536.31
1 Mar	Balance b/d	427.91		

(b)

Dr		Sales Ledger Control Account		Cr
1997		£ p	1997	£ p
1 Feb	Balances b/d	2,012.43	28 Feb Sales returns	221.67
28 Feb	Credit sales	1,288.76	28 Feb Cheques received from debtors	911.43
			28 Feb Cash discount allowed	23.37
			28 Feb Set-off	364.68
			28 Feb Bad debts written off	59.28
			28 Feb Balances c/d	1,720.76
		3,301.19		3,301.19
1 Mar	Balances b/d	1,720.76		

(c)

Reconciliation of sales ledger control account with debtor balances

	1 February 1997	28 February 1997
	£ p	£ p
Arrow Valley Retailers	826.40	338.59
B Brick (Builders) Limited	59.28	–
Mereford Manufacturing Company	293.49	nil
Redgrove Restorations	724.86	954.26
Wyvern Warehouse Limited	108.40	427.91
Sales ledger control account	2,012.43	1,720.76

10.7 (a)

Dr			**Apple Supplies Limited**				Cr
1997		£ p		1997			£ p
14 Feb	Purchases returns	157.20		1 Feb	Balance b/d		1,843.22
17 Feb	Bank	2,646.15		3 Feb	Purchases		1,027.98
17 Feb	Discount received	67.85		27 Feb	Purchases		849.36
28 Feb	Balance c/d	849.36					
		3,720.56					3,720.56
				1 Mar	Balance b/d		849.36

Dr			**Beatty Brothers**				Cr
1997		£ p		1997			£ p
1 Feb	Balance b/d	51.47		3 Feb	Purchases		150.68
28 Feb	Balance c/d	99.21					
		150.68					150.68
				1 Mar	Balance b/d		99.21

Dr			**J Johnson**				Cr
1997		£ p		1997			£ p
24 Feb	Bank	978.51		1 Feb	Balance b/d		675.38
24 Feb	Discount received	25.09		10 Feb	Purchases		328.22
		1,003.60					1,003.60

Dr			**Mereford Manufacturing Company**				Cr
1997		£ p		1997			£ p
28 Feb	Set-off	364.68		1 Feb	Balance b/d		478.29
28 Feb	Balance c/d	113.61					
		478.29					478.29
				1 Mar	Balance b/d		113.61

Dr		Newtown Equipment Limited			Cr
1997		£ p	1997		£ p
11 Feb	Bank	684.86	1 Feb	Balance b/d	684.86
18 Feb	Purchases returns	105.68	28 Feb	Balance c/d	105.68
		790.54			790.54
1 Mar	Balance b/d	105.68			

Dr		W Wright			Cr
1997		£ p	1997		£ p
6 Feb	Bank	962.52	1 Feb	Balance b/d	987.20
6 Feb	Discount received	24.68	10 Feb	Purchases	476.38
28 Feb	Balance c/d	476.38			
		1,463.58			1,463.58
			1 Mar	Balance b/d	476.38

(b)

Dr		Purchases Ledger Control Account			Cr
1997		£ p	1997		£ p
1 Feb	Balance b/d	51.47	1 Feb	Balances b/d	4,668.95
28 Feb	Cheques paid to suppliers	5,272.04	28 Feb	Credit purchases	2,832.62
28 Feb	Cash discount received	117.62	28 Feb	Balance c/d	105.68
28 Feb	Purchases returns	262.88			
28 Feb	Set-off	364.68			
28 Feb	Balances c/d	1,538.56			
		7,607.25			7,607.25
1 Mar	Balance b/d	105.68	1 Mar	Balances b/d	1,538.56

(c)   **Reconciliation of purchases ledger control account with creditor balances**

	1 February 1997	28 February 1997
	£ p	£ p
Apple Supplies Limited	1,843.22	849.36
Beatty Brothers	*(51.47)	99.21
J Johnson	675.38	nil
Mereford Manufacturing Company	478.29	113.61
Newtown Equipment Limited	684.86	*(105.68)
W Wright	987.20	476.38
Net balances	4,617.48	1,432.88

* debit balances

Purchases ledger control account:

Debit	(51.47)	(105.68)
Credit	4,668.95	1,538.56
Net balance	4,617.48	1,432.88

CHAPTER 11: THE JOURNAL

11.1   (b)

11.2   *business transaction*

- credit sale of a fixed asset
- credit purchase of goods from a supplier
- returned credit purchases to the supplier
- customer returns goods sold on credit
- cheque received from a debtor
- credit sale of goods to a customer

primary accounting record

- journal
- purchases day book
- purchases returns day book
- sales returns day book
- cash book
- sales day book

11.3   (a)

11.4

	primary accounting record	*debit*	*credit*
(a)	purchases day book	purchases account	Temeside Traders
(b)	sales day book	Malvern Models	sales account
(c)	journal	office equipment account	A-Z Computers Ltd
(d)	sales returns day book	sales returns account	Johnson Bros
(e)	cash book	bank account	Melanie Fisher
(f)	cash book	cash account	sales account
(g)	cash book	drawings account	cash account
(h)	cash book	Stationery Supplies Ltd	bank account
(i)	journal	bad debts written off account	J Bowen
(j)	purchases returns day book	I Johnson	purchases returns account

11.5 (a) *error of omission*

Date	Details	Folio	Dr	Cr
			£	£
	J Rigby	SL	150	
	Sales account	GL		150
	Sales invoice no .... omitted from accounts			

(b) *mispost/error of commission*

Date	Details	Folio	Dr	Cr
			£	£
	H Price Limited	PL	125	
	H Prince	PL		125
	Correction of mispost – cheque no .... to H Price Limited			

(c) *error of principle*

Date	Details	Folio	Dr	Cr
			£	£
	Delivery van account	GL	10,000	
	Vehicle expenses account	GL		10,000
	Correction of error – vehicle no .... invoice no			

(d) *reversal of entries*

Date	Details	Folio	Dr	Cr
			£	£
	S Mortimer	PL	55	
	Purchases returns account	GL		55
	S Mortimer	PL	55	
	Purchases returns account	GL		55
	Correction of reversal of entries, credit note received no		110	110

(e) *compensating error*

Date	Details	Folio	Dr	Cr
			£	£
	Purchases account	GL	100	
	Purchases returns account	GL		100
	Correction of under-cast on purchases account and purchases returns account on .....(date)......			

(f)   *error of original entry*

Date	Details	Folio	Dr	Cr
			£	£
	L Johnson	SL	98	
	Bank account	CB		98
	Bank account	CB	89	
	L Johnson	SL		89
	Correction of error – cheque for £89 received on ......(date)........			
			187	187

11.6

	Date	Details	Folio	Dr	Cr
				£	£
(a)		Wyvern Supplies	PL	85	
		Suspense account	GL		85
		Omission of entry in purchases ledger – payment by cheque no			
(b)		H Barton	PL	87	
		Suspense account	GL		87
		Suspense account	GL	78	
		H Barton	PL		78
		Purchases invoice no .... for £78 entered in purchases ledger as £87 in error		165	165
(c)		Suspense account	GL	100	
		Sales returns account	GL		100
		Over-cast on .....(date).... now corrected			
(d)		T Jarvis	SL	25	
		Suspense account	GL		25
		Credit note no .... entered twice in sales ledger, now corrected			

Dr			**Suspense Account**		Cr
1997		£	1997		£
30 Sep	Trial balance difference	19	(a)	Wyvern Supplies	85
(b)	H Barton	78	(b)	H Barton	87
(c)	Sales returns	100	(d)	T Jarvis	25
		197			197

CHAPTER 12: RECEIVING AND RECORDING PAYMENTS

12.1

Customer	Change	Notes & coin given in change
1	£1.50	1 x £1 coin, 1 x 50p coin
2	£6.70	1 x £5 note, 1 x £1 coin, 1 x 50p coin, 1 x 20p coin
3	£2.49	2 x £1 coins, 2 x 20p coins, 1 x 5p coin, 2 x 2p coins
4	£3.21	3 x £1 coins, 1 x 20p coin, 1 x 1p coin
5	£0.66	1 x 50p coin, 1 x 10p coin, 1 x 5p coin, 1 x 1p coin
6	£3.78	3 x £1 coins, 1 x 50p coin, 1 x 20p coin, 1 x 5p coin, 1 x 2p coin, 1 x 1p coin
7	£7.24	1 x £5 note, 2 x £1 coins, 1 x 20p coin, 2 x 2p coins
8	£0.58	1 x 50p coin, 1 x 5p coin, 1 x 2p coin, 1 x 1p coin
9	£3.46	3 x £1 coins, 2 x 20p coins, 1 x 5p coin, 1 x 1p coin
10	£1.92	1 x £1 coin, 1 x 50p coin, 2 x 20p coins, 1 x 2p coin

12.2

	£
cash float at start of day	28.71
plus sales made during the day	46.46
equals amount of cash held at end of day	75.17

12.3 (a) 2 x £13.99 = £27.98; 2 x 85p = £1.70; total £29.68 + VAT £5.19 = £34.87

(b) £149.95 + 99p = £150.94; add VAT of £26.41 = £177.35

(c) 2 x £35.99 = £71.98; add VAT of £12.59 = £84.57

12.4 (a) A & S Systems Ltd (G Brown signs as director – an authorised signatory)

(b) Southern Bank PLC

(c) Electron Games Limited

For explanations see page 186.

12.5 A crossed cheque must be paid into a bank account; it cannot be cashed (except by an account holder making a cheque payable to him/herself). A cheque without a crossing – an 'open' cheque – may be cashed by the payee. It is therefore a security risk and is very rare.

12.6 (a) The cheque has to be paid into an account.

(b) The cheque has to be paid in at Barclays Bank, Hanover Square.

(c) The same as (a) – the phrase '& co' no longer has any significance.

(d) The cheque must be paid into the account of the payee.

(e) The same as (d).

(f) The cheque *can* be endorsed over by the payee, but in practice banks will only accept the cheque for the account of the payee – they stand to lose if the cheque has been stolen.

12.7 (a)   It should be paid into *Sandra Lobbs* account.

(b)   This entitles *anyone* who comes into possession of the cheque to pay it into his/her account.

12.8   See page 187 of text.

12.9   See page 190 of text.

12.10   See page 192 of text.

12.11   (c)

12.12   False

12.13   (b)

12.14   (d)

12.15   See page 195 of text.

12.16   (a) the bank (b) large purchase where cash or near cash is required, eg car purchase, house purchase

12.17   Cheques received through the post, cash sales at the counter.

CHAPTER 13: PAYING INTO THE BANK

13.1   See page 207 of text.

13.2   See page 207 of text.

13.3   False. Debtor

13.4   False. Creditor

13.5   (a) ... mortgagor ... mortgagee

(b) ... bailee ... bailor

(c)   agent

13.6   (a)   Loan account

(b)   Overdraft

(c)   Deposit account

13.7   (a)   3 days

(b)   24 hours (or as long as first class post takes)

Yes, the business could obtain same day clearance (the two accounts are at the same branch)

13.8   *'Refer to Drawer, Please Represent'*: the cheque will be put through the bank clearing system again <u>by the bank</u>, so there is nothing the business can do with the cheque. The business will be alerted, however, to a possible bad debt and will review carefully credit given to the customer in question.

'Refer to Drawer' : in this case the cheque will be returned to the business which can then make strenuous efforts to recover the money from the customer. This answer is normally very bad news for a supplier as it normally means the buyer is in serious financial difficulties.

13.9   See page 215 of text.

13.10   See page 218 of text.

13.11   (a) credit (b) debit

13.12

Cheques:		Cash:		
	£20.00		2 x £20 notes	£40.00
	£18.50		5 x £10 notes	£50.00
	£75.25		8 x £5 notes	£40.00
	£68.95		2 x £1 coins	£2.00
	£182.70		6 x 50p coins	£3.00
			4 x 10p coins	£0.40
			2 x 2p coins	£0.04
				£135.44

Total amount of credit: £318.14

13.13 Total of sales vouchers £396.94 less refund voucher £13.50, total of summary £383.44.

CHAPTER 14: MAKING AND RECORDING PAYMENTS

14.1 False. No cheque is involved in a BACS payment.

14.2 For security reasons: to prevent fraudulent alterations.

14.3 (d)

14.4 To establish the legal relationship between the bank and the business. The bank has to know *who* can sign cheques, and for what amounts. It also needs specimen signatures so that it can verify written instructions, eg cheque signatures and other payment instructions.

14.5 (a) See text page 235 (b) Standing order (c) Direct debit

14.6 (a) Bank draft (b) CHAPS

14.7 (a) He/she doesn't have to rely on carrying his/her own money; or he/she doesn't have to pay!

(b) Monitoring of expenditure, or control of expenditure.

14.8 Note that the cash discount is not available – the period has expired. Total £15,255.34.

14.9 Total £4,083.05

14.10 Bank giro completed as below:

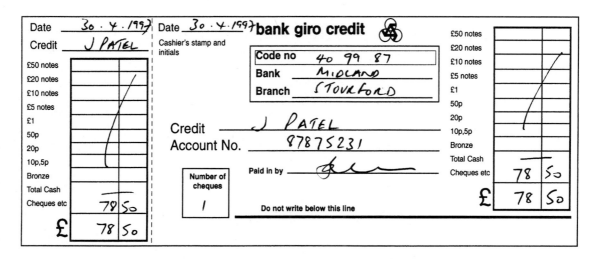

STANDING ORDER MANDATE

To _____ *NATIONAL* _____ Bank

Address ___ *10 CATHEDRAL STREET MEREFORD MR1 5DE* ___

PLEASE PAY TO

Bank _*BARCLAYS*_   Branch _*EVESMORE*_   Sort code | *30 98 15* |

Beneficiary   Account number | *726 27161* |

The sum of | £ *350* | Amount in words _*THREE HUNDRED AND FIFTY POUNDS*_

Date of first payment ___ *15 MAY 1997* ___   Frequency of payment ___ *MONTHLY* ___

Until ___ *15 APRIL 1998* ___   Reference ___ *BE/ 6637* ___

Account to be debited | *NIMROD DRAINAGE LTD* | Account number | *1203 4875* |

SIGNATURE(S)   ....

         .... date...........................

14.11 (a) Standing order completed as shown above.

(b) The form will be sent to the National Bank, as they will set up the payments.

(c) The standing order will have to be signed by an authorised signatory (or two) within the business. It should also be noted that details of the due payments will be passed to the person in charge of entering up the cash book as the payments will form part of the double-entry book-keeping of the company.

For details of the direct debit – see the next page.

```
──────────────── direct debit instruction ────────────────

                                    Tradesure Insurance Company
                                         PO Box 134, Helliford, HL9 6TY

                                    Originator's Identification Number  914208
                                          03924540234
        Reference(tobecompletedbyTradesureInsurance)........................................................

Please complete the details and return this form to Tradesure Insurance

name and address of bank/building society          Instructions to bank/building society

  _ _ _ NATIONAL_ BANK_ _ _ _ _        • I instruct you to pay direct debits from my account at
                                          the request of Tradesure Insurance Company
  _ _ _ 10_ CATHEDRAL_ STREET_ _ _      • The amounts are variable and may be debited on
                                          various dates
  _ _ _ MENEFORD_ _ _ _ _ _ _ _        • I understand that Tradesure Insurance Company may
                                          change the amounts and dates only after giving me
         MN 5DE                           prior notice
                                        • I will inform the bank/building society if I wish to
account name                              cancel this instruction
                                        • I understand that if any direct debit is paid which
  NIMROD DRAINAGE LIMITED                 breaks the terms of this instruction, the bank/building
                                          society will make a refund.
account number         sort code        signature(s)                      date

  1203 4875           35.09.75
```

14.11 (a) Direct debit form completed as shown above.

(b) The form will be sent to Tradesure Insurance, as they will set up the payments.

(c) The direct debit will have to be signed by an authorised signatory (or two) within the business. It should also be noted that details of the due payments are normally advised by the originator of the direct debit (here the insurance company). These will be passed to the person in charge of entering up the cash book as the payments will form part of the double-entry book-keeping of the company.

CHAPTER 15: CASH BOOK

15.1   (d)

15.2   (d)

15.3   *Main responsibilities of the cashier*

- Preparing remittance lists (see page 198) for cheques received in the post
- Recording receipts and payments by cheque and in cash in the firm's cash book
- Issuing receipts for cash (and sometimes cheques) received
- Making authorised cash payments (except for low-value expenses payments which are paid by the petty cashier)
- Preparing cheques for authorised payments – to be signed by those permitted to sign on behalf of the company
- Paying cash and cheques received into the bank
- Controlling the firm's cash, either in a cash till or cash box
- Issuing cash to the petty cashier who operates the firm's petty cash book
- Ensuring that all transactions passing through the cash book are supported by documentary evidence
- Checking the accuracy of the cash and bank balances at regular intervals
- Checking expenses claims and seeking authorisation before making payment
- Liaising with the other accounts staff – accounts clerks and petty cashier

Qualities of a cashier

- Accuracy – in writing up the cash book, in cash handling, and in ensuring that payments are made only against correct documents and appropriate authorisation
- Security – of cash and cheque books, and correct authorisation of payments
- Confidentiality – that all cash/bank transactions, including cash and bank balances, are kept confidential

15.4

Dr | | | | | | | | | | | Cr

Cash Book

Date	Details	Folio	Disc allwd	Cash	Bank	Date	Details	Folio	Disc recd	Cash	Bank
1997			£	£	£	1997			£	£	£
1 Aug	Balances b/d			276	4,928	5 Aug	T Hall Ltd		24		541
1 Aug	Wild & Sons Ltd				398	8 Aug	Wages			254	
11 Aug	Bank	C		500		11 Aug	Cash	C			500
12 Aug	A Lewis Ltd		20		1,755	18 Aug	F Jarvis				457
21 Aug	Harvey & Sons Ltd				261	22 Aug	Wages			436	
29 Aug	Wild & Sons Ltd		15		595	25 Aug	J Jones		33		628
29 Aug	Bank	C		275		27 Aug	Salaries				2,043
						28 Aug	Telephone				276
						29 Aug	Cash	C			275
						31 Aug	Balances c/d			361	3,217
			35	1,051	7,937				57	1,051	7,937
1 Sep	Balances b/d			361	3,217						

15.5

Dr | | | | | | | **Cash Book** | | | | | | Cr

Date	Details	Folio	Disc allwd	VAT	Cash	Bank	Date	Details	Folio	Disc recd	VAT	Cash	Bank
1997			£	£	£	£	1997			£	£	£	£
1 Apr	Balance b/d				85		1 Apr	Balance b/d					718
7 Apr	J Bowen	SL	5		85		3 Apr	Travel exp	GL			65	
10 Apr	Sales	GL		70		470	4 Apr	Telephone	GL		35		235
18 Apr	J Burrows	SL	25			575	14 Apr	M Hughes	PL	10			180
21 Apr	Sales	GL		28	188		17 Apr	Purchases	GL		14		94
22 Apr	Bank	C			200		22 Apr	Cash	C				200
30 Apr	Balance c/d					627	24 Apr	Wilson Ltd	PL	10			245
							25 Apr	Wages	GL			350	
							30 Apr	Balance c/d				143	
			30	98	558	1,672				20	49	558	1,672
1 May	Balance b/d				143		1 May	Balance b/d					627

GENERAL LEDGER

Dr   **Discount Allowed Account**   Cr

1997		£	1997		£
30 Apr	Cash Book	30			

Dr   **Discount Received Account**   Cr

1997		£	1997		£
			30 Apr	Cash Book	20

Dr   **Value Added Tax Account**   Cr

1997		£	1997		£
30 Apr	Cash Book	49	30 Apr	Cash Book	98

15.6 Dr (Receipts)

Date	Details	Folio	Cash	Bank	Disc allwd	VAT	Sales	Sales ledger	Sundry
1997			£ p	£ p	£ p	£ p	£ p	£ p	£ p
12 May	Balances b/d		205.75	825.30					
12 May	Sales	GL		534.62		79.62	455.00		
13 May	Sales	GL	164.50			24.50	140.00		
13 May	T Jarvis	SL		155.00	2.50			155.00	
14 May	Sales	GL		752.00		112.00	640.00		
15 May	Cash	C		250.00					
15 May	Sales	GL	264.37			39.37	225.00		
16 May	Wyvern District Cncl	SL		560.45	5.00			560.45	
			634.62	3,077.37	7.50	255.49	1,460.00	715.45	–

Cr (Payments)

Date	Details	Folio	Cash	Bank	Disc recd	VAT	Purchases	Purchases ledger	Sundry
1997			£ p	£ p	£ p	£ p	£ p	£ p	£ p
12 May	Shop rent	GL		255.50				*258.90*	255.50
13 May	Terry Carpets Ltd	PL		363.55	4.65			363.55	
14 May	Stationery	GL	28.20			4.20			24.00
15 May	Bank	C	250.00						
15 May	Longlife Carpets Ltd	PL		291.50	4.30			295.80	
16 May	Wages	GL	314.20						314.20
16 May	Balance c/d		42.22	2,166.82					
			634.62	3,077.37	8.95	4.20	–	659.35	593.70
								554.70	

Transfers to general ledger

- *discount allowed* column total of £7.50 is debited to discount allowed account
- *discount received* column total of £8.95 is credited to discount received account
- *Value Added Tax* columns, the total of £255.49 is credited to VAT account, while the total of £4.20 is debited to the VAT account
- *sales* column total of £1,460.00 is credited to sales account
- *sundry* column – the individual payments are debited to shop rent account, £255.50, stationery account, £24.00, and wages account, £314.20

The transactions in the columns for sales ledger and purchases ledger are respectively credited and debited to the individual accounts of the debtors and creditors.

CHAPTER 16: PETTY CASH BOOK

16.1 (d)

16.2 (c)

16.3 *Allow:* (a), (b), (d), (f), (g), (h), (j) – all subject to an appropriate receipt being attached to the petty cash voucher, and payment being in accordance with the company's policies – eg amount, authorisation.

Refer:

(c) travel to work – not normally a business expense, except for emergency call-outs

(e) staff tea and coffee – check if it is company policy to pay for this personal expense of the office staff

(i) shelving for the office – this expense is, most probably, too large to be put through petty cash; check with the accounts supervisor who is likely to say that it should go through the main cash book

16.4 *Security and confidentiality aspects of petty cash*

- On taking over, check that the petty cash book has been balanced and that the amount of cash held agrees with the balance shown in the book.
- Start each week with the imprest amount of cash which has been agreed with the office manager.
- Keep the petty cash secure in a locked cash box, and keep control of the keys.
- Provide petty cash vouchers (in numerical order) on request.
- Pay out of petty cash against correctly completed petty cash vouchers ensuring that:
  - the voucher is signed by the person receiving the money
  - the voucher is signed by the person authorising payment (a list of authorised signatories will be provided)
  - a receipt (whenever possible) is attached to the petty cash voucher, and receipt and petty cash voucher are for the same amount
- Write up the petty cash book (including calculation of VAT amounts when appropriate); it is important that the petty cash book is *accurate*.
- Store the completed petty cash vouchers safely – filed in numerical order. They will need to be kept for at least six years in the company's archives, together with completed petty cash books.
- The office manager will carry out a surprise check from time-to-time – the cash held, plus amounts of completed petty cash vouchers, should equal the imprest amount.
- At the end of each week (or month) balance the petty cash book and draw an amount of cash from the cashier equal to the amount of payments made, in order to restore the imprest amount.
- Prepare a posting sheet for the book-keeper with the totals of each analysis column, so that he/she can enter the amount of each expense into the double-entry system.
- Present the petty cash book and cash in hand for checking by the office manager.
- Deal with any discrepancies promptly, eg:
  - a receipt and petty cash voucher total differing
  - a difference between the totals of the analysis columns and the total payments column in the petty cash book

– a difference between the cash in the petty cash book and the balance shown in the petty cash book

- Where discrepancies and queries cannot be resolved, they should be referred to the office manager.

- Remember that all aspects of petty cash are confidential and should not be discussed with others.

16.5

petty cash voucher		No. 851
date *today*		

description	amount (£)	
Postage on urgent parcel of spare parts to Evelode Supplies Ltd	4	45
	4	45
VAT		
	4	45

signature   *Jayne Smith*

authorised   *A Student*

Documentation will be a post office receipt for £4.45, being the amount of postages paid.

petty cash voucher		No. 852
date *today*		

description	amount (£)	
Airmail envelopes	2	00
	2	00
VAT	0	35
	2	35

signature   *Tanya Howard*

authorised   *A Student*

Documentation will be a till receipt (or handwritten receipt) from the stationery shop for £2.35.

16.6

	Expense (excluding VAT) £	VAT £	Total £
(a)	8.00	1.40	9.40
(b)	4.00	0.70	4.70
(c)	2.00	0.35	2.35
(d)	2.09	0.36	2.45
(e)	4.77	0.83	5.60
(f)	2.96	0.51	3.47
(g)	7.45	1.30	8.75
(h)	0.80	0.14	0.94
(i)	0.85	0.14	0.99
(j)	8.01	1.40	9.41

16.7

Petty Cash Book

Receipts £	Date	Details	Voucher No	Total Payment £	Analysis columns					
					VAT £	Travel £	Postages £	Stationery £	Meals £	Misc £
75.00	1997 1 Aug	Balance b/d								
	4 Aug	Taxi fare	39	3.80	0.56	3.24				
	6 Aug	Parcel post	40	2.35			2.35			
	7 Aug	Pencils	41	1.26	0.18			1.08		
	11 Aug	Travel expenses	42	5.46		5.46				
	12 Aug	Window cleaner	43	8.50						8.50
	14 Aug	Envelopes	44	2.45	0.36			2.09		
	18 Aug	Donation	45	5.00						5.00
	19 Aug	Rail fare/meal allow	46	10.60		5.60			5.00	
	20 Aug	Postage	47	0.75			0.75			
	22 Aug	Tape	48	1.50	0.22			1.28		
	25 Aug	Postage	49	0.55			0.55			
	27 Aug	Taxi fare	50	5.40	0.80	4.60				
				47.62	2.12	18.90	3.65	4.45	5.00	13.50
47.62	29 Aug	Cash received								
	29 Aug	Balance c/d		75.00						
122.62				122.62						
75.00	1 Sep	Balance b/d								

GENERAL LEDGER

Dr   **Value Added Tax Account**   Cr

1997		£ p	1997		£ p
29 Aug	Petty Cash Book	2.12			

Dr   **Travel Expenses Account**   Cr

1997		£ p	1997		£ p
29 Aug	Petty Cash Book	18.90			

Dr   **Postages Account**   Cr

1997		£ p	1997		£ p
29 Aug	Petty Cash Book	3.65			

Dr   **Stationery Account**   Cr

1997		£ p	1997		£ p
29 Aug	Petty Cash Book	4.45			

Dr   **Meals Account**   Cr

1997		£ p	1997		£ p
29 Aug	Petty Cash Book	5.00			

Dr   **Miscellaneous Expenses Account**   Cr

1997		£ p	1997		£ p
29 Aug	Petty Cash Book	13.50			

CASH BOOK

Dr   **Cash book**   Cr

	Cash	Bank		Cash	Bank
1997	£ p	£ p	1997	£ p	£ p
			29 Aug Petty Cash Book	47.62	

16.8   **Petty Cash Book**

Receipts	Date	Details	Voucher No	Total Payment	Analysis columns				
					VAT	Postages	Travel	Meals	Sundry Office
£	1997			£	£	£	£	£	£
100.00	2 Jun	Balance b/d							
	2 Jun	Postages	123	6.35		6.35			
	3 Jun	Travel expenses	124	3.25			3.25		
	3 Jun	Postages	125	1.28		1.28			
	4 Jun	Envelopes	126	4.54	0.67				3.87
	4 Jun	Window cleaning	127	5.50	0.81				4.69
	5 Jun	Taxi fare/meals	128	15.41	2.28		3.89	9.24	
	5 Jun	Post/packing	129	11.81	0.48	8.56			2.77
	5 Jun	Taxi fare/meals	130	11.95	1.77		3.83	6.35	
	6 Jun	Pens/envelopes	131	6.35	0.94				5.41
				66.44	6.95	16.19	10.97	15.59	16.74
66.44	6 Jun	Cash received							
	6 Jun	Balance c/d		100.00					
166.44				166.44					
100.00	7 Jun	Balance b/d							

GENERAL LEDGER

Dr		**Value Added Tax Account**		Cr	
1997		£ p	1997		£ p
6 Jun	Petty Cash Book	6.95			

Dr		**Postages Account**		Cr	
1997		£ p	1997		£ p
6 Jun	Petty Cash Book	16.19			

Dr		**Travel Expenses Account**		Cr	
1997		£ p	1997		£ p
6 Jun	Petty Cash Book	10.97			

Dr	Meals Account		Cr
1997		£ p	1997	£ p
6 Jun Petty Cash Book	15.59		

Dr	Sundry Office Expenses Account		Cr
1997		£ p	1997	£ p
6 Jun Petty Cash Book	16.74		

CASH BOOK

Dr			Cash book			Cr
	Cash	Bank		Cash	Bank
1997	£ p	£ p	1997	£ p	£ p
			6 Jun Petty Cash Book	66.44	

CHAPTER 17: BANK RECONCILIATION STATEMENTS

17.1 (a)

17.2 (c)

17.3

TOM REID

BANK RECONCILIATION STATEMENT AS AT 31 DECEMBER 1997

	£
Balance at bank as per bank statement	207
Less: unpresented cheque	
B Kay cheque no. 345126	20
	187
Add: outstanding lodgement	
J Hill	13
Balance at bank as per cash book	200

17.4 (a)

Dr	Cash Book (bank columns)				Cr
1997		£ p	1997		£ p
1 Jan	Balance b/d	415.15	23 Jan	Direct debit: Omni Finance	207.95
13 Jan	BACS credit: T K Supplies	716.50	31 Jan	Balance c/d	923.70
		1,131.65			1,131.65
1 Feb	Balance b/d	923.70			

(b)

P GERRARD

BANK RECONCILIATION STATEMENT AS AT 31 JANUARY 1997

		£	£
Balance at bank as per bank statement			1,076.45
Less: unpresented cheques			
Bryant & Sons	cheque no. 001354	312.00	
P Reid	cheque no. 001355	176.50	
			488.50
			587.95
Add: outstanding lodgement			
G Shotton Limited			335.75
Balance at bank as per cash book			923.70

17.5 (a)

Dr	**Cash Book** (bank columns)			Cr

1997		£	1997			£
1 May	Balance b/d	300	2 May	P Stone	867714	28
7 May	Cash	162	14 May	Alpha Ltd	867715	50
16 May	C Brewster	89	29 May	E Deakin	867716	110
23 May	Cash	60	16 May	Standing order: A-Z Insurance		25
30 May	Cash	40	31 May	Bank charges		10
			31 May	Balance c/d		428
		651				651
1 Jun	Balance b/d	428				

(b)

JANE DOYLE

BANK RECONCILIATION STATEMENT AS AT 1 MAY 1997

	£
Balance at bank as per bank statement	326
Less: unpresented cheque:	
cheque no. 867713	80
	246
Add: outstanding lodgement	54
Balance at bank as per cash book	300

(c)

BANK RECONCILIATION STATEMENT AS AT 31 MAY 1997

	£
Balance at bank as per bank statement	498
Less: unpresented cheque	
E Deakin cheque no. 867716	110
	388
Add: outstanding lodgement	
cash	40
Balance at bank as per cash book	428

17.6

MEMORANDUM

TO: ....

FROM: Accounts Clerk

DATE: ....

SUBJECT: Bank Reconciliation Statements

Reconciliation of the bank statement balance with that shown in the cash book is carried out at the month-end as follows:

1. From the bank columns of the cash book tick off, in both cash book and bank statement:

    - the receipts that appear in both

    - the payments that appear in both

2. Identify the items that are unticked on the bank statement and enter them in the cash book on the debit or credit side as appropriate. These will be things such as BACS receipts, standing order and direct debit payments, bank charges and interest, unpaid cheques debited by the bank. However, if the bank has made a mistake by debiting or crediting our account in error, don't enter them in the cash book; instead, notify the bank for them to make the correction.

3. Balance the bank columns of the cash book to find the up-to-date balance.

4. Start the bank reconciliation statement with the final figure shown on the bank statement.

5. In the bank reconciliation statement:

    - *deduct* the unticked payments shown in the cash book – these are unpresented cheques

    - *add* the unticked receipts shown in the cash book – these are outstanding lodgements

6. The resultant money amount on the bank reconciliation statement is the balance at bank as per cash book.

7. Date the reconciliation statement and file it away for future reference. Note that, if the balances of the bank statement and the cash book (bank columns) were not identical *at the beginning of the month,* then you will need to refer to the previous bank reconciliation statement prepared at the end of last month. Items appearing on that bank reconciliation statement must also be ticked off at step 1. Anything remaining unticked will be included in this month's reconciliation statement (step 5).

A Student

CHAPTER 18: COMMUNICATING FOR ACCOUNTING

18.1 Types include data relating to banking, sales ledger management, purchase ledger management and stock.

18.2 Paper back-up (in case computer system fails and for audit purposes), computer data back-up (in case computer data is corrupted or system fails).

18.3 Data may be filed in the following way:
- alphabetic: sales ledger, purchase ledger
- numeric: invoices, credit notes
- date order: bank statements, correspondence

The main reason, in each case, is for ease of storage and reference. Students should be made aware that these categories of filing system are very flexible: there are no 'hard and fast' rules.

18.4 (a) a Web Site is an information source accessed via a computer internet link, Viewdata is telephone /screen based

(b) microfilm is a record stored on continuous film, microfiche is on separate sheets ('fiches')

18.5 The note must be correctly addressed and marked with the date and time, must indicate urgency, and must provide information about the tasks to be done and the appropriate deadlines. The note should also include an apology.

18.6 The memorandum should be correctly headed and addressed. The message should be brief and clear. The memorandum can be signed, although this is not essential. The memorandum should include an 'enc.' (enclosure) marker.

18.7 Examples of chasers are reproduced on pages 303 (mild) and 305 (stronger). The important details to include are invoice amount, number and date (a copy should ideally be enclosed [nb 'enc.' marker]) and terms. The tone should not be too strong – remember that the invoice may even have been lost, or the cheque already be in the post (both common excuses!). The letter should be marked for signature by the Accounts Manager.

18.8 A letter of complaint should be drafted (see page 306). It must contain full details of the problems and ask for a full explanation. The tone should remain polite but firm. Problem (a) would suggest that a refund should be requested and problem (b) that full details should be provided of the interest calculations.

18.9 A letter of apology is required here (see page 307). The error may well be the customer's fault, but on no account should this be suggested in the letter (she is 'a valued customer'). The letter should acknowledge the problem, state what corrective action has been taken and finish on a positive note. The tone should be conciliatory but not 'grovelling' (which sounds insincere). The letter should be correctly addressed and signed off.

CHAPTER 19: BUSINESS CONTRACTS

19.1   The definition must contain the message that a contract is an agreement that is legally binding and enforceable in a court of law.

19.2   Agreement, bargain, intention to create legal relations. See text on pages 312 to 316.

19.3   (a)   Yes. A contract can be oral. A purchase order is just part of the paperwork confirming the agreement.

   (b)   Yes. The purchase order and despatch of the goods constitute the agreement, bargain and commercial nature of the transaction.

   (c)   No. When the job was done there was no intention to create legal relations or to involve consideration (payment) – it was done as a favour. The £10 followed the job and was just incidental.

   (d)   Yes. The fact that the person is a friend is not relevant. There was an agreement, consideration and an intention to create legal relations.

19.4   The cashier is right. The price on the shelf is just an invitation to treat. The price is agreed at the till.

19.5   No. The stipulation that the goods are received by 4 April amounts to a counter-offer to the supplier's terms and does not constitute an acceptance. It would only be a valid contract if the supplier had agreed to the revised terms.

19.6   17 March. The postal rule applies – as long as the letter is correctly addressed stamped and posted.

19.7   He is wrong. He is liable under the Sale of Goods Act which states that goods sold must be of 'satisfactory quality … fit for the purpose … as described.' The purchaser is entitled to a replacement or a refund as long as the problem is reported without delay.

19.8   No. The Trades Descriptions Act states that it is illegal to make false statements about goods offered for sale. The chair is advertised as having an adjustable back; if it does not, you are entitled to your money back. You could also report the matter to Trading Standards Department who can pursue the matter.

INDEX

Proforma
Invoice 231